Jane Austen
and Discourses
of Feminism

JANE AUSTEN
AND DISCOURSES
OF FEMINISM

Edited by
Devoney Looser

MACMILLAN

First published 1995 by
MACMILLAN PRESS LTD
Houndmills, Basingstoke, Hampshire RG21 6XS
and London
Companies and representatives
throughout the world

ISBN 0–333–63872–7

A catalogue record for this book is available from the British Library.

10   9   8   7   6   5   4   3   2   1
04 03 02 01 00 99 98 97 96 95

Printed in the United States of America by
Haddon Craftsmen
Scranton, PA

To Alison Sulloway

Contents

III. FEMINIST DISCOURSES IN DIALOGUE

Preface and Acknowledgments

When my mother first presented me with *Pride and Prejudice*, I was 13 and not very inclined to read "old books." On the third attempt at reading it, I was "hooked." Indeed, my love for Austen's novels brought me directly to the professional study of literature. Her novels were not, however, primarily responsible for my seeking out training in women's studies and feminist theories—at least as far as I am able to trace these influences from where I stand now.

Austen, then, did not "lead me" to feminism; conversely, it was not usually feminists who led me to Austen. Somewhere along the line, however, the link between these two interests did converge—through a professor's suggestion, through a key phrase in *Persuasion*, and finally, through a belated discovery of the vast array of second-wave feminist criticism of Austen. Work by Sandra Gilbert and Susan Gubar, Elaine Showalter, and Janet Todd served as an impetus for many of us to think through (and rethink) how we made sense of Austen among women writers and alongside feminist theorizing. As I suspect has been the case for other readers who share a love for Austen and a passion for feminism, I sometimes came upon difficulties in trying to bring together the two interests. In the initial stages of planning for this anthology, I discovered that many other readers and critics of Austen were struggling with similar questions and concerns.

In putting together this collection, I feared the too-easy pull for reconciliation—claiming Austen for feminism and encouraging feminists to claim Austen. I wanted very much to avoid that pull and to bring together original works that significantly complicated the versions of Austen and feminism we've seen in the last several decades. What has resulted, I believe, is a collection of essays that is wide-ranging, provocative, and often conflicting—something certainly true of Austen studies *and* feminist studies more generally. I hope *Jane Austen and Discourses of Feminism* will provide a springboard for further critical discussion about Austen as we enter feminism's so-called third wave.

Work on this anthology would not have been possible without early encouragement and advice from Nancy Armstrong, Julia Prewitt Brown, Margaret Doody, Claudia Johnson, Deborah Kaplan, Juliet McMaster, Susan

Morgan, and Elaine Showalter. Catherine Nicholl was among the first to teach me that there was more to Austen than just a "good read." Other professors—Pat Belanoff, Helen Cooper, Drucilla Cornell, E. Ann Kaplan, Ira Livingston, Adrienne Munich, Clifford Siskin, Michael Sprinker, Susan Squier, Kathleen Wilson, and Rose Zimbardo—provided valuable feedback and support in matters personal and professional over the years. Martha Heller, Catherine Ingrassia, Linda Frost, Mary Jo Kietzman, Greg Laugero, Pamela Moore, Mona Narain, and Tony Vaver also gave crucial advice and professional support to this project.

Paula Backscheider's National Endowment for the Humanities 1994 summer seminar entitled "Biography and the Uses of Biographical Evidence" at the Public Record Office, London, helped to further my thinking on women's authorial practices. I also thank colleagues at Indiana State University for their feedback on my work on Austen and feminism presented in the department colloquium series—especially to Jim Broaddus, Madelyn DeGaetano, Myrna Handley, and Darlene Hantzis. The audience at the Jane Austen Society of North America's 1994 conference, where I was a featured speaker, must also be thanked; the valuable comments of Rachel Brownstein, Gene Koppel, Juliet McMaster, and Ruth Perry deserve mention. Those whose help is often of the most thankless kind—administrative and research supporters—made this project possible: Mari Abdullah, Chaun Daniels, Heather Hairston, Lisa Hickman, and most of all, Mary Ann Duncan. I would also like to thank my editor, Jennifer Farthing, for her expert guidance and assistance. Final thanks must go to Alison Sulloway, to whom this book is dedicated, for her unflagging support and optimistic spirit at a time when such professional relationships seem all too rare.

I gratefully acknowledge *Persuasions* for permission to reprint from my "Jane Austen, Feminist Literary Criticism, and a Fourth 'R': Reassessment," 16 (1994): 125-134. Portions of Glenda Hudson's essay have appeared previously in her *Sibling Love and Incest in Jane Austen's Fiction* (New York: St. Martin's Press, 1992).

Introduction:
Jane Austen and Discourses of Feminism

Devoney Looser

In the thriving industry of Jane Austen criticism, the driving force is arguably feminist. Park Honan, for one, has claimed that in recent Austen scholarship "feminism ceases to be an 'ism' and informs our way of understanding the novels."[1] I would not be so quick to consider feminism fully assimilated, however, or to deem its use-value as a term in Austen studies at an end. Feminism has altered the ways in which we are able to see Austen today, to be sure, but these "ways of seeing" are by no means settled, despite the fact that certain insights may have become mainstream. *Jane Austen and Discourses of Feminism* involves—among other things—a reassessment of these versions of Austen's relationship to feminisms. This volume aims implicitly and explicitly to recap feminist attention to Austen and to suggest new directions that criticism on Austen might take.

June Dwyer has claimed that though much has been written on Austen, none of it is ridiculous.[2] Scholarship on Austen tends to be of a high quality, as Austen attracts devotees willing to spend their lives studying her six novels, her Juvenilia and letters, and her familial and cultural minutiae. Most readers of Austen are quite at ease talking about the Jane Austen we praise un-complicatedly for her "genius" or the Austen of the New Critics or the "Great Tradition." Fewer readers are well prepared to discuss the Jane Austen of feminisms and cultural studies. These latter Austens, though not without relation to the aforementioned groups of readers and readings, seem to stand alone, looking unlike the author whom others have described. Not simply "genius" or "spinster," this Austen, as Janet Todd has suggested, "has been an awkward subject for feminist criticism to cope with."[3]

As Todd's statement suggests, and as those familiar with the last several decades of criticism on Austen must know, a good deal of debate has centered around whether we should call Austen's novels—or Austen herself—"feminist." This is not a debate peculiar to Austen studies, of course. Many women writers have become the focus of similar "identity crises." Second-wave feminist literary criticism of the 1970s and '80s devised litmus tests for discerning feminist authors in centuries past. As we reassess this work, we can't help but notice that those women writers who have been dubbed "feminists" may have had precious little in common. Strange and unlikely sisterhoods have been devised within and across generations. Grouped together for feminist study, for example, were royalist eccentric Margaret Cavendish and pious Puritan Lucy Hutchinson; unabashed usurper of so-called male territory playwright Aphra Behn and properly feminine poet Katharine Philips; and finally vindicator of rights Mary Wollstonecraft and self-professed writer of little bits of ivory Austen herself. These unlikely pairings of feminist precursors would seem to imply that *any* woman who wrote is likely to be a feminist—that she has more in common with any *other* woman who wrote than she has with any other man.

For those of us now studying British women writers from the Restoration to the Romantic era, questions about the "commonality" of women continue to provoke argument. Some critics remain lobbyists for the efficacy of the categories "woman author" and "feminist author," often maintaining that these categories are necessarily synonymous during the period in question. Those espousing this argument would have it that women who wrote in the difficult cultural climate of the long eighteenth century in England (roughly 1660 to 1830) must *automatically* be classed as feminists. Picking up the pen—regardless of to what end—makes a woman author an activist of sorts; she is said to break with the strictures for "proper" gendered behavior in her day solely through the act of writing. However, as more early modern British women authors are read, studied, and (happily) taught, the differences among them strike today's feminist critics as much as the similarities did feminists of the second wave. Flattening woman writer into feminist writer no longer seems critically savvy, particularly as women writers come to the fore whose views appear patently antifeminist to today's sensibilities. In short, it is no longer easy to celebrate the achievements of a woman writer solely on the basis of her sex.

Though some might lament this lack of ease, I think we would do better to welcome it. Feminist struggles over naming our historical authorial precursors demonstrate that we haven't reached a consensus about what it means to "do" feminist literary criticism on women writers—something that shows both the variety and vitality of our tasks. Austen cannot easily be deemed a "protofeminist," a "feminist," or an "antifeminist," as is illustrated by what Alistair Duckworth has called "the conflict of interpretations" in Austen scholarship.[4]

The conflicts surrounding Austen are echoed in more recent statements by other prominent critics. Claudia Johnson has claimed that "Jane Austen enjoys a peculiar status in academic studies. Her position in the canon is secure, but she is beloved in part because she seems to invite us to suspend our customary critical procedures."[5] Johnson claims that Austen's novels "are one—perhaps the only—place where academics may enjoy high art without suffering the rigors and risks of thought, as if criticism were somehow uncouth, like spitting or smoking in front of the ladies."[6] As Johnson would agree, however, just because readers have resisted using recent literary and cultural theories on Austen's texts does not mean that our readings of her novels wouldn't be enriched by these critical endeavors.

Recent feminist theories have significantly complicated the terms "political" and "social." These traditionally have been slippery terms in Austen criticism. Scholarship dealing with Austen could meet this slipperiness head on by engaging with contemporary literary theoretical innovations concerning gender, history, genre, authorship, resistance, and complicity. These theories allow us to grasp more firmly the possibilities for understanding Austen's texts in a sophisticated critical frame. Not all readers of Austen—and not all feminists—agree with this position vis à vis theory. Some remain skeptical about whether feminist theories are appropriately brought to bear on Austen's works. The contributors to this anthology, however, employ recent theoretical scholarship in furthering their "risks of thought" on Austen (a risk that, as I hope readers will agree, is well worth taking).

Of course, what constitutes a risk today is very much determined by the critical standards of yesteryear. The version of Austen that was handed down from one critical generation to another—from the late Victorian period up until the work of Marilyn Butler in the mid-1970s—is that of an apolitical author.[7] Austen was said to be uninvolved and perhaps uninterested in the ✗ historical events of her day. She was presented as a woman who lived a life in which nothing happened. If all of us agreed with these portraits, feminists would seem to have a *misplaced* interest in such a detached disinterested author. Fortunately, these versions of Austen have been widely debunked and have allowed for conversations quite different from those that scholars of 20 or more years ago might have envisioned.

These changed conversations bring about difficult—often painful—questions. Evidence of the difficulty of discussing Austen in today's cultural climate can be found in the poem, "The Stranglehold of English Lit." (1961) by Felix Mnthali—a poet and a professor of literature at the University of Botswana. Mnthali wonders if readers had questioned why Jane Austen's people "carouse" and "do no work," rather than simply adoring her novels as they were taught in the colonizers' schools, would colonialism ("Europe in Africa") have lasted as long as it did?[8] At some level, I think it is unfortunate that Mnthali chose Austen to stand in for what is obviously a much larger tradition (literary and otherwise) of imperialist practices. But today we have no choice but to take Mnthali's visions and versions of Austen quite seriously. They provide serious charges. Feminists, interested as we are in issues of social justice, must also enter into these difficult conversations including, but not limited to, questions of colonialism.

In what follows, I attempt to introduce these difficult conversations about Austen, discourses of feminism, and history as they have played out in recent literary criticism. A review of second-wave feminist arguments about Austen provides a necessary starting point; at least five critical positions, often intersecting and overlapping, might be charted for scholarship on Austen and feminism. First, there is an Austen who has been linked more closely to what Juliet Mitchell has called "The Longest Revolution" (the women's movement) than to the French Revolution.[9] This feminist position maintains (as I suggested earlier) that any woman writing in early modern England must—as a matter of course—"be" a feminist, as a result of her rebellious foray onto the manuscript page or into print. The woman author's lack of ostensible political involvement doesn't matter in the face of her writing, which is seen in itself as a political act.

Austen, though she published anonymously, is labeled a feminist because of the risks to which she was exposed in seeking an audience for her writings. This Austen inherited and perpetuated the feminist tradition of a long line of women authors, who were unrecognized until recently. This is the version of feminist literary history offered by the likes of Dale Spender in her *Mothers of the Novel: 100 Good Writers Before Jane Austen*.[10] This version, I think, has seen its heyday of critical fashion come and go, primarily because of its inattention to certain kinds of historical detail. It is perhaps ironic that critics such as Spender, in the name of increased attention to history, created feminist ahistoricisms of their own. As Janet Todd has noted, this critical paradigm "made sisterhood across time but not within it."[11]

A second version Austen's feminism provides a reversal of the first. Some have argued that we cannot rightly use the word "feminist" in early modern British contexts because it would be anachronistic. The *Oxford English Dictionary* shows the emergence of the word "feminism" in 1851, but the word "feminist" does not come into the language until the 1880s and '90s.[12] This adherence to linguistic history, then, would exempt *all* authors of the so-called Romantic era and earlier from being considered for the label "feminist," though we might still talk about the development of these ideas in the work of seventeenth-century writer Mary Astell or in the late eighteenth-century bluestocking circle. This version has attracted little support, and most of us refer to Enlightenment feminisms with relative complacency.

A third feminist paradigm involves those who have located Austen's feminism as far more surreptitious. In this version of Austen's gender politics, she is seen as enacting a "sneaky feminism," using traditional romance plots to soften her ironic and perhaps more radical feminist messages. Austen's feminism is guarded, but it is the job of this critic to find these traces under the surface of the text. This Austen just plain doesn't say what she means.[13] In general, when feminists have made this argument for Austen, it hasn't been to see her as a lone example but rather to see her as part of a tradition of partially expressed feminism, of madwomen's languages. The feminist critics most associated with the version of Austen's subversive feminism include Sandra Gilbert and Susan Gubar and Mary Poovey (particularly her early work).[14] Again, this method has been taken to task for its ahistoricism. As Christine Marshall writes of Gilbert and Gubar's work, "their approach does not place Austen in an historical context other than as a closet rebel in an oppressive male-dominated society."[15] Most now concede that too much from Austen's works needs to be created between the lines or simply explained away to make her fit this mold.

A fourth feminist version of Austen gives her to us as a Tory proponent of the political and cultural status quo—a picture that does not see her novels as particularly liberatory for women. Austen's insistence on marrying off and domesticating her heroines runs counter to these critics' ideas about what feminist literature is or should be. The novelistic imperative of heterosexual coupling is seen as inherently patriarchal. Austen, therefore, is deemed a partial or an unrealized feminist at best and a patriarchal pawn or a sellout at worst. For Virginia Woolf, Austen's conservatism and ladylike qualities show us that she had simply not yet come into her own strident, feminist voice, at least in part because of the influences of her conservative society and her close-knit family.[16] Critics of this school often point to Austen's elegant, confined stylistic qualities as well. We might think here of Charlotte Brontë's disdain for Austen's "carefully fenced, highly cultivated garden, with near borders and delicate flowers." Elaine Showalter uses this 1848 quotation to note that by midcentury, "Austen's name had become a byword for female literary restraint."[17] Such a restrained quality, for some, is part and parcel of a conservatism not likened to forthright or proper feminism, such as Wollstonecraft's. This image of Austen, according to LeRoy Smith, has been discarded as well.[18] Evidence of its once holding critical sway still abounds— though perhaps not so much among feminists.

ϟ   A fifth version of Austen and feminism emerged with the notion that her central focus on women characters—and intelligent, strong women at that— proved her feminism. Any author who could create an Elizabeth Bennet or an Emma Woodhouse, it might be argued, must be promoting a feminist cause. This idea of a feminist Austen, in its more recent formulations at least, has worked from far more historically based critical ground. Here we might think of the work of Margaret Kirkham, who likens Austen to Wollstonecraft and argues that both writers were committed to principles of Enlightenment humanism.[19] These principles included the belief in women's capacity to reason and the need for women's education.

Also in this camp might be placed Claudia Johnson and Alison Sulloway, both of whom highlight Austen's possibilities and place in the aftermath of Wollstonecraft's fallen reputation.[20] Johnson argues for an Austen who—as a result of what we might now be tempted to call the "backlash" of the 1790s—fashioned a message that was of necessity far less didactic in its tone. Unlike their more anachronistic predecessors, these critics do not see Austen's messages as covering up her "true feminism" (a dubious, static category—especially as it is understood by the proponents of the subversive Austen). Rather, this version seeks to label Austen in a far more historically based manner. Some of these feminist critics continue to place Austen in a politically conservative camp; others, such as Mary Evans, prefer to label Austen a social critic—perhaps even a proto-Marxist. Arguments for Austen's Marxism, however, have not seemed to take hold.[21] All told, it is this fifth version, and the permutations, additions, and revolutions it has been spawn-ing, that seems to be leading us to newer answers to the "Is Jane Austen a feminist?" issue—as well as to entirely different questions.

Instead of simply weighing the pro and con arguments of these five positions or the merits of the (admittedly partial) divisions I've outlined, I think it would be more productive to step back at this point and to ask what is at stake in formulating answers to these questions, in taking positions on Austen and feminism. What are the ramifications of asking and answering the question, "Is she or isn't she a feminist?" Of course, as with every critical revolution, lives—and careers—may hang in the balance. This would be one level on which to examine the effects of Austen and discourses of feminism, to be sure. There have been and will be Internet flame wars waged, book contracts gained and lost, and tenure won or denied over such seemingly moot questions as

Austen's feminism. In the greater scheme of things, then, whether this generation or the next deems Austen a feminist matters most to only a few lives—those of professional academics and of other interested readers. I raise this point not just to be clever or to abuse ourselves for not talking instead about the "real world," but rather to contextualize and characterize these debates over Austen even further. To step away from these professionalized critical effects involves asking why these questions have become so important *now*.

The matter of Austen's feminism is one that still generates a good deal of critical anger. In 1993 John Halperin published a scathing review of Deborah Kaplan's *Jane Austen Among Women* in the journal *Nineteenth-Century Literature*.[22] Kaplan's book fashions an Austen who is a feminist not just because she wrote about strong women but because she participated in what Kaplan calls a "women's culture." Kaplan describes Austen's relationships with her sister Cassandra, with her nieces, and with other important female confidantes as what drives her artistic productions. Halperin calls Kaplan's book "a good (or perhaps a bad) example of what happens when ideology and the politics of the moment are allowed to take over and control the critical act. Something always goes wrong."[23]

I think it is important that we not accept Halperin's own divisions and definitions. His statements might rather lead us to ask if there are indeed nonpolitical or nonideological ways of reading Austen. If there are not, as many maintain, then are we always, as Halperin puts it, "going wrong"? Perhaps there is something to Halperin's claim that it is misleading to downplay the importance of the men in Austen's life by accentuating the importance of the women. His statement rankles, however, in that it seems to exclude *itself* from ideology and politics. Surely, Halperin's response is a political statement of the moment as well. His contribution is perhaps best characterized as one that laments the increasing *visibility* of ideology and politics in criticism on Austen—and one that longs for the day of its unacknowledged force.

From all appearances, the days of the unacknowledged presence of politics in literature are behind us; the political/social ramifications of literary study are now widely examined. It is in this respect that scholarship dealing with Austen—feminist and otherwise—must come to terms with contemporary literary theoretical innovations concerning authorship, class, complicity, gender, genre, history, nationality, race, resistance, and sexuality in order to give us a more sophisticated picture of the possibilities for understanding Austen's texts in a critical frame. Amid all of the arguments, what feminist criticism offers us is a way to talk about the gendered implications of Austen's writings and of our readings of her.

A focus on gender politics is the strength all feminist work on Austen exemplifies—and it's a strength that one also finds in Austen's own writings. Issues of gender do not comprise the only struggle in which her texts are embroiled. In this sense, then, the isolation of gender as a discourse presents critical problems; in contemporary feminist scholarship, gender is rarely considered without theorizing related issues, such as those just named. ✗Gender in Austen's texts therefore must be considered in tandem with other discourses. It seems important here to offer at least one example. The defense of novels that the narrator offers at the end of chapter five in *Northanger Abbey* has intrigued and even puzzled literary critics for decades. Some have read it as a straightforward position statement. Others have seen it as loaded with doses of Austen's masterful irony. Still others have criticized its inclusion in critical discussions at all—calling it representative of the immature Austen and therefore not worthy of much comment. The narrator's comments continue to be worthy of our attention. Austen writes:

> Yes, novels;—for I will not adopt that ungenerous and impolitic custom so common with novel writers, of degrading by their contemptuous censure the very performances, to the number of which they are themselves adding—joining with their greatest enemies in bestowing the harshest epithets on such works, and scarcely ever permitting them to be read by their own heroine, who, if she accidentally take up a novel, is sure to turn over its insipid pages with disgust. Alas! If the heroine of one novel be not patronized by the heroine of another, from whom can she expect protection and regard? I cannot approve of it. Let us leave it to the Reviewers to abuse such effusions of fancy at their leisure, and over every new novel to talk in threadbare strains of the trash with which the press now groans. Let us not desert one another; we are an injured body.[24]

When interpreting this passage, some feminists have been quick to claim this injured body is an injured female body. They point to Austen's subsequent statement, the "'Oh! it is only a novel!'" section, in which the young lady lays down her book with "affected indifference or momentary shame" (*NA*, 38). The narrator proclaims: "'It is only Cecilia, or Camilla, or Belinda;' or, in short, only some work in which the greatest powers of the mind are displayed, in which the most thorough knowledge of human nature, the happiest delineation of its varieties, the liveliest effusions of wit and humour are conveyed to the world in the best chosen language" (*NA*, 38). This section, with its references to the writings of Frances Burney and Maria Edgeworth, has been used by some to argue that Austen is in fact invoking a women's literary tradition—that she is creating a bond with her sister authors.

As recent work has shown us, however, it is also possible that Austen invokes Burney and Edgeworth because they would not claim their productions as novels. Edgeworth called *Belinda* (1801) "a moral tale," labeling novels (as was the wont of many) as immoral in themselves. Austen, then, may be castigating her fellow female authors or even poking fun at them. It is possible that Austen purposefully took up their texts (and claimed for them something other than what they claimed to be) in order to advance her own classificatory cause—though she may not have been primarily motivated by the politics of gender to do so. Perhaps her motives were more closely linked to the politics of genre.[25] What seems on the face of it to be sisterhood may not be quite so simply categorized. These are the kinds of distinctions that feminist Austen scholars will continue to grapple with in years to come.

Despite the long-standing tradition of seeing Austen as "apolitical" and her novels and her life as texts in which "nothing happens," her texts contain significant commentary on what it means to perform the subject position "woman" (primarily British white heterosexual "middle-class" woman) in her day. Recent feminist theories have only begun to complicate the terms of debate to include questions that discuss gender not as an isolated or historically unchanging category but as one that can be understood *only in relation to other discourses.* Austen cannot easily be deemed a "protofeminist" or a "feminist," and simply celebrated for that stance. Recent work on colonialism, for instance, has begun considering the privileges of empire alongside the oppressions of gender and class—has begun, in other words, to consider the kinds of questions Felix Mnthali raised for Austen studies (and for English literature more generally) in his poem over 30 years ago.

Rather than continuing to struggle over whether Austen "was" or "was not" a feminist, our time might be better spent describing more intricately the workings of gender politics in her novels—without a primary troubling over what to label her. Feminist literary critics have more pressing tasks today than determining whether Austen (or any author, for that matter) was or is a "proper" feminist. Furthermore, whether Austen's feminism seems "proper"—seems worth celebrating or worth taking to task—depends very much on where one is standing when viewing Austen's world. As Edward Said puts it, "interpreting Jane Austen depends on *who* does the interpreting, *when* it is done, and no less important, from *where* it is done."[26]

From where I stand, it appears that future discussions of Austen's relation to feminist politics (or of the discourses of feminism emergent in her culture more generally) will allow us to consider her texts in tandem with discourses of other identities and practices at issue in her own time—as well as in our own. Unlike Halperin, I am not bothered by the fact that "politics and ideologies of the moment" shape the questions that we bring to literature. In fact, I share the view that it could not be any other way. But this does not mean our only option is utter relativism. The ways in which "we" define feminism—both historically and in our own time—are crucially important not just to a handful of academics but to lives more generally. How will feminism be represented to and/or taken up by subsequent generations? How will we understand the debates and the struggles in which Austen's texts participated? Will we continue to read Austen at all, and if so, what might we gain or lose in the process?

The original essays included in *Jane Austen and Discourses of Feminism* offer us not only new ways of reading Austen but renewed reasons to continue our explorations of gender in her work. In the following pages the gains are seen to far outweigh the losses, and each author has given us provocative questions with which to return to Austen's writings. The anthology is divided into three sections. The first group of essays, "Changing Histories," sees Austen in relation to historical issues and social context; new research on early modern British life has changed the ways in which we understand Austen's milieu. All of the authors contribute to and/or make use of these insights. The second section, "Critical Re-examinations," reassesses some of the central arguments (feminist and otherwise) in Austen criticism today, investigating constructions of her as an author and suggesting possibilities for change. These essays extend the divisions I've drawn for feminist readings of Austen—furthering some interpretations and taking issue with others. A final section, "Feminist Discourses in Dialogue," gives critical attention to what might be considered less-often-theorized novels (*Mansfield Park* and *Northanger Abbey*) and in the process serves as an enactment of the feminist critical debates being waged today. Throughout the anthology, Austen is reconsidered in light of recent scholarship on previously lesser-known authors writing (and events occurring or practices emerging) before, during, and after her time.

ƴ Gary Kelly's essay, "Jane Austen, Romantic Feminism, and Civil Society," distinguishes among kinds of feminism available in Austen's day: Enlightenment, "bluestocking," Sentimental, and Revolutionary feminisms. Defining "civil society" as "a network of relations existing between subjectivity and domesticity on one hand and the state on the other," Kelly demonstrates how Austen's writings provide a specifically feminized version of civil society. In readings of each of her novels, Kelly finds Austen critical of Romantic feminisms; he also argues that her novels contain elements that could be seen as feminist, in that they "emplot a reconstruction of civil society for the Revolutionary aftermath, centered critically on the role of women." Throughout his essay, Kelly accounts for the "field of conflict" into which any "feminism" must be exercised.

In her "'Invention Is What Delights Me': Jane Austen's Remaking of 'English' History," Antoinette Burton investigates Austen's early foray into history writing. Using the well-known but less-often-examined piece from Austen's Juvenilia, *The History of England From the Reign of Henry IV to the Death of Charles I*, Burton compares Austen's production to Oliver Goldsmith's. Her essay looks particularly to each author's representations of women and to the politics of history writing. Burton sees Austen's history as a "collaborative feminist text" that "plays with the question of what happens when a historian reveals herself as a gendered subject deeply invested in the project of unmasking history *and* history-writing both as the exclusive domains of men." Finally, Burton discusses the ways in which we might deem such a project "feminist" today.

Clifford Siskin's "Jane Austen and the Engendering of Disciplinarity" hypothesizes that Austen poses not just an individual enigma but a disciplinary one, tied to historicizing our understandings of "Literature." He argues that the discipline ("English") that, during the nineteenth century, took the newly restricted category of literature as its field of knowledge was "founded in an extraordinary act—in scope and in speed—of gendered exclusion and forgetting." Likening what he calls the "Great Forgetting" to F. R. Leavis's "Great Tradition," Siskin focuses on market and on genre—on "the mode of publication" (specifically considering Austen's relation to periodical publication) and "the mode of writing." He concludes that Austen's writings were valued for their levels of "comfort," for "taming" the threat of writing, and thus they helped to turn writing into a discipline, concomitantly entailing the disciplinary disappearance of many women writers.

Laura Mooneyham White's "Jane Austen and the Marriage Plot: Questions of Persistence" argues that "the marriage plot persists in the fictive imagination for some compelling reasons." While acknowledging that feminist attacks on the marriage plot in Austen are in some ways well justified, Mooneyham White suggests that feminist critics might benefit from "seeing beyond the historical and cultural dimensions to marriage." Using structuralist and psychoanalytic approaches provides us with another way into the element of marriage in Austen's novels. Mooneyham White's essay explores a range of Austen's novels, ending with extended consideration of her unfinished *Sanditon*. She suggests that a feminist reinterpretation of the marriage plot, based on its persistence, is in order.

In Jocelyn Harris's "Jane Austen and the Burden of the (Male) Past: The Case Reexamined," we are provided with an extended critique of Gilbert and Gubar's readings of Austen. Harris argues that applying the oedipal model to Austen is "anachronistic and unhelpful" and that we might understand

Austen's responses to her predecessors as more eroticized than violent. She sees Austen as drawing on male and female authors alike, though particularly from Milton, Richardson, Shakespeare, and Chaucer. Following the critical lead of Anne Mellor, Harris argues that Austen "regenders" Romantic ideas. According to Harris, Austen "re-visions the entire history of Western culture when she denies its traditional assumptions that women are vain, inconstant, necessarily mute, ignorant, and unequal." Rather than seeing Austen as a victim of the past, Harries argues for an Austen who places herself proudly within a great tradition of literature and who "shows herself even more congenial to feminists than we knew."

Austen's gender politics in relationships based on fraternal qualities are Glenda Hudson's focus in "Consolidated Communities: Masculine and Feminine Values in Austen's Fiction." Drawing on sociohistorical work investigating networks of kinship and affinity, Hudson sees Austen's novels in relation to other eighteenth-century novels that present endogamous unions. The fantasy of incest is prevalent in earlier novels, and Austen both draws on and refashions this motif, according to Hudson. She sees Austen's endogamous relations as "microcosmic paradigms of her aesthetic and moral vision" and suggests that feminist critics have unfortunately overlooked these aspects to concentrate on political and economic realities instead. Hudson offers historical reasons for such a focus, suggesting that Austen's "depiction of symmetrical, concordant sibling relations may be viewed as a means to restore the vitality of the home or the estate during a time of transition and moral chaos." She concludes by discussing Austen's inadvertent contributions to restrictive Victorian formulations of the "angel in the house."

Diane Hoeveler and Maria Jerinic consider *Northanger Abbey* with quite different critical aims and ends. Hoeveler's essay, "Vindicating *Northanger Abbey*: Wollstonecraft, Austen, and Gothic Feminism," looks at Austen's novel as a fictionalization of Wollstonecraft's treatise *A Vindication of the Rights of Woman*. Hoeveler sees Wollstonecraft as the inventor of "gothic feminism"— a form of feminism that sees women as morally superior and that encourages passive aggression, that creates "willing victims" who expect to be rewarded for their suffering. Austen, however, both constructed and deconstructed gothic feminism, according to Hoeveler. *Northanger Abbey* provides a blank-slate heroine (Catherine Morland) who "needs" to be educated at the hands of a man (Henry Tilney). The novel suggests an Austen who "was as attracted to the potential for evil in life as she was compelled to finally deny its power and allure" and who wanted to be "one of the boys." Hoeveler's essay illustrates Austen's ambivalence toward the gothic tradition and its feminist permutations.

Though she agrees with Hoeveler about Catherine's status as "everywoman" and with the power of writing in *Northanger Abbey*, Maria Jerinic's essay, "In Defense of the Gothic: Rereading *Northanger Abbey*," provides us with a quite different version of Austen and feminism. Viewing *Northanger Abbey* against the backdrop of the transformation to print culture and the "moral corruption" of novels, Jerinic sees an Austen who celebrates the figure of the reading woman rather than condemning print technology or textually induced moral corruption for women. Austen, according to Jerinic, exhibits instead "a discomfort with men and conversations about reading with them." In Jerinic's reading of *Northanger Abbey*, Catherine reads texts and situations astutely and resists the words of men who would mold her (but also on occasion gives in). Comparing *Northanger Abbey* to Radcliffe's *The Mysteries of Udolpho*, Jerinic, like Hoeveler, sees the gothic novel as providing critics with ambiguities. Jerinic concludes, however, that Austen's novel provides a strong social critique of the eighteenth-century positioning of the female reader.

Ellen Gardiner's and Misty G. Anderson's essays on *Mansfield Park* investigate the role of Fanny's voice and use of language in that novel, but from there their arguments diverge. For Gardiner, *Mansfield Park* is of interest as an example of the "power relationships that develop between women as writers and as readers, and the institutions that reduce their options and make them marginal, especially in the field of letters." In her essay, "Privacy, Privilege, and 'Poaching' in *Mansfield Park*," Gardiner uses the theories of Michel de Certeau to see Fanny as a "poacher"—that is, as someone who "learns to use for her own ends and gain the education she is provided." Gardiner argues for a Fanny who is an adept literary critic, "a nomad who travels across the linguistic and moral fields of the Bertram circle of actors." Both Fanny and Austen, Gardiner concludes, make use of the "privileges of privacy" to gain their society's sanction as readers. She suggests that the new direction for Austen studies lies in a cultural studies approach to her writings.

Misty G. Anderson's "'The Different Sorts of Friendship': Desire in *Mansfield Park*" turns to the writings of Eve Kosofsky Sedgwick and others to discuss the "remarkable ways in which Mary and Fanny are drawn to one another." Historicizing the term "lesbian" and investigating the ways in which same-sex attractions were textualized in Austen's day, Anderson argues for a reading of *Mansfield Park* that recognizes the homoerotic potential just beneath the surface. Anderson suggests that such desires, such "friendships," threaten social and narrative convention, and that attraction to another woman cannot be articulated directly—especially by a woman writer. Her essay argues that Austen could not have carried that homoerotic plot any further than she did, though women's desire remains part of the palimpsestic quality of Austen's text. Anderson's work illustrates the ways in which "queer theory" might be used productively to further and perhaps overturn feminist insights about Austen's writings.

All of the essays included here show that both "Austen" and "feminism" are very much alive as critical terms that deserve further conversation. At a time when a book titled *Who Stole Feminism?* is getting a lot of press, it is worth troubling over precisely what "feminism" is and does as a contemporary and a historical concept. Various discourses of feminism have co-existed (though not always peacefully), as a look at the debates of either the early nineteenth century or the late twentieth century will show. Most feminists, however, have spent some of their energies exposing the inadequacies and partiality of those who claim objectivity, a project that Austen seemed to share. Our projects cannot begin and end with Austen, of course. Feminists—concerned with the ways women have been and are still devalued and caricatured in literature and in life—must continue to articulate how we got where we are today and where we hope to move in the future. Reassessing questions of Austen's relation to feminist discourses (historically and currently) reveals this articulation to be sometimes more simple but usually more difficult than we may formerly have thought.

Jane Austen and Discourses of Feminism puts itself firmly in the middle of today's debates and concerns in order to provide readers of Austen—and those who study British Romanticism or women's literature more generally—with a sourcebook for new research on Austen and feminist studies. Such a sourcebook is not, to be sure, the "last word." History writing, as Catherine Morland naively suggests in *Northanger Abbey*, may be made up of partially rendered truths. Our ability to speak about the histories of gender politics in partial truths, however, should not stop our conversations; it should spur them on. After all, how we see feminism in history has everything to do with how we see the "evolution" of feminist studies, of Austen studies, and, ultimately, of their respective (and, I trust, productive) futures.

Notes

1. Park Honan, *Jane Austen: Her Life* (London: Weidenfeld and Nicholson, 1987), 417-18.
2. June Dwyer, *Jane Austen* (New York: Continuum, 1989).
3. Janet Todd, "Jane Austen, Politics, and Sensibility," in *Feminist Criticism: Theory and Practice*, ed. Susan Sellers (Toronto: University of Toronto Press, 1991), 71.

4. Alistair M. Duckworth, "Jane Austen and the Conflict of Interpretations," in *Jane Austen: New Perspectives*, ed. Janet Todd (New York: Holmes and Meier, 1983), 39-52. See also Alistair Duckworth, "Jane Austen and the Construction of a Progressive Author," *College English* 53, no. 1 (1991): 77-90.

5. Claudia Johnson, "Rev. of John Wiltshire's *Jane Austen and the Body: 'The Picture of Health,'*" *Nineteenth-Century Literature* 48, no. 4 (1994): 532.

6. Johnson, "Rev.," 532.

7. See Marilyn Butler, *Jane Austen and the War of Ideas* (Oxford: Clarendon Press, 1975) and her *Romantics, Rebels, and Reactionaries: English Literature and Its Backgrounds, 1760–1830* (Oxford: Oxford University Press, 1981).

8. Felix Mnthali, "The Stranglehold of English Lit.," in *Literature: The Human Experience.*, ed. Richard Abcarian and Marvin Klotz, 6th ed. (New York: St. Martin's Press, 1994), 493. Many scholars have taken up questions of colonialism in Austen and in British literature more generally since Mnthali's poem was penned. The writings of Meenakshi Mukherjee, Suvendrini Perera, and Maaja Stewart come to mind.

9. Juliet Mitchell, *Women: The Longest Revolution* (London: Virago), 1984. Thanks to Susan Groag Bell for her formulation of this comparison in her remarks, "Letters as Literature in Eighteenth-Century France and England," presented at the Western Association of Women Historians' Conference, San Marino, CA, Huntington Library, 30 May 1992.

10. Dale Spender, *Mothers of the Novel: 100 Good Writers Before Jane Austen* (London: Pandora Press, 1986).

11. Todd, "Jane Austen," 71.

12. The *OED* shows that in its earliest use (1851), the word "feminism" signified "the qualities of females." The definition of feminism as "advocacy of the rights of women (based on the theory of equality of the sexes)" emerges in the *Athenaeum* in 1895. It is interesting to note that an 1882 definition of feminism involved "the development of female secondary sexual characteristics in a male."

13. Todd, "Jane Austen," 71.

14. See Mary Poovey, *The Proper Lady and the Woman Writer: Ideology as Style in the Works of Mary Wollstonecraft, Mary Shelley, and Jane Austen* (Chicago: University of Chicago Press, 1984) and Sandra M. Gilbert and Susan Gubar, *Madwoman in the Attic: The Woman Writer and the Nineteenth-Century Literary Imagination* (New Haven, CT: Yale University Press, 1979).

15. Christine Marshall, "'Dull Elves' and Feminists: A Summary of Feminist Criticism of Jane Austen," *Persuasions* 14 (1992): 41.

16. See Virginia Woolf, *The Common Reader: First Series*, ed. Andrew McNeillie (New York: Harcourt Brace Jovanovich, 1984), 144-45.

17. Elaine Showalter, *A Literature of Their Own: British Women Novelists from Brontë to Lessing* (Princeton, NJ: Princeton University Press, 1977), 102.

18. LeRoy W. Smith, *Jane Austen and the Drama of Womanhood* (New York: St. Martin's Press, 1983), 19.

19. See Margaret Kirkham, "Jane Austen and Contemporary Feminism," in *The Jane Austen Companion* ed. J. David Grey (New York: Macmillan, 1986), 157, as well as her *Jane Austen: Feminism and Fiction* (Totowa, NJ: Barnes & Noble, 1983).

20. Claudia Johnson, *Jane Austen: Women, Politics, and the Novel* (Chicago: University of Chicago Press, 1988), and Alison G. Sulloway, *Jane Austen and the Province of Womanhood* (Philadelphia: University of Pennsylvania Press, 1989).

21. Mary Evans, *Jane Austen and the State* (London: Tavistock Publications, 1987).

22. Deborah Kaplan, *Jane Austen Among Women* (Baltimore: Johns Hopkins University Press, 1992).

23. John Halperin, "Rev. of Deborah Kaplan's *Jane Austen Among Women*," *Nineteenth-Century Literature* 48, no. 1 (1993): 99.

24. Jane Austen, *Northanger Abbey and Persuasion*, vol. 5 of *The Novels of Jane Austen*, ed. R. W. Chapman, 3d ed. (London: Oxford University Press, 1932 - 34). Subsequent references are cited parenthetically in the text as *NA*.

25. I do not mean to suggest that issues of gender are separable from issues of genre. On the contrary, critics today see them as intimately linked. I only mean to suggest that perhaps Austen's primary goal was not to suture them in her references to fellow female authors—that her interests were primarily that of a novelist among novelists (as she would have it) rather than as a woman among women.

26. Edward Said, "Jane Austen and Empire," in *Raymond Williams: Critical Perspectives*, ed. Terry Eagleton (Boston: Northeastern University Press, 1989), 161.

I

Changing Histories

1

Jane Austen, Romantic Feminism, and Civil Society

Gary Kelly

Recent years have seen much discussion of Jane Austen's feminism, its nature, degree, and relation to present-day feminist concerns.[1] My contribution to this debate assumes that feminism is always socially and historically particular, advancing the rights and claims of women within specific historical, social, and cultural conditions.[2] Thus if Austen were considered a feminist, it would be by her participating in a feminism of her time, and not of ours. I argue that Austen was a feminist in this sense: she participated in a feminism conditioned by the circumstances of what has come to be called the Romantic period, and she did so by addressing one of the central concerns of at least the early part of that period. This was the role of women in creating and sustaining civil society in the aftermath of a political, social, and cultural cataclysm. I advance this argument first by outlining the rise of "civil society" in the social theory and practice of Enlightenment and Sensibility. I go on to describe the feminism created to address concerns that dominated culture and politics until the 1820s, if not longer, and especially the class-based reconstruction of civil society in the aftermath of Revolutionary cataclysm. I then show how Austen's novels participate in this form of feminism.

"The rise of civil society" was a central theme of Enlightenment political thought, social theory, and critical historiography.[3] In general terms, civil society was represented as a network of relations existing between subjectivity and domesticity on one hand and the state on the other, and mediating between these spheres. It was represented as the field of operations for the autonomous and independent individual, or the modern economic and political agent—that is, the agent no longer bound by tradition. It was seen as a society governed by law and social convention, or "civility," rather than by violence and main force. Civil society was also portrayed as the transformation of feudalism in the "progress of civilization," or economic, social, and cultural modernization.[4] Conceived primarily in masculine terms, it was to serve what were understood to be the character, needs, activities, and interests of men. Yet women were supposed to have a central role in its development, mostly by leading men into society through their "natural" desire for female company and, once men had joined such society, by "polishing" their otherwise rough and too-masculine manners. ("Manners" here meant the entire range of social practice, and not just social etiquette.)[5] Though this relationship was couched in terms of gender, it had obvious and predominant, if mostly unstated, implications in terms of class by excluding, as "savagery" and "barbarism," both residual elements of feudal aristocratic culture and "uncivilized" elements of plebeian culture and sociality.

The class basis of "civil society" was complex. Enlightenment social theorists posited civil society as mixed, informal, and "polite." Enlightenment "philosophical historians" assigned this society a lineage going back through Renaissance court culture to feudal and chivalric culture. This was an aristocratic culture. Its incorporation in models and practices of civil society could be seen as either dependent emulation or critical *embourgeoisement*, or something of both. Enlightenment histories of feudalism and chivalry and the "rise of civil society" offer a critique of medieval feudalism and chivalry as oppressive and irrational.[6] Yet they also appropriate chivalry by redefining it in terms of contemporary upper middle-class culture, as elevated subjectivity, or nobility of soul, and gentrified "manners," or social relations. This redefinition eventually took the form of what Mark Girouard calls "the return to Camelot," or the Romantic and Victorian ideology of the "gentleman" (and "lady").[7]

The idea of civil society was a form of the social imaginary, enabling the constitution of an "imagined community," but there were also material institutions and practices of civil society.[8] In the mid-eighteenth century these institutions and practices were mostly for men, and included academic and professional clubs, coffeehouse society, associations such as the Freemasons, and socializing at meetings for local government, church management, or administration of the justice system. Mixed-society counterparts developed in the public spaces and events associated with these operations of the state apparatus and in public social spaces at health spas or tourist resorts, where members of the "political nation," or those directly implicated in government and the state, mixed with their professional middle-class associates and agents. Also important, however, especially in intellectual and cultural life, were the mixed-society counterparts of male civil society that developed in half-public, half-domestic spaces including visiting circles, salons, coteries, correspondence networks, and the so-called bluestocking clubs. All but the last of these provide the settings for the late eighteenth-century novel of manners, including Austen's novels, which might therefore be considered novels of the specifically feminized aspect of civil society.

Toward the latter part of the century many of these coteries tended to be socially and culturally progressive. One of their leading traits was suspension of courtly ritual and formality and the rights and prerogatives of rank, so that those of different classes but entitled to be considered "gentlemen" and "ladies" could associate on equal footing, with emphasis on common rather than divergent or conflicting interests. Increasingly, then, such practices of civil society facilitated development of middle-class identity and interests against a state dominated by the upper classes and their emulators in other classes. Another implicitly oppositional trait of these practices was that through them, women were ostensibly accepted on equal social and intellectual terms with men, thereby rejecting what were seen as the trivialization and eroticization of women in court society and culture.

Furthermore, such practices of civil society facilitated dissemination of the culture of Sensibility—a feminized development of the Enlightenment, circulating Europe-wide by the later eighteenth century. In Britain, Sensibility had strong support in the provinces and among marginalized social groups such as religious Dissenters. The Lichfield circle around the leading Sentimental poet Anna Seward, for example, had connections with the Midlands Enlightenment based in Birmingham and such major centers of Dissenting education and intellectual culture as the Warrington academy. On the other hand, Sensibility was seen by some rather as a transmuted and disguised form of courtly aristocratic culture, displacing social identity of ascribed rank and status to subjective identity, in a discourse of merit.

More important, after 1789 the social critique of the Enlightenments and the more belletristic culture of Sensibility were claimed or blamed as inspirations for both the French Revolution and British reform movements. In addition, political unrest seemed centered in forms of civil society, especially clubs with overt or indirect political aims, open to middle- and lower-class men and—more scandalously—sometimes to women.[9] Forms of civil society hitherto relatively apolitical, such as provincial "literary and philosophical" societies, became politicized by the Revolution debate. The implication of ideas and forms of civil society in Revolutionary conflict then caused them to suffer from the reaction against the Revolution, especially in various counter-Revolutionary conspiracy theories. In the Revolutionary aftermath, forms of civil society ranging from Freemasonry to "bluestocking" assemblies were discredited by their association with Revolutionary insubordination and violence.[10] So too were related movements, such as Revolutionary feminism, which was a feminism designed to address the debate on the French Revolution and its consequences for Britain.

This discrediting of certain forms of civil society had several consequences. First was the construction of a coalition of gentry and upper middle class, based in renewed kinds of civil society and designed to stand apart from both courtly civil society and plebeian and lower middle-class forms of civil society. It is the construction of this form of civil society that Austen represents in her novels. Another consequence was government-sponsored proscription and harassment of the plebeian and petty bourgeois forms of politicized civil society, together with the closer self-policing and censoring of upper- and middle-class forms of civil society, with more formal organizational structures, overt links to established authority, and banning of certain topics, especially politics and religion. Secular forms of civil society were displaced by formal organizations under the aegis of religious Evangelicals both inside and outside the established church. A domestic, aestheticized, and intellectualized form of civil society developed in the cultural movement later called Romanticism (of which Pantisocracy was one version).[11] This contribution to the renewal of civil society was also represented in Austen's novels, though critically and selectively. Finally, there was increased policing of social boundaries, with greater separation of the classes and sexes, including renewed emphasis on the restriction of women to the domestic and local spheres. Austen's novels engage critically with this development too, and from a perspective that can be construed as feminist in terms of the possibilities of the moment.

Thus ideas and practices of civil society were extended and made overtly political during the Revolutionary crisis and were ostensibly depoliticized and subjected to greater regulation in the Revolutionary aftermath. In this process women were paradoxically restricted to domesticity and thus virtually excluded from the kinds of civil society imagined by Enlightenment social theorists and practiced in Sentimental culture and moderate Revolutionary coteries, such as those of the Girondins in Paris or the Godwin circle in London. Yet in such influential post-Revolutionary polemics as Hannah More's *Strictures on the Modern System of Female Education* (1799) women were also called to heroic defense of the "national" culture, identity, and destiny within and from the ideological and cultural bastion of the home.[12] Woman (hypostatized and made transcendent and transhistorical, as the general noun indicates) was made the presiding genius of a domain outside a public sphere now characterized as antidomestic, of a domain figured as the source and inspiration for reform of extradomestic civil society and the public and political sphere.[13] As with the pre-Revolutionary culture of Sensibility, women writers were quick to seize this opportunity to enter the public sphere and civil society under cover of pursuing their conventional areas of exper- tise, though now they were more careful to maintain their cover by insisting on the predominance of their *domestic* identity, knowledge, and role.

This move, in which Austen was but one of many participants, was feminist in a particular sense, though one that may seem merely feminist today. If feminism in a general sense is advocacy of the rights and claims of women (but feminisms are always historically specific), one could argue that there were Enlightenment, "bluestocking," Sentimental, and Revolutionary feminisms, conditioned by yet intervening in their particular historical circumstances. Like other movements of its time, Romantic feminism ad- dressed a post-Revolutionary situation, but in ways appropriate to women's interests. First, Romantic feminists subsumed elements of the Revolutionary feminism of the 1790s led by Mary Wollstonecraft and Mary Hays. Though Romantic feminists abandoned Revolutionary feminists' claims for women's direct participation in the public and political sphere, they continued their predecessors' critique of court culture and the courtization of women and repeated their call for greater access by women to technologies of the self, or disciplines of subjectivity (then encoded as "reason" and "virtue"), thought necessary for men but not for women because men had to face the rigors of professional life in the public sphere, whereas women did not. Second, Romantic feminists addressed the post-Revolutionary crisis in social rela- tions, national unity, economy, culture, and empire by specifying a strong, even central, role for women, working directly only in the domestic and local spheres, but indirectly in the wider public and political sphere. It was here that Romantic feminists contributed to the post-Revolutionary reconstruc- tion of civil society. Third, Romantic feminists retrieved some of the gains made by women in Sensibility's feminization of culture. This act of retrieval unfortunately left much women's literary work open to charges of "sentimen- talism" in the remasculinization of culture and literature that became the dominant strain in Romanticism—and in interpretations of Romanticism down to the present. Finally, by participating in post-Revolutionary attempts to repair Revolutionary disruption of society, culture, and discourse, Roman- tic feminists mediated between pre-Revolutionary feminisms and such later forms as Victorian "women's mission" feminism.

Austen's attitude toward this Romantic feminism was necessarily a critical one because of her ideological, cultural, and social commitment to the established church, the established professional middle class, and the dominant class, the landed gentry. These institutions had been strongly challenged during the Revolution debate and continued to be challenged by those aspects of Romantic culture that subsumed elements of Revolutionary critique. Thus Austen's attitude to Romantic culture and to Romantic feminism was critical in the sense of being analytical, evaluative, and selective. For one thing, her novels reject or even attack aspects of the post-Revolutionary sublation of Sensibility. This fact helped her work survive the Romantic remasculinization of culture and literature and allowed her to be claimed, then and later, as an antiRomantic.[14] Her novels also avoid the post-Revolutionary feminization—through novelization and popularization—of discourses otherwise gendered "masculine," including historiography, philosophy, theology, and science. Her novels avoid formal and stylistic claims to originality and "genius," thereby rejecting an important post-Revolutionary device for aestheticizing the political. Similarly, Austen's novels offer no representations of excessive and transgressive selfhood, and they eschew temporal and spatial exoticism to insist on domestic and quotidian settings and relationships, thereby producing the effect of "realism" for which her novels became celebrated in nineteenth- and twentieth-century criticism. In fact, Austen's novels purposely look rather old-fashioned for the 1810s, like a reprise of the pre-Revolutionary novel of manners but purged of "sensibility" and reduced in social and cultural scope to accord with a post-Revolutionary aesthetic of retrenchment and consolidation (opposed to a post-Revolutionary and "romantic" aesthetic of extravagance, excess, and "gusto"). Then there is her use of narratorial irony, a device considered antithetical both to "sentimental" and "romantic" modes and to revolutionary enthusiasm and overstatement.

Yet Austen's novels, like much post-Revolutionary women's writing, do contain elements that could be seen as feminist.[15] They protest, however mutedly, against the social, legal, and economic injustice of male primogeniture, restriction of women's property rights, and female economic dependence. They show, however indirectly, how courtly culture trivializes and eroticizes women, leaving them with little alternative access to power but through intrigue and coquetry, and with few personal resources beyond indolence, immediate self-gratification, and self-centeredness. Austen's novels do criticize the too-active female, thereby following the line of conservative eighteenth-century conduct books for women—books reprinted in the 1790s as a counter-Revolutionary move. But they also illustrate the limits of passivity, a "female virtue" widely celebrated in the earlier conduct books and newly emphasized and glorified in post-Revolutionary domestic ideology.

More important, however, Austen is one of many women writers to represent an important or central role for women of the upper middle classes in a specifically post-Revolutionary model of civil society. This model is more domestic, local, and rural than public and metropolitan and comprises a dialectic and coalition of gentry and upper middle class—the class to which Austen and most of her readers belonged. Like those readers, Austen had good opportunity to become acquainted, at least indirectly, with earlier ideas of civil society. It is true that these ideas had been developed mainly in the Scottish, French, and English Nonconformist Enlightenments, which were different from and partly opposed to the established church that shaped Austen's ideology, culture, and social experience. But a "progressive" element in Anglicanism did support social, economic, and institutional modernization of a kind called for by the Enlightenments. Furthermore, in the Revolutionary aftermath, this kind of progressive Anglicanism could offer continuity with the past, suturing Revolutionary disruption while avoiding association with Enlightenment ideas of civil society, now contaminated by Revolutionary associations, and with Anglican Evangelicalism, now aggressively pursuing embourgeoisement of church, state, and society. More important, ideas of civil society had become widely diffused among the gentry and professional middle class through forms of print including books and magazines, but especially novels, and particularly the novel of manners that was Austen's chosen form of fiction.

Austen's version of post-Revolutionary civil society was carefully constructed to avoid association with other versions discredited during the 1790s by association with French Revolutionary politics and the politics promoted by such groups as English Dissenters, middle- and lower-class sympathizers with the French Revolution, and Revolutionary feminists. Accordingly, Austen's novels represent a version of civil society residing in the domestic, local, feminized spheres, embodying a proto-Romantic English nationalism, and underwritten by central principles of Anglican theology. This post-Revolutionary idea of civil society is represented clearly in the novel Austen finished during the early Revolutionary aftermath. In *Northanger Abbey*, sold to a publisher in 1802 but not published until after Austen's death, Henry Tilney rebukes Catherine Morland for her gothic imaginings:

"Dear Miss Morland, consider the dreadful nature of the suspicions you have entertained. What have you been judging from? Remember the country and the age in which we live. Remember that we are English, that we are Christians. Consult your own understanding, your own sense of the probable, your own observation of what is passing around you—Does our education prepare us for such atrocities? Do our laws connive at them? Could they be perpetrated without being known, in a country like this, where social and literary intercourse is on such a footing, where every man is surrounded by a neighbourhood of voluntary spies, and where roads and newspapers lay every thing open? Dearest Miss Morland, what ideas have you been admitting?" (197-98)[16]

The passage presents a prescription for post-Revolutionary civil society that echoes leading counter-Revolutionary arguments still fresh from the political and cultural debates of the 1790s. It insists on the "national" character of civil society ("we are English") and argues that it is based in Christian ethics, is secured by the law, is guaranteed by social convention and surveillance ("neighbourhood of voluntary spies"), is diffused by material forms of modernization ("roads and newspapers"), is incompatible with "ideas" of other kinds of social reality, especially the "atrocities" that Revolutionary sympathizers attributed to the *ancien regime* in France and to courtly society in Britain, is extended locally and nationally (from "neighbourhood" to "newspapers"), and above all is constructed in cultural and social interaction of particular kinds ("social and literary intercourse").

The foundation of civil society in the "natural" power and position of the gentry, reinforced by the merit of the professional middle class, is illustrated more fully in *Sense and Sensibility*, which was probably written in its first form just at the point in the mid-1790s when the intense and divisive Revolution debate was giving way to the search for post-Revolutionary forms of mediation. The novel uses a familiar device of didactic, moralistic fiction—the contrasting sisters—to illustrate the danger to self and society of excessive sensibility, or reliance on "instinct," feeling, or "genius" (as unique subjectivity), rather than "sense." The novel also uses disciplined subjectivity as the basis for properly ethical conduct, ranging from social interchange to choice of a marriage partner, in quotidian as well as permanent forms of civil society. But most readers at that time, whether when the novel was first written or when it was first published, would know that "sense" and "sensibility" were also recurring figures in the Revolution debate, as writers both for and against the Revolution evinced their sensibility, or moral and intellectual sensitivity, in order to authorize their political arguments.[17] Like Frances Burney's *Camilla* (1796), written at around the same time, *Sense and Sensibility* declines to make overt political connections, and in any case was probably revised before being published in 1811. Characteristically, it takes terms that had had currency in the Revolution debate and deploys them exclusively at the local, domestic level of experience, thereby suggesting that this is the basic, foundational level of social experience and of a stable yet open social order. *Sense and Sensibility* is also post-Revolutionary in emphasizing the dangers posed to civil society by residual elements of court culture, ranging from male and female "gallantry" (Lucy Steele and Willoughby) to material selfishness (Mrs. Jennings). The closure of the novel represents, in the unions of Elinor and Edward Ferrars and Marianne and Colonel Brandon, the confirmation and renewal of civil society based on the integration of gentry and professional middle class centered in domestic life and spreading over the country in a network as a civil society should do, countering the socially disruptive decadence and selfishness represented by most of the other characters and couples. That this network may seem a fragile security for civil society reflects the continuing crisis of national political confidence in the early 1810s.

In *Pride and Prejudice* an apparently stable civil society, again predominantly rural in location, is revealed to be dangerously vulnerable to disruption because of complacencies produced by that stability. Mr. Bennet's social values and practices clearly represent the best of an intellectualized or professionalized gentry, but he has been insufficiently attentive to the necessity of ensuring a stable succession of those values and practices. He has given in to courtly gallantry in choosing a merely beautiful wife, who accordingly behaves like a merely courtly woman, intriguing for her family's social advance and therefore meddling in matters beyond her intellectual and moral capacity. Mr. Bennet has also allowed his family's destiny to be overtaken by the accidents of mortality. Having produced only daughters when his estate is entailed on a male heir, his neglect of these daughters' moral and intellectual education opens the moral, political, economic, and national order that his family estate represents to disruption or subversion by other inadequate social elements. These include the courtly gallantry of Wickham, the middle-class emulativeness and toadying of Mr. Collins, the *nouveau-riche* class sensitivity and unassertiveness of Bingley and ambition and snobbery of his sister, and the courtly arrogance of Darcy and Lady Catherine de Bourgh. Significantly, the failures of these elements are repaired partly by an alliance of upper-class responsibility (in the chastened Darcy) and middle-class competence (the retired tradesman Mr. Gardiner), and partly by the tendency of the courtly and emulative to countermine themselves. (This was a cliché of 1790s literary critiques of courtliness, such as the gothic novels of Ann Radcliffe.) More significant in Austen's envisioning or revisioning of civil society is the way that this alliance of virtuous gentry and meritorious bourgeoisie is motivated by a woman—Elizabeth, who is admired and then loved by Darcy, apparently because she is also the intellectual and moral child of the Gardiners. Paradoxically, it is Elizabeth's merit, or her consciousness of it, that first leads her to reject Darcy, drawing forth his self-vindication, which in turn forces her to recognize the dangerous excess of her sense of self-worth. This excess is much smaller in scale but similar in kind to that of the men of merit who pushed through the Revolution in France and called for a revolution in Britain during the 1790s, confident of their own rightness—and "rights"—in the face of real or apparent upper-class arrogance like Darcy's.

Pride and Prejudice is not a novel of the 1790s, however. Like its predecessor, it was first written during the 1790s, and in its rewritten and published form it still bears marks of the anxieties about the ability of the old order to survive subversion by its own weaknesses. But these anxieties were revived in the period just before and when the notoriously courtly Prince of Wales, then widely thought to support new and disruptive forces of social and political ambition, assumed the regency in 1811, as Britain also faced renewed Revolutionary challenge in the form of Napoleonic imperialism. This was just the period in which Austen was rewriting her two manuscript novels of the 1790s for publication.

Mansfield Park more obviously addresses the question of the survival of a stable yet open civil society in the context of an apparent recrudescence, under the Regency, of the disastrous courtly decadence that had made possible the Revolution as a movement uniting socially disaffected and socially ambitious elements that had been unleashed by earlier and, to those like Austen, incorrect forms of civil society. The business of *Lovers' Vows* unites at once familiar representations of both court government and Revolution as merely theatrical, while giving particular emphasis to the novel's exhibition of how ambitious *parvenus*, from Mrs. Norris to the Crawfords, use the unsuspecting hospitality of the upper class to push their own interests in a way that disrupts a stable social order. (This was a favorite theme of English Anti-Jacobin novelists.) Sir Thomas Bertram's convenient absence, tending to his plantations in Antigua, serves to remind the reader of how the global crisis of empire during the engagement with Napoleonic France could distract "natural" authority from its weakness on the home front. At the same time, it is clear that Sir Thomas's first mistake was succumbing to courtliness by marrying mere beauty, for as in *Pride and Prejudice* this error allowed the introduction of forces of bourgeois ambition disruptive of a too-complacent and gentry-dominated civil society. The prospective match between Edmund Bertram and Mary Crawford raises the possibility of further weakening country-based civil society by detaching church from state (precisely one of the aims of Revolutionaries and their English sympathizers). The self-interested patronage by Henry Crawford of the noble young sailor William Price, in order to seduce Fanny Price's affections, represents the potentially powerful alliance of middle class and plebeian merit and ambition, while the growing appreciation of Fanny's merit by the inhabitants of Mansfield Park and the union of Fanny and Edmund represent the accession of merit to an established (or reestablished) order based on a coalition of gentry and professional middle class in an expressly English and Anglican civil society. This coalition was prefigured in Fanny's intellectual education by Edmund, in a neat reversal of the seduction-by-education at the center of Jean-Jacques Rousseau's *La Nouvelle Héloïse*, the most influential novel of Sensibility in European literature and a novel widely discussed, imitated, and condemned during the 1790s and 1800s for its protorevolutionary influence, especially on women readers and young readers of either sex.[18] Austen was, of course, not the first writer to use the novel to counter the supposedly disruptive effect of certain novels, or of novels in general.

Emma returns to the dangerous saliency of the overconfident woman, though Emma Woodhouse has the social and material standing that Elizabeth Bennet lacks, while lacking the intellectual if not moral merit of the latter. Emma's interference in the civil society of Hartfield is motivated by a paradoxical combination of the same upper-class arrogance that many blamed for arousing Revolutionary resistance and the same self-generated bourgeois enterprise that Burke had condemned as the disruptive driving force of the Revolutionaries in France and their sympathizers in Britain. By contrast Mr. Knightley, her mentor, then lover, and eventually husband, clearly understands civil society as a socially cohesive practice, based on estate management, directing the dominant class to proper exercise of their power in the interests of all classes and thus of social stability, continuity, and prosperity. He also understands the importance of women to this form of civil society, as wives and domestic managers, seen in his concern to find a proper match for his tenant and eventually for himself, in his appreciation of the merits of Jane Fairfax and his contempt for the courtly fecklessness of Frank Churchill, and in his concern that Emma exercise her social leadership in proper ways.

Nowhere in Austen's œuvre, however, is the need for reconstruction of civil society in a post-Revolutionary context, and the importance of women to that reconstruction, more sharply presented than in *Persuasion*. The upper class's arrogance, shallowness, improvidence, and susceptibility to manipulation by ambitious upstarts are made clear in the novel's first chapter and reiterated at key points in the course of the novel, such as the concert scene at Bath. More damaging still is the upper class's inability to recognize useful merit, not only in class outsiders, but within its own ranks. This failing is found not only in the vain and unintellectual, such as Sir Walter Elliot, but also in the apparently humane and discriminating, such as Lady Russell. The civil society practiced by these people is typically courtly—formal, hierarchical, superficial, theatrical, emulative, alienating, and dangerously vulnerable to infiltration and subversion by ambitious intriguers such as Mrs. Clay and William Walter Elliot. By contrast, the civil society practiced by the novel's model professional people—the naval officers and their wives and fiancées—is informal, egalitarian, genteelly intellectual, candid, inclusive, and discriminating. What Austen does not have to point out to readers of the 1810s is that these are also the heroes of Britain's resistance to Revolution militant, despite the notorious incompetence and corruption of Britain's upper-class leaders. What she does point out is that the naval society is about to renew, strengthen, and stabilize Britain's social order by assuming their place among the historic ruling class, with the financial proceeds of their military heroism—shares from the sale of captured French ships. Perhaps surprisingly, Austen also insists that the civil society of the navy people includes women, if not as equals then as essential supports in their domestic role, not only on land but even at sea, as in the case of the Crofts.

Thus all of Austen's novels emplot a reconstruction of civil society for the Revolutionary aftermath, centered critically on the role of women. This centering is not emplotted but represented structurally in Austen's chosen narrative mode—third-person centered narration with extensive use of "free indirect discourse," or reported inward speech and thought of the protagonist. The protagonist is a young woman moving from parental family world to her own "establishment" in society as a wife, or agent in the reproduction and maintenance of local civil society from her base in the home. For Austen, as for many post-Revolutionary social critics, that sphere was the foundational unit of nation, state, and empire. The protagonist's reproduction of civil society is not depicted in the novel but rather prefigured in the crucial act of the plot—the protagonist's choice of (or comical stumbling upon) a husband. This is the major ethical choice of her life, but only one of many that constitute agency in civil society lived daily, at the local level (thereby bypassing demands for constitutional and institutional change). The protagonist is only a figure, however; for a man could as easily read himself into her, as we know many have. Thus the protagonist's situation speaks to all members of the novel-reading classes, who were precisely those faced with the task of reconstructing civil society in the Revolutionary aftermath. Ultimately, Austen's dramatization of this situation is based on the Arminian theology of her liberal Anglicanism, with its stress on both true faith and good works, and the necessary connection between the two, as the path to salvation.

Austen dramatizes the protagonist's qualification to refound civil society by subjecting her to a crucial exercise in what might be called social reading. This exercise involves the mental operations described by Henry Tilney in his rebuke to Catherine Morland: observing, remembering, considering, having a sense of the probable, consulting the understanding, entertaining, judging. Significantly, though unobtrusively, in Austen's novels the protagonist's success in this exercise is shown to be commensurate with her degree of experience in reading books, as well as in reading society and herself. The exercise is crucial in that it is the precondition for successful negotiation between social expectation and personal desire—those of others as well as of the protagonist herself. Thus, in a move characteristic of Romantic literature, Austen displaces the site for originary production of civil society from the sociability of Enlightenment, Sentimental, and Revolutionary theory and practice to an educable subjectivity necessarily engaged in ethical practice in daily life. This is a readerly self because it is addressed to the professional middle class to which Austen herself belonged and whose identity, culture, and material prosperity were heavily dependent on reading of particular kinds. Implicitly, as Austen's readers would know well from the literature of the Revolution debate, and even before, the success or failure of the female social reader is a metaphor and metonymy for success or failure of readers of all kinds, for whole classes of readers. In the same way, success or failure of the reader at the personal, domestic, and local level is a metaphor and metonymy for success or failure at the national and imperial level. In an age of national and international crisis, such reading is clearly critical, in every sense of the word.

Yet Austen addresses the reading classes in a form—the novel—widely considered subversive of those classes' interests and by depicting the kind of reader—a woman—widely considered incapable of sustaining those interests if left to herself to do so. Significantly, Austen's immediate post-Revolutionary novel, *Northanger Abbey*, contains the best-known defense of novel-reading in English, in the narrator's outburst, "only a novel . . ." In using the novel to exemplify for the reading classes the basis of civil society in a reading process, Austen greatly furthered the cultural, aesthetic, and ideological reclamation of what had been considered a "feminine" and therefore subliterary form. This in itself could be seen as a feminist act. It also points to a major link between Austen and the Revolutionary feminists. The ability of and necessity for women to acquire intellectual training if domestic and social order were to be maintained was a central argument of Revolutionary feminism, set forth most clearly in Mary Wollstonecraft's *A Vindication of the Rights of Woman* (1792). Austen's staging of female reading and its relationship to domestic and local social stability, order, and continuity—to a civil society—is based on that argument and addresses post-Revolutionary concern with the role of women in reasserting and reforming civil society, based on a dialectic and coalition of landed gentry and upper middle class, dominated by the latter. This coalition assumed hegemony during the early nineteenth century and retained it into the twentieth century. Not surprisingly, its members made Austen a "classic," in the sense of a rereadable text, or a text that reproduces through rereading the conditions of its own production. Austen novelized these conditions in an acceptably "feminine" form of cultural and ideological work. Yet in doing so she both represented and exemplified the power of women to create and sustain civil society, if given appropriate opportunity to do so.

The problem for modern feminists is that Austen's vision of what is "appropriate" now seems contradictory. Like the Revolutionary feminists of the 1790s, Austen critiques court culture's trivialization of women and the marginalization of women under the property system of gentry capitalism. But like the counterfeminists of the Revolution debate and the Revolutionary aftermath, Austen also accepts the predominantly domestic and local roles of women. These roles were represented in late eighteenth- and early nineteenth-century political theory as important, or even essential to the creation and maintenance of civil society. Such a position can be seen as a feminism, like other feminisms conditioned by and addressed to particular social and historical circumstances. Informed by Anglican theology and in intense dialogue with the changing feminisms and ideas of civil society advanced during her time, Austen gave a powerful though not unique representation of this form of feminism. One task of feminist scholarship and criticism is to bring to the present, however defined, an understanding of how feminisms and counterfeminisms were constructed in a past, however defined, that has no meaning unless conceived as different from the present. In the recent revival and transformation of ideas of civil society in the aftermath of the Cold War and in post-Marxist theory, an important role has been assumed by and assigned to feminisms of various kinds. In this context, a historicist argument for Austen as a feminist within post-Revolutionary ideas of civil society should have interest and value. Thus Austen's feminism, like other feminisms of the past, is relevant to the present not directly but in the way it demonstrates how feminisms are constructed by individual and collective exercise of social, discursive, and artistic options within a structured yet open and changing field of social and cultural practice, a field that is also and always a field of conflict.

Notes

1. Notably in Margaret Kirkham, *Jane Austen, Feminism and Fiction* (Brighton, Sussex: Barnes & Noble, 1983); Alison Sulloway, *Jane Austen and the Province of Womanhood*

(Philadelphia: University of Pennsylvania Press, 1989); and Claudia L. Johnson, *Jane Austen: Women, Politics, and the Novel* (Chicago: University of Chicago Press, 1988).

2. For a recent account of contemporary materialist feminist practices, see Donna Landry and Gerald MacLean, *Materialist Feminisms* (Oxford: Blackwell, 1993).

3. For general accounts of Enlightenment theories of civil society, see Jean L. Cohen and Andrew Arato, *Civil Society and Political Theory* (Cambridge, MA: MIT Press, 1992).

4. On the civilizing process see, Norbert Elias, *The Court Society*, trans. Edmund Jephcott (Oxford: Blackwell, 1983).

5. See, for example, the account in David Hume's essay "Of the Rise and Progress of the Arts and Sciences," in *Essays: Moral, Political, and Literary*, ed. Eugene F. Miller, Rev. ed. (Indianapolis, IN: Liberty Classics, 1985).

6. See, for example, William Robertson's long prefatory essay to his *History of the Reign of Charles the Fifth, Emperor of Germany, and King of Spain* (1771).

7. Mark Girouard, *The Return to Camelot: Chivalry and the English Gentleman* (New Haven: Yale University Press, 1981).

8. Keith Tester, *Civil Society* (London: Routledge, 1992), chap. 1; Benedict Anderson, *Imagined Communities: Reflections on the Origin and Spread of Nationalism*, rev. ed. (London: Verso, 1991); Margaret C. Jacob, "The Enlightenment Redefined: The Formation of Modern Civil Society," *Social Research* 58:2 (Summer 1991): 475-95.

9. Joan B. Landes, *Women and the Public Sphere in the Age of the French Revolution* (Ithaca, NY: Cornell University Press, 1988).

10. See J. M. Roberts, *The Mythology of the Secret Societies* (London: Secker and Warburg, 1972); Sylvia Harcstark Myers, *The Bluestocking Circle: Women, Friendship, and the Life of the Mind in Eighteenth-Century England* (Oxford: Clarendon Press, 1990).

11. There is an extensive literature on the relation between Romanticism and Revolution, but for a detailed study in the transformation from one to the other see Nicholas Roe, *Wordsworth and Coleridge: The Radical Years* (Oxford: Clarendon Press, 1988).

12. See Gary Kelly, *Women, Writing, and Revolution 1790-1827* (Oxford: Clarendon Press, 1992).

13. See *The Ideology of Conduct: Essays on Literature and the History of Sexuality*, ed. Nancy Armstrong and Leonard Tennenhouse (New York: Methuen, 1987); Lenore Davidoff and Catherine Hall, *Family Fortunes: Men and Women of the English Middle Class 1780-1850* (London: Hutchinson, 1987).

14. See, for example, the views of Sir Walter Scott in Brian Southam, *Jane Austen: The Critical Heritage* (London: Routledge & Kegan Paul, 1968).

15. See the comments of Rebecca West in Southam, *Jane Austen: The Critical Heritage 1870-1940* (London: Routledge & Kegan Paul, 1987).

16. Jane Austen, *Northanger Abbey and Persuasion*, vol. 5 of *The Novels of Jane Austen*, ed. R. W. Chapman, 3d ed. (London: Oxford University Press, 1932-34).

17. Marilyn Butler, *Jane Austen and the War of Ideas* (Oxford: Clarendon Press, 1975).

18. See Nicola J. Watson, *Revolution and the Form of the English Novel, 1790–1825* (Oxford: Clarendon Press, 1994).

2

"Invention Is What Delights Me": Jane Austen's Remaking of "English" History

Antoinette Burton

If readers of Jane Austen's novels were asked what her view of history was, there are few, I suspect, who would not refer to the now-infamous characterization she articulated through the heroine of *Northanger Abbey*, Catherine Morland. "But history, real solemn history, I cannot be interested in . . . ," Catherine tells Mr. and Miss Tilney. "I read it a little as a duty, but it tells me nothing that does not either vex or weary me. The quarrels of popes and kings, with wars or pestilences, in every page; the men all so good for nothing, and hardly any women at all—it is very tiresome; and yet I often think it odd that it should be so dull, for a great deal of it must be invention. The speeches that are put into the heroes' mouths, their thoughts and designs—the chief of all this must be invention, and invention is what delights me in other books."[1] This extract from the novel has proven a popular tag recently for a variety of feminist practitioners trying to introduce the problem of "women and/women in history"—Karen Offen, Susan Bell, Michelle Perrot and Georges Duby among them.[2] I privilege it here because it enunciates with precision and prescience the basic themes of late-twentieth-century feminist historiography. Morland's lament about the exclusivities of traditional history offers historically minded practitioners of feminism the opportunity to read Jane Austen as a fellow traveler. This opportunity is particularly welcome since, when it comes to understanding Austen's relationship to history, she has proven to be, in the words of one critic, "a particularly hard nut . . . to crack."[3]

Foregrounding Catherine's frustration with the absence of women in traditional histories is just one of the ways in which Austen anticipates the assumptions that have governed modern feminist history-writing. In addition to adding women to history, feminists engaged in the work of excavating women's historical experience have subjected History (capital H) to scrutiny, chiefly by calling its truth claims—its objectivity—into question.[4] Austen makes clear, through her heroine Catherine, that gender is not the only struggle in which her texts, or feminism more generally, are embroiled.[5] History itself is a field of representation, and hence of power and struggle. She therefore has Catherine insist that history is but "invention," a kind of stage upon which apparently invisible playwrights script "speeches" and put them "into heroes' mouths." Catherine's vexation stems not just from the absence of heroines, but from historians' failure to countenance fully the contingencies of the truths they purport to tell, as well as to imagine narratives that entertain their readers. By issuing this complaint, Austen demands that historians imagine and endeavor to play to an audience that includes young women like herself as consumers of historical spectacle and drama. In doing so she requires readers to concede that women are capable of being critical history-readers and that History itself is a right and proper site of feminist intervention. She also makes way for the possibility that to be (a) feminist is to engage with the writing of history—to demand that it re-create the conditions of the past for use by women in the present.[6]

In addition to questioning the conventions of late-Georgian history-writing, Austen invented a history of her own. Less well known than the passage cited earlier, except perhaps among readers of Austen juvenilia, is Austen's *History of England From the Reign of Henry IV to the Death of Charles I*, written in the fall of 1791 when the author was just 16 years old—a year younger than Catherine Morland when she announced her boredom with conventional history in *Northanger Abbey*. Austen's *History* (reprinted as a facsimile edition in 1993) is a parody of Oliver Goldsmith's four-volume work, *The History of England from the Earliest Times to the Death of George II* (1771), which was commonly used as a schoolroom text in the late eighteenth century. It was part of the household library during Austen's adolescence and remains in the family archive, complete with marginalia scribbled by Jane, her siblings, and later generations of pupils. Austen's determination to satirize these ponderous tomes and their historical conventionality is clear from the very outset: although she did not sign her name to the manuscript, she described the author as "a partial, prejudiced and ignorant Historian" and promised gleefully that "there will be very few dates in this History" (frontispiece). In fact what dates there are in Austen's *History* were carefully chosen to enhance the dramatic movement of the narrative, to persuade the reader to embrace Austen's avowedly "partial and prejudiced" interpretation of early modern English history, and above all, to dispel the myth that history-writing must be "tiresome" or worse, "solemn," in order to qualify as History at all.[7]

That Austen should have undertaken to reconstitute such a traditional historical narrative as the rise of the English nation-state, however parodically, suggests a feminist sensibility unusual in one so young as well as a canniness about the politics of history-writing that has been a characteristic of English feminist production through the centuries.[8] Although Austen's *History* has been examined in the context of her Juvenilia, most notably by Christopher Kent, there has been little or no evaluation of it as an instance of *feminist* cultural production.[9] By this I mean that the ways in which the *History* represents Austen's belief that the past was not just useful for but essential to the woman reader's consciousness in the present have yet to be sufficiently addressed. Given the renewed concern over the myth of Austen's "extrahistoricity,"[10] as well as the attention in this volume to the nature and parameters of her feminism, analysis of her *History of England* as a feminist text is warranted. Indeed, late-twentieth-century western feminist criticism, driven as it is by the impulse to historicize, both requires and enables such an analysis. How Austen enacted a feminist narrative of English history, how women figure in that narrative as agents and objects, and what her newly invented *History of England* tells us about the relationship between historical consciousness and a feminist politics are the subject of this essay.

There may be some who will hesitate to see what were undoubtedly the playful musings of the young Jane Austen being overdetermined as a pioneer piece of feminist historiography. I agree that it would be unwise to read the work of several afternoons' amusement, whose audience was the immediate family and which was not published during the author's lifetime, as evidence of scholarly intent or sustained intellectual preoccupation. Her *History* cannot, for example, compare to that of the premier English female historian of the eighteenth century, Catharine Macaulay, whose *History of England from the Accession of James I to that of the Brunswick Line* (1783) ran to eight volumes and took 20 years to complete.[11] And yet we should not necessarily dismiss Austen's adolescent preoccupations as tangential to the kind of woman writer she became. The juvenilia of Charlotte Brontë and her siblings, for example, has yielded important insights into their life's work—less, as Firdous Azim has recently argued, for advancing the search for "new and more authentic facts about their lives" and more for providing the opportunity to explore the origins of later trends and to throw some light on the micro-history of the female writer's subjectivity.[12] As with Charlotte Brontë's short stories, Austen's *History* helps to complicate the question "What sort of teenager was this?"[13] by revealing the rambunctious roots of her later social commentary and by enlarging our vision of the social contexts in which she nurtured her first ideas into prose. Like Brontë's early work, Austen's *History* too was a joint project: she wrote the text while her sister Cassandra drew the accompanying "historical portraits." The various segments of the *History*, which was in three short "volumes," were moreover dedicated to her sister and to her brother James, who also figures in the historical narrative by allusion (x). The *History* is therefore not simply "the beginnings of her feminism" in any self-evident way: it is rather part of a large corpus of early work (27 pieces in all) that signals how well read, how well written, and how well practiced in collaboration she was by the time she articulated a full-fledged novelist's voice.[14] It also represents her claim as a woman writer to a space that was at once among the most "domestic" and the least available to women—the domain of English "national" history—thereby vindicating Virginia Woolf's observation that she was not only writing "to the parsonage" but to worlds and to historical eras beyond her own.[15]

Although celebrated chiefly for his novels, his plays, and his extended lamentation on the decline of village life in the eighteenth century, Oliver Goldsmith also produced several different histories in his lifetime. His *History of England from Earliest Times to the Death of George II*, which served as Austen's "antihistory," was first published three years before his death in 1774. Much more popular at the time was his *History of England, in a Series of Letters from a Nobleman to His Son* (1764), though at least one twentieth-century critic deemed all Goldsmith's attempts at history writing nothing short of "worthless and unreadable."[16] If Goldsmith was elsewhere a master of fancy, wit, gaiety, and humor—*She Stoops to Conquer* is surely one of the deftest parodies in the English language—his *History of England* is nothing but solemnity and high seriousness. Over the course of several dozen chapters Goldsmith narrates the emergence of the English monarchy beginning with William the Conqueror and ending just before the accession of the sovereign reigning while Goldsmith wrote, George III. Despite Samuel Johnson's conviction that Goldsmith was skilled in "the art of . . . saying everything he has to say in a pleasing manner,"[17] this is a plodding narrative driven by the inexorable march toward the House of Tudor and, ultimately, toward the House of Hanover.[18] The fate of the throne and its occupants is, rather unimaginatively, the chief organizing principle in his *History*, with all the chapter titles save the first three named for each individual monarch.

The fact that he was paid £400 to produce this history and that he did so while writing *The Deserted Village* and *She Stoops to Conquer* may explain the workmanlike quality of Goldsmith's prose.[19] According to one eighteenth-century commentator, all his history-writing projects gained him "more money than fame."[20] Goldsmith's *History* is not, of course, without either its drama or its editorial commentary. The assassination of Richard II, the murder of the princes in the Tower, the marriages of Henry VIII, the execution of Mary Queen of Scots, and the tyrannies of Charles II are detailed in all their intrigue and pageantry. Goldsmith's great hero is Henry VII, founder of the House of Tudor, the king who not only quelled the "mutineers" who opposed his quest for power but succeeded in "civilizing" the country. Goldsmith writes, "Since the time of Alfred, England had not seen such another king. He rendered his subjects powerful and happy, and wrought a greater change in the manners of the people than it was possible to suppose could be effected in so short a time."[21] Goldsmith had little admiration for his successor Henry VIII, though he tended to see his brutality as necessary for what he called "our holy redemption,"—the establishment of the national (Anglican) church. For Goldsmith as for many later historians of the period, the ascendancy of the House of Tudor was synonymous with the rise of England to nationhood and, with it, to the status of world power.[22]

Given Catherine Morland's declaration, we might expect a radical rewriting of English history from the young Jane Austen. In fact, there is much that is conventional about her *History*. In structural terms, she adheres to a chronological progression and a dynastic scheme. As with Goldsmith, her chapters mark the devolution of monarchical power from Henry IV through Charles I, with each one narrating the biographies of kings, queens, princes or princesses, their rise to power, and their demise. Some personalities are more detailed and more heavily dramatized than others, with Henry VIII and his heirs, not surprisingly, monopolizing the story. Strictly speaking, the men are not neglected in favor of the women. Austen gives proportionate weight to each character regardless of gender: the chapter on Edward VI, for instance, has a brevity commensurate with his reign, and although the one dealing with Elizabeth I is the longest of them all, Austen's purpose, as we shall shortly see, is not to glorify her but rather to use the space given over to "the Virgin Queen" to clinch her arguments about the injustices done to Mary Queen of Scots. When all is said and done, Austen's *History* has much in common with Goldsmith's. In spite of her hatred for the Tudors, by emphasizing their villainy she could not but make their fortunes as central to her narrative as did he.

At the same time, the reader knows almost immediately on picking up Austen's *History* that this is not "business as usual" as history writing goes. Flippancy, together with a certain lightheartedness about the whole project of history-writing, characterizes much of Austen's tone throughout the narrative. Where Goldsmith announces in his preface that his sources are Rapin, Carte, Smollett, and Hume, Austen references Shakespeare—hardly a historical authority—or else scoffs at the need for citation or detailed evidence at all (stanza 4).[23] The very first chapter signals her impatience with the details of traditional narrative. Henry IV, we are told, did not merely ascend to the throne, he did so "much to his own satisfaction" in 1399, after having "prevailed upon his cousin and predecessor Richard the 2nd to resign it to him." According to Austen, Richard was also persuaded by Henry to "retire for the rest of his life to Pomfret castle, where he happened to be murdered." With this single irreverent sentence Austen explains away one of the foundational dynastic struggles of the pre-Tudor monarchy. There is no blood, no gore, scarcely a hint of scandal—just a tidy rendition of a political crisis that Goldsmith, for his part, spends several pages on. Austen is nothing if not blunt about her philosophy. If you want more detail, she tells us, "you had better read some other History" (stanza 5). Not only is she willing to announce her unconcern with the details of this particular monarchical coup (Henry IV has been described as "the first usurper"[24]), Austen is equally ready to reveal her impatience with the facts and figures of dynastic marriages: "It is to be supposed that Henry was married, since he had certainly four sons, but it is not in my power to inform the reader who was his wife." In fact Henry had two wives, Mary of Bohun and Joan of Navarre. Although it seems improbable, Austen may have been trying to imply that Henry's sons were bastards. Or she may have wanted to satirize the fact that while Henry's progeny effectively established the beginnings of the Tudor line, his sons appear from the sources available to her to have been miraculously produced without benefit of mothers. More likely still, she was enacting her distaste for "the quarrels of popes and kings" by relegating this traditionally pivotal episode in the history of English kingship to something of a footnote.

One might expect Austen to perform this same recalibration—privileging the heretofore marginal while sidelining the conventionally central—when it comes to addressing the role of women in her *History*. In practice, she is not as concerned with re-materializing forgotten women as she is with challenging Goldsmith's characterizations of both minor and major female characters. She defends Anne Boleyn, for example, against insinuations that she was a whore, an adulterer, and (hence) a heretic. For Boleyn's fate, the king's brutality and licentiousness are to blame: "it is . . . but Justice and my Duty to declare that this amiable woman was entirely innocent of the crimes with which she was accused, of which her Beauty, her elegance, and her sprightliness were sufficient proofs, not to mention her solemn protestations of Innocence, the weakness of the charges against her, and the King's character" (stanza 13). Lady Jane Grey (the teenage daughter-in-law of the Duke of Northumberland who through the accidents of fate, lineage, and political intrigue was queen of England for nine days) provides another occasion for reinterpretation. Significantly, she is not a character whom Goldsmith has slighted. He describes her as "a lady every way accomplished for government, as well as by the charms of her person, as the virtues and accomplishments of her mind." Note Goldsmith's studied equilibrium here between her personal "charms" and her intellectual attainments (she was reported to have read Greek). "All historians agree," he says, "that the solidity of her understanding, improved by continual application, rendered her the wonder of her age."[25]

Austen is not nearly so obsequious in her reading. In fact, she seems to be taking Goldsmith to task for failing to see the real Lady Jane. Echoing her assessment of Anne Boleyn, Austen describes Lady Jane Grey as "amiable" and even clever because of her capacity for foreign languages, though she was not ready to say unequivocally whether such capacity was fact or hearsay. "Whether she really understood that language (Greek) or whether such a study proceeded from an excess of vanity for which I believe she was always rather remarkable, is uncertain. Whatever might be the cause, she preserved the same appearance of knowledge, and contempt of what was generally esteemed pleasure, during her whole Life, for she declared herself displeased with being appointed queen, and while conducting to the Scaffold, she wrote a Sentence in Latin and another in Greek on seeing the dead Body of her husband accidentally passing that way" (stanza 17). Here Austen is almost Machiavellian. What estimation she has for Lady Jane is rooted in an appreciation for the ways in which the young and fleeting queen was able to *appear* learned and virtuous, rather than in any certainty that she was either or both. I suspect that this somewhat mocking comment about Lady Jane reflects on Jane Austen, too; Lady Jane had her brief moment in the spotlight of English history when she was approximately the same age as Austen was when she wrote her *History*. It is Austen parodying, in other words, her own efforts to appear sufficiently equipped to undertake a history of the nation. Their common names must have struck Austen and no doubt encouraged her to linger over the relatively minor role played by the young queen. Her playfulness toward this particular Jane is but one example among many in the *History* of what A. S. Byatt calls Austen's "wild early irony" (vi).

Austen's characterization of Lady Jane announces that her "recovery" of women is not necessarily flattering to the female sex and her grasp of their characters can be more cynical and perhaps more realistic than Goldsmith's—

whose reputation as an antisentimentalist is as common now as it was among his contemporaries.[26] Of the minor female personages whom Austen attends to, none is more interesting in terms of how she is dealt with than Jane Shore, the mistress of Edward IV. While Goldsmith spends considerable time detailing her exposure as an adulterer, the accusations of witchcraft against her, and her subsequent public humiliation, Austen turns her eyes and ours away from this whole scenario with another single, definitive line: "one of Edward's mistresses was Jane Shore, who has had a play written about her, but it is a tragedy and therefore not worth reading." As with the stories of other figures in the narrative, Austen chooses not to repeat what was a well-worn tale. In her introduction to the chapter on Henry VIII, for example, she wrote—again with disarming bluntness—"It would be an affront to my readers were I to suppose that they were not as well acquainted with the particulars of this King's reign as I am myself. It will therefore be saving *them* the task of reading again what they have read before, and *myself* the trouble of writing what I do not perfectly recollect" (stanzas 11-12). Ever conservative of her own historical energies and always concerned to produce a good read, Austen sidelined Shore in order to sustain the whimsical tone that she was intent on writing into her *History*.

The quest for whimsy, as it turns out, is difficult if not impossible to maintain, especially once Austen's narrative brings her to the two chief protagonists of her story: Elizabeth I and Mary Queen of Scots. It is here, while wrestling with the legacy of the Henrician Reformation and the foundation of the Protestant English nation represented by the cousins' dynastic conflict, that Austen stakes her biggest claim against Goldsmith. In part, it is a question of rehabilitating Mary and making Elizabeth out to be the "Murderess" and the "pest of society" Austen believes her to be—a dimension of Austen's "full-blooded Stuart partisanship" that scholars of the Juvenilia have not really dwelt on.[27] Hence in Austen's rendition, Mary's death was "untimely, unmerited and scandalous"; any "imprudencies" she may have committed (such as her involvement in the murder of Darnley or her sexual indiscretions) were the result of her naïveté and her betrayal by false friends; and her steadfastness in the face of death can be ascribed to "a magnanimity that alone could proceed from conscious innocence" (stanzas 21-22). Austen's Mary echoes her Anne Boleyn. In addition to being "amiable" ("a favorite eighteenth-century anodyne," according to Kent), Mary and Anne are both the victims of evil Tudor monarchs, and dates pertaining to their execution are, significantly, two out of the three mentioned in Austen's *History*.[28] But Austen makes it clear that both have also unjustly been the victims of historians' scorn. Mary Queen of Scots especially has been wronged by chroniclers who have resisted seeing the righteousness of her cause—partly out of a commitment to highlighting the march of English Protestantism and progress that her death and Elizabeth's reign were held to have inaugurated. Righting the public record is the chief purpose of Austen's *History*, and vindicating Mary is nothing less than the sole purpose of the text, so much so that Austen's narrative of the two Jameses and Charles I and II that follow is anticlimactic.

Austen makes no apology for this; it is the inevitable effect of her unabashedly partial story. "Indeed," she tells us, "the recital of any events (except what I make myself) is uninteresting to me; my principle reason for undertaking the History of England being to prove the innocence of the Queen of Scotland, which I flatter myself with having effectually done, and to abuse Elizabeth tho' I am rather fearful of having fallen short in the latter part of my scheme" (stanza 33). Austen is a shrewd critic of her own work: three-quarters of her chapter on Elizabeth is given over to Mary Queen of Scots. When Austen does stop to characterize her, it is in the section devoted to "Bloody Mary," whose failure to produce an heir guaranteed Elizabeth's succession. Thus are the biographies of both Mary Tudor and Elizabeth, two women undoubtedly important in their own right, given over almost entirely to an explanation of how Mary of Scotland was cheated out of the throne. Mary's Stuart descendants suffer the same fate at Austen's hands. She tells us they interest her as subjects worthy of vindication against accusations of tyranny simply because they were Stuarts—an interpretation that underscores the extent to which, however playfully, Austen was determined to make an argument about the inevitability of a "partial and prejudiced" history for its own sake, and apparently at any cost (stanza 34).

It would be easy, and even self-evident, to argue that part of what makes this history "feminist" is that it insists on placing a wronged woman at its center. Like Mary Wollstonecraft, Austen centered her later fiction on ostensibly unempowered women, enabling her, as Claudia Johnson has observed, "to expose and explore those aspects of traditional institutions . . . which patently do not serve her heroines well."[29] In many ways, Mary Queen of Scots is the quintessential sentimental and aristocratic heroine—one whose rank brings not power but "delicious powerlessness."[30] This is not to say that a feminist history requires a female victim, but rather that it privileges stories of how institutional oppression (in this case, the operations of monarchical succession and more specifically, patrilineal heredity, at a particular historical moment) exclude women from political power. That it does not essentialize the category of "Woman" by casting all women as good and all men as evil (Austen does not hesitate to name Elizabeth the party responsible for Mary's death) also makes the *History* a certain kind of feminist text. That Austen is additionally willing to implicate "sisterhood" (loosely understood) in the operations of patriarchy makes her *History*, in my view, not just a feminist text, but a courageous one at that. As in her later fiction, Austen was not hesitant about showing that "oppressed women might be as bitter or bad as dominating men."[31] A sense of outrage at the violation of sisterly solidarity that Mary's execution represents smolders unarticulated beneath the surface of Austen's *History*, diminishing the claim that her adolescent writings taken as a whole display the kind of spectatorial detachment that may be said to characterize her "mature" novels. And if her laughter is "unengaged" throughout the rest of the *History*, it is not audible at all when it comes to Mary's fate.[32] Even if Mary was not meant to be Queen, Austen insists, she nonetheless deserved the "assistance and protection" of Elizabeth, and she implies that not to have offered these made her "the destroyer of all comfort" and "the deceitful betrayer of trust reposed in her." (stanzas 21, 19). She does not go so far as to say that Elizabeth betrayed her sex, yet there is an implicit critique of Elizabeth's femininity that was by no means original to Austen.[33]

I would like to argue here that what makes this *History* a feminist one is not just that the power struggle between two women is featured as the heart of the narrative of Tudor ascendancy and hence of English nation-building. Such a staging is clearly an audacious critical intervention in the performance of English history insofar as it suggests that women were the motor forces behind the rise of the English nation-state. More important still is the way that Austen insists on the inevitability of historians' own biases—even and especially her own—in accounts of "what happened in the past." In comparing Austen's *History* with Goldsmith's, it is difficult not to conclude that what she objected to was his pretension to objectivity as much as the misreading of Mary that was one of its effects. For Goldsmith is quite explicit about his conviction that historians can be impartial recorders of fact. Of the contest between the two cousins he writes: "in contemplating the contentions of mankind, we find almost ever both sides culpable; Mary, who was stained with crimes that deserved punishment, was put to death by a princess who had no just pretensions to inflict punishment on her equal."[34] Goldsmith gives equality of status to Mary and hence perhaps may be said to recognize the legitimacy of her claims to the throne. But at the same time he insists on universalizing from this episode a kind of theory of historical judgment—that both sides of any given argument have equal merit, the kind of merit that disinterested historians are in a position to represent. Toward the close of his *History*, Goldsmith elaborates on and reiterates this theory when he ends his chapter on Charles I. "As for his character," writes Goldsmith, "the reader will decide it with more precision and satisfaction to himself from the detail of his conduct, than from any summary given of it by the historian.[35] It is surely to this claim that Austen is responding in her *History* when she writes, apropos of the War of the Roses (which, not incidentally, secured the supremacy of the House of Tudor over that of York): "I suppose you know all about the wars between [Henry VI] and the Duke of York who was of the right side; if you do not, you had better read some other History, for I shall not be very diffuse in this, meaning by it only to vent my Spleen *against*, and shew my hatred *to* all those people whose parties or principles do not suit with mine, and not to give information" (stanza 5).

This is more than a petulant whine about a dull and monotonous history. It is an impassioned and politically engaged declaration of the impossibility of impartiality, as well as an embrace of the personal pleasure (Goldsmith's "satisfaction") experienced by the female historian as she witnesses her own historical judgments in action. Austen is not content simply to "decide for herself" on the basis of what Goldsmith has told her. She has seized the reins and is out to remake his story into one that is more believable because it does not shrink from bold strokes and "prejudiced" readings. Not only is Austen's *not* a factual history (it does not purport to "give information"), but the author's likes and dislikes, her heroes, heroines, and especially villains drive the whole enterprise. Before any of the violence, betrayal, murder, and intrigue of the Tudors is even exposed, then, we see Austen's bile ("meaning by it only to vent my Spleen") and her self-confessed hatred for some of her characters splashed across the page. If she does nothing else in this *History*, she moves the center of the action away from the historical figures in question and brings us back time and again to her—not just as the purveyor of historical adventure, but as the self-interested inventor and the clearly delighted consumer of a national historical drama.[36] In doing so she makes it clear that her own consciousness as a resistant female reader in the present is the product of critical engagement with women's condition in the historical past.

Austen does rely on "Duty" as one justification for rescuing wronged heroines from the clutches of traditional historians. And yet hers is not exactly a genteel history—mainly because of her determination to reject, in often combative and contemptuous terms, any historical narrative that does not declare its own colors. Austen's are irreverence, vengeance, and above all a kind of populist heroism that make Mary of Scotland seem like an ordinary, if majestic, woman seeking what was due her. Austen's sister Cassandra's drawings, which depict English sovereigns as if they were common people, mock the high seriousness of historical illustrations just as Jane's gibes at Goldsmith do, and help in their own way to underscore the ordinariness and the familiarity of what was in essence a family squabble in the wealthiest domicile of the land. The illustrations and the text together suggest the availability of standardized, public versions of the English past for appropriation and reformulation in the privacy of the middle-class home. Cassandra's participation in the project also suggests a more utopian faith in the possibilities of sisterhood than the *History* ends up telling.

As a collaborative feminist text, then, Austen's *History* enacts a series of refusals: of post-Enlightenment presumptions about the rationality of history and historians, of the transparency of historical narrative, of the univocality of the author, of the immutability and elitism of the public record, of the deadening effect of the past on those who wish to make critical use of it in the present. Austen plays with the question of what happens when a historian reveals herself as a gendered subject deeply invested in the process of unmasking history *and* history-writing both as the exclusive domains of men. When she does so she articulates one of the underlying convictions of modern feminist criticism: that history *is* "invention" but that it cannot merely be dismissed as such—because history-writing itself is one of the most influential exercises of power in the public sphere.[37] She also testifies to the power of history to allow women to reinvent the past and so too perhaps to imagine differently their own futures. Among the most interesting results of Austen's playful admonition about the power of historiography is that the long march of English national progress is thrown into doubt. The gist of her narrative is that the Elizabethan settlement upon which notions of Englishness (especially Englishness as Protestantism) are built is itself unstable, explicable not in terms of historical destiny but grounded rather in the murder of a queen by her kinswoman. That Mary was of Scotland and a Catholic rematerializes the instabilities and the violence at the heart of "Englishness" hegemonically conceived as well. Critics have debated the relative invisibility in Austen's novels of events such as the industrial revolution and especially the French Revolution, both of which were in the process of unfolding onto the world historical scene as Jane composed her *History* in 1791.[38] Austen's championing of the Scottish princess as the rightful Queen of England reminds us how recently England had been consolidated into a "nation" by union with Scotland (1707) and that "Englishness" was not necessarily a self-evident category, either historically or contemporaneously for Austen, as Linda Colley's monograph *Britons: Forging the Nation* has recently demonstrated.[39] Austen's insistence on Mary as the legitimate queen places a most "unnatural" figure at the heart of an English order of her own design, even as it questions the naturalness of the historical landscape on which Tudor majesty appears as the right and logical culmination of "English" history.[40]

Austen's *History of England* occupies an interesting cusp. It suggests links between Austen's "childhood," her "adolescence," and her "adulthood," even while it undoes the very distinctions those categories impose; and it challenges the "classificatory enterprise," to use Devoney Looser's phrase, involved in differentiating History from Literature in late eighteenth-century women's writing, even while it contains elements of, and helps to constitute, both of those domains.[41] Given the confluence of chronological organization and high political narrative strategy on the one hand and comedic timing, flippancy, and satirical voice on the other, it would be difficult to categorize Austen's *History* as either "fact" or "fiction," strictly speaking. Nor, I think, does Austen ask us to. The *History* aims to be at once education, entertainment, and "impolite knowledge," insofar as it challenges what were the linear ascendant tendencies of Whig history and makes women the center of a less sanitized version of the story of the nation than was elsewhere available. What makes Austen's *History* subversive and, finally, feminist in the most expansive sense of the term is that it dares to suggest that traditional representations of English history were (and are) so vulnerable to reinterpretation, and the imaginative powers of women readers so great, that the mischievous work of two teenage girls scribbling in the family parlor could easily render "the History of England" a not so innocuous parody of itself. And if we need further evidence that Jane Austen is the indubitable heroine of her own *History*, we need only revisit Catherine Morland's cautious hopefulness about the possibility of a different kind of historiography from that on offer in the late eighteenth century schoolroom: "I have often wondered at the person's courage that could sit down on purpose to do it."[42]

Notes

I wish to thank Devoney Looser for inviting me to consider Jane Austen's feminism, and for challenging me to refine my understandings of both the novelist and feminism itself. This chapter has also benefited from conversations with Maura O'Connor and Mike Kugler.

1. Quoted in Jane Austen, *The History of England from the Reign of Henry the 4th to the Death of Charles the 1st*, introduction by A. S. Byatt (Chapel Hill, NC: Algonquin Books, 1993), ix. All subsequent references are cited parenthetically in the text and refer to this facsimile edition, with the printed text of the *History* referenced by stanza number.

2. For a discussion of these usages, see Devoney Looser, "Rethinking Women/History/Literature: A Feminist Investigation of Disciplinarity in Lucy Hutchinson, Lady Mary Wortley Montagu, Charlotte Lennox, and Jane Austen," Ph.D. diss., State University of New York at Stony Brook, 1993. I will confess here that Catherine Morland's lament has also graced the first page of my syllabi for more than one women's history and feminist historiography course.

3. Nancy Armstrong, "The Nineteenth-Century Jane Austen: A Turning Point in the History of Fear," *Genre* 23 (Summer/Fall, 1990): 227.

4. Joan Scott's *Gender and the Politics of History* (New York: Columbia University Press, 1988) remains a foundational text for outlining a feminist critique of history as a discipline. For more recent articulations of this epistemological intervention, see Judith P. Zinsser, *History and Feminism: A Glass Half Full* (New York: Twayne Publishers, 1993) and Ann-Louise Shapiro, ed., *Feminists Revision History* (New Brunswick, NJ: Rutgers University Press, 1994).

5. See Looser's introduction to this volume.

6. See Christina Crosby, *The Ends of History: Victorians and "the Woman Question"*(New York: Routledge, 1991) and Mrinalini Sinha, "Gender in the Critiques of Colonialism and Nationalism: Locating the 'Indian Woman,'" in Shapiro, ed., *Feminists Revision History*, 269. I am grateful to Rachel Tanguay for helping me to articulate this formulation.

7. For a discussion of how fluid the boundaries were between History and Literature in this period, see Devoney Looser, "(Re)Making History and Philosophy: Austen's *Northanger Abbey*," *European Romantic Review* 4 (Summer 1993): 34-56.

8. For an account of the significance of history-writing to the Victorian feminist movement, see Antoinette Burton, *Burdens of History: British Feminists, Indian Women and Imperial Culture, 1865–1915* (Chapel Hill: University of North Carolina Press, 1994), chap. 3.

9. Christopher Kent, "'Real Solemn History' and Social History," in *Jane Austen in a Social Context*, ed. David Monaghan (New York: Macmillan, 1981), 86-104, and "Learning History with, and from, Jane Austen," in *Jane Austen's Beginnings: The Juvenilia and Lady Susan*, ed. J. David Grey (Ann Arbor, MI: UMI Research Press), 59-72. For a different, almost psychoanalytic, discussion of Austen's *History* see Brigid Brophy, "Jane Austen and the Stuarts," in *Critical Essays on Jane Austen*, ed. B. C. Southam (London: Routledge and Kegan Paul, 1968), 21-38.

10. The term is Kent's. See his, "Learning History," 59.

11. See Bridget Hill, *The Republican Virago: The Life and Times of Catharine Macaulay, Historian* (Oxford: Clarendon Press, 1992), especially chap. 2.

12. Firdous Azim, *The Colonial Rise of the Novel* (New York: Routledge, 1993), chap. 5.

13. John Halperin, "Unengaged Laughter: Jane Austen's Juvenilia," in Grey, ed., *Jane Austen's Beginnings*, 30.

14. See Halperin, "Unengaged Laughter," and John McAleer, "What a Biographer Can Learn About Jane Austen," both in Grey, ed., *Jane Austen's Beginnings*, 29 and 7, respectively.

15. Virginia Woolf, *The Common Reader*, cited in McAleer, "What a Biographer Can Learn," 24.

16. This evaluation is attributed to J. H. Plumb by Ricardo Quintana, *Oliver Goldsmith: A Georgian Study* (New York: Macmillan 1967), 186.

17. John Buxton, "Goldsmith's Classicism," in Andrew Swarbrick, ed., *The Art of Oliver Goldsmith* (London: Vision Press, 1984), 77.

18. In contrast, Goldsmith's other English history, *An History of England, In a Series of Letters from a Nobleman to His Only Son* (1764), departs from what Christopher Kent calls this "monarch-to-monarch trudge." See his "Learning History," 63.

19. Kent, "Learning History," 63.

20. Robert Anderson, *The Works of British Poets* (1795), quoted in G. S. Rousseau, ed., *Oliver Goldsmith: The Critical Heritage* (Boston: Routledge and Kegan Paul, 1974), 219.

21. Oliver Goldsmith, *An Abridgment of the History of England, from the Invasion of Julius Caesar to the Death of George the Second* (Boston: T. Bedlington, 1825), 96.

22. This was an equation the Tudors themselves invented and helped to nurture. For a critical assessment, see John Guy, *Tudor England* (Oxford: Oxford University Press, 1988).

23. For Goldsmith, see Quintana, *Oliver Goldsmith*, 187.

24. Ralph A. Griffiths, "The Later Middle Ages, 1290–1485," in *The Oxford Illustrated History of Britain*, ed. Kenneth O. Morgan (Oxford: Oxford University Press, 1989), 197.

25. Goldsmith, *History*, 114.

26. See, for example, Harold Bloom, ed., *Oliver Goldsmith* (New York: Chelsea House Publishers, 1987) and Rousseau, ed., *Oliver Goldsmith*, 115-28.

27. See, for example, Brophy, "Jane Austen and the Stuarts," in Southam, ed., *Critical Essays*, 21-38.

28. The third is that of Elizabeth's councilor, the Earl of Essex.

29. Claudia L. Johnson, *Jane Austen: Women, Politics, and the Novel* (Chicago: University of Chicago Press, 1988), xxiv.

30. Janet Todd, "Jane Austen, Politics and Sensibility," in *Feminist Criticism: Theory and Practice*, ed. Susan Sellers (Hertfordshire, UK: Harvester Wheatsheaf, 1991), 77.

31. Todd, "Jane Austen, Politics and Sensibility," 86.

32. Halperin, "Unengaged Laughter," 30 and passim.

33. For a carefully historicized analysis of the gendering of Elizabeth I, see Carole Levin, *The Heart and Stomach of a King: Elizabeth I and the Politics of Sex and Power* (Philadelphia: University of Pennsylvania Press, 1994).

34. Goldsmith, *History*, 126.

35. Goldsmith, *History*, 159.

36. Christopher Kent calls Austen "a dissatisfied consumer of history" and Northanger Abbey, a "consumer history." See his "Learning History," 95 and 98.

37. For one of the clearest articulations of this viewpoint to date, see "Recasting Women: An Introduction," in Kumkum Sangari and Sudesh Vaid, ed., *Recasting Women: Essays in Colonial History* (New Delhi: Kali Press, 1989), 1-26.

38. For these critiques, see Armstrong, "Nineteenth-Century Jane Austen," 227-46; Todd, "Austen, Politics and Sensibility," 71-88; and Kent, "'Real Solemn History' and Social History," 86-104. For the colonial context, see Edward Said, "Jane Austen and Empire" in his *Culture and Imperialism* (New York: Knopf, 1993), 80-86; Maaja A. Stewart, *Domestic Realities and Imperial Fictions: Jane Austen's Novels in Eighteenth-Century Contexts* (Athens: University of Georgia Press, 1993); and Ruth Vanita, "*Mansfield Park* in Miranda House," in Rajeswari Sunder Rajan, ed., *The Lie of the Land: English Literary Studies in India* (Delhi: Oxford University Press, 1992), 90-98.

39. Linda Colley, *Britons: Forging the Nation 1707-1837* (New Haven, CT: Yale University Press, 1992); see also Michael Hechter, *Internal Colonialism: The Celtic Fringe in British National Development, 1536-1966* (Berkeley: University of California Press, 1975).

40. In making this observation I have borrowed from Said's reading of *Mansfield Park*. See *Culture and Imperialism*, 87.

41. Looser, "(Re)Making History and Philosophy," 34.

42. Jane Austen, *Northanger Abbey*, in R. W. Chapman, *The Novels of Jane Austen* (Oxford: Oxford University Press, 1960), 109.

3

Jane Austen and the Engendering of Disciplinarity

Clifford Siskin

The collection of essays you are reading, as well as the Modern Language Association convention session from which this particular contribution emerged, belong to an increasingly popular scholarly genre: the "So what?" genre—a formal effort to take stock of the past decade or two of theoretical, historical, and cultural critiques. In its more pessimistic versions, the "So what?" carries overtones of "Enough already"; the more optimistic ones ask "What's next?" The difference turns upon the sense of difference—how much, and of what importance, is the change occasioned by these critical flurries?— and thus a feature of the "So what?" genre is the centering of an apparently continuous object to measure the discontinuity. "Despite the prolonged and earnest application of ideological approaches to Austen's work," wrote the organizer of the MLA session in a strategically successful appeal to the Program Committee, "she *remains* as enigmatic as ever."[1] Our charge, both in that session and, in important ways, now in this present volume, is to figure out how Jane Austen "can be used to examine, interrogate, and revise certain premises and practices of feminist and cultural criticism."

Unless we read "enigmatic" as impenetrable genius (in which case we should simply bow and withdraw) this is a call not to abandon but to recontextualize earlier inquiries. At least I hope it is, since the considerable time and effort I've spent on Austen in the past can easily be pushed to the "So what?" abyss: "So what if Austen was a Romantic?"[2] To a critic such as Claudia Johnson, one might similarly ask: "So what if Austen was a feminist?"[3] Because critics have provided such different answers, what these questions often query is not so much the integrity of the key terms such as "Romantic" and "feminist" but the agendas of those who insist on employing them. The term "ideology" sometimes surfaces as shorthand for the suspicion that Austen is being used to make a political power play that she has been enigmatically able to resist. As the title of the MLA session, "Out of Bounds," may at first seem to suggest, should we, or can we, contain Austen within ideological boundaries?

Let me repose that question so as to spread the politics around a bit; after all, we should not reproduce what Janet Todd identifies as a "device" of the 1790s: "if one held radical or liberal views, this was a political stance, but if one expressed proper conservative ones, this was a moral position."[4] Within what bounds, I would ask, does Austen continue to function ideologically as an enigma? She remains a puzzle, that is, only in relationship to the particular context in which we try to understand her. That context, I will argue, is the discipline of Literature. The acts of labeling her in regard to period and gender have transpired within efforts to produce literary knowledge, and whatever the results of those acts, we need to address Austen's enigmatic status as a problem within that field. My hypothesis, in other words, is that she poses not just an individual enigma but a disciplinary one.

Let me paint the problem with broad brushstrokes. On the one hand, thanks to the efforts of such critics as Moira Ferguson and Roger Lonsdale, Jane Spencer, and Janet Todd,[5] we now know that during the late-eighteenth and early-nineteenth centuries many women wrote in many different genres with a considerable degree of popular and often critical success. On the other hand, Raymond Williams, Alvin Kernan, and others[6] have worked on the historicity of the notion of "literature" in England, showing how a term that had once embraced all kinds of writing came, during this same period of time, to refer more narrowly to only certain texts within certain genres. In ways that we are only beginning to explore, these acts of narrowing were also acts of gendering, largely leaving out writing by women. The discipline that, during the next century, took this newly restricted category of literature as its field of knowledge was thus founded in an extraordinary act (in scope and in speed) of gendered exclusion and forgetting.

Within this Great Forgetting that became the Great Tradition, Austen appeared as a very rare turn to the worlds and concerns of women and women writing, and became the subject of aesthetic appreciations. In recent years, however, she has attracted (as evidenced by the current "So what(s)?") more and more efforts to label her in terms of history and gender. But as those same *kinds* of inquiries helped restore our disciplinary memory, Austen has become a different type of object: "she who was celebrated for being one of the few who wrote and was remembered," has a different spin than "she who, for some reason, was not forgotten *when all the others who wrote were.*"

The critical stakes regarding these different Austens have been raised even higher by recent work on the eighteenth-century novel that suggests that the relationship between that genre and the gender category of "women" was more complex than had been thought and in fact basic. Wallace Flanders, for example, acknowledges links based on "the increasing literacy of women," but finds what he sees as a more fundamental connection in content: The novel is *about* women, more specifically, it dwells on the "severe contradiction between the dictates of egalitarian enlightenment thought on the status of the individual in society and the position of women." While for Flanders, then, "the characteristic modern consciousness of the 'woman problem' forms one of the underlying strata of the novel from its beginnings,"[7] Michael Danahy constructs the same linkage in other ways. Arguing that "discourse about the novel [is] a disguised form of prescriptive discourse about women," he locates the novel "both vertically, as part of an ascending order or hierarchy of genres in which the novel is invariably assigned woman's place in a man's world, and horizontally, as part of a synchronous system of binary oppositions once again equating it with women."[8] For Deborah Ross, this equating of women and the novel proceeds by appropriating the terms of older, masculinist literary histories. Arguing that "it was not at all clear to women readers that romances were any less true than what was normally called reality," she reconceives Ian Watt's notion of "realism" to include the adventures of romance, since, as she wryly notes, "'Adventure' literally denotes events that come to one from without, and therefore the lives of the unempowered [for example, women] are full of it."[9]

If these eighteenth-century connections between gender and genre are accurate, then Austen's canonical early nineteenth-century fit between the Founding Fathers, Henry Fielding and Samuel Richardson, and the Romantic and Victorian heroics of Sir Walter Scott and Charles Dickens may not simply signal a positive, if momentary, turn *to* women. In fact, the almost immediate welcome accorded her by Scott and other male critics could be construed as signaling a crucial moment in the Great Forgetting: the moment that some of the fundamental links between women and the novel—links that we are only now recovering—were first detached, or at least obscured. I want to begin now to sort through these possibilities, for here is where Austen functions as a disciplinary enigma. The problems with attempts to classify her in *individual* terms either as a Romantic or as a feminist point to the problematic nature of the classification system itself: what we think of as, and what we do with, Literature. What's finally at stake in the "So what(s)?"

is the disciplinary identity of those who pose and engage the questions. Austen, I shall argue, has been a figure of such confused concern to us—and is especially so now in literary study's current identity crisis—because of her (ongoing) role in the engendering of modern disciplinarity.

Here is my response to those "So what(s)?" and my sense of what we can do to rethink that system by recontextualizing Austen. Let us first take her out of the standard "rise of the novel" narratives that bind her to Fielding and Richardson within essentialistic assumptions about the novel. In The Historicity of Romantic Discourse I differentiated her work from theirs by isolating the innovative feature of "development," but I see now that other kinds of ruptures—both generic and statistical—can be recovered. In regard to the continuity of form, for example, epistolary novels like Richardson's begin to wane after the 1780s, and imitators of Fielding's formal strategy of authorial interruptions dwindle at that same moment; as models to imitate, in other words, the works of both authors turned out, by the end of the century, to be dead-ends.[10] But (and this is why the "rise" narratives, and the system of Literature they inhabit and perpetuate, produce enigmas) that was precisely the moment when the novel actually did rise—rise literally in quantitative terms.

As I have detailed elsewhere,[11] this disciplinary confusion has derived not from an inability to count, or a failure to connect genre to history, but rather from the power of the connections that already do count. Our associations have been firmly fixed: Once we supposedly rise novelistically along with Fielding, Richardson, and Lawrence Sterne, and the 1780s and 1790s come into view, disciplinary attention shifts to the supposedly lyrical advent of Romanticism. But those were precisely the decades when the novel took off, with publication reaching, in James Raven's words, "unprecedented levels in the late 1780s." Growth until that point in the century had been slow and erratic. From an annual rate of between four to 20 new titles through the first four decades, and remaining—despite Fielding's and Richardson's popularity—within a range of roughly 20 to 40 for the next three, new novel production peaked briefly near 60 in 1770 before a steep decline to well below 40 during the latter half of that decade. Within the next seven years, however, the output jumped to close to 90, and continued to increase sharply into the next century.[12]

"Was Austen a Romantic?" becomes a newly compelling question in this light, where Fielding and Richardson are not the "rise," and Romanticism is not simply lyrical. Scott, Richard Whately,[13] and others brought the category of "new" to their judgments of Austen because her work participated in this new wave of novel writing—a wave that transformed both the market for, and the status of, that genre. Similarly, "Was Austen a feminist?" becomes a newly compelling question when we recognize that this altered market for the novel—and its shift in status—signaled the disciplinary advent of Literature, and thus the start of the Great Forgetting. Categorizing Austen's beliefs about, and representations of, women remains an important task in considering her link to feminism, but this new context points to other work to be done. My focus here will be both on market and on genre: the mode of publication, on the one hand, and the mode of writing, on the other.

Explanations of Austen's strange publication history—prolific writing in the 1790s but no publishing until the second decade of the nineteenth century—have provided us with often fascinating biographical, psychological, and sociological insights. They have failed, however, to engage the one market option that was both crucial to the Romantic rise of the novel and that was itself reconfigured by that rise. Even Jan Fergus's groundbreaking study of Austen's literary life largely ignores the activity that fueled the take-off in publication rates that made such a life possible: the proliferation of periodicals. That proliferation was itself fueled by the late eighteenth-century phenomenon of readers becoming authors by submitting often anonymous, and almost always free, material to editors and prospective editors, allowing new periodicals to be launched and sustained with very little capital.

As I argue in detail elsewhere,[14] this transformation of readers into authors was a dual act of fiction. First, they formed, or "fiction-ed," themselves into authors. Second, authorial activity itself in periodicals was already (whether tattling to female readers, or, assuming, for the benefit of those seeking improvement, what Robert Mayo calls a "courtly and deferential air") a form of fiction. Thus the very act of writing was, for these readers, at least partly an experience *in* fiction, making it an increasingly natural category for their growing reading/writing habit. Mayo has catalogued 1,375 works of novel (over 12,000 words) and novelette (5,000-12,000) length, most of them published after 1770.[15]

Raven's figures juxtaposed with Mayo's illuminate two important aspects of this growth of the novel market. First, although the initial increases in magazine novels through early 1770s correspond with some growth in new novel titles, the most striking rise—not surprisingly, given the availability of texts and the likelihood of profit—was in reprints. In fact, the gap between the number of new titles and total novel production widens during those decades. Second, after 1775, Raven's new title numbers, in his words, show "striking similarities" (34, 40) to Mayo's magazine counts, their mutual strong growth both closing the gap I have just described and confirming the advent, by the 1790s, of a two-tier market—one in which the popularity of one product supports rather than cannibalizes the sales of the other.

Although, as Todd observes, "women writing in magazines and reviews for the general public became relatively common" by the end of the century,[16] Austen did not contribute any kind of writing to the periodicals. She did send out letters regarding publication under assumed names, but not, like so many other aspiring writers of fiction, to magazine editors. Having sold *Susan,* later retitled *Northanger Abbey,* to a publisher who refused to bring it out, Austen resorted after six years (1803-1809) to sending him letters from a Mrs. Ashton Dennis signed M.A.D.[17] Despite her anger, her clear desire to get into print, and her production of a considerable quantity of new and revised fiction, she remained unpublished until 1811, with *Northanger* not even appearing until after her death in 1817.

Why the long wait for publication when Austen was not only aware of, but intimately familiar with, the opportunities opened up by the proliferation of periodicals? When she was thirteen, in fact, her brothers launched their own weekly periodical *The Loiterer,* which lasted through the sixtieth number. Jan Fergus does argue that "*The Loiterer* conclusively demonstrated" to Austen "that publication was a real, available goal for a writer," particularly since the first issue offered itself as evidence: "from reading to writing," wrote James Austen, "is but one step, from writing to publishing it is less." If, as Fergus suggests, Jane "took these words as a challenge," then why did she not meet it in the form it was issued?[18] Doing so did not preclude additional publication in other forms; anonymity was the norm, and Austen was writing pieces (for example, *Love and Friendship, Catharine*) of precisely the length—12,000 words—that Mayo identifies as the normal range for a magazine novel. The desire to be paid was certainly an issue for Austen, but these shorter pieces were never offered for sale, and the copyright for *Susan* was sold for only £10.

Austen's turn from periodicals is even thematized in the revised version of that work, in the famous defense of the novel at the end of chapter 5 of *Northanger Abbey.* Her praise of that form has drawn the most critical attention, but it is, in fact, buttressed by a concluding denunciation not of romances or of inferior novels but of the *Spectator* as a "coarse" object of "disgust."[19] What this comparative judgment and her publication decisions—whatever the other factors that influenced them—point to is Austen's apparent participation in the historical transformation of the two-tier market into a hierarchical system of what we now know as high versus low culture—a hierarchization that in narrowing the range of proper writing ushered in the disciplinary advent of the new category of Literature. I say "apparent participation" because the historical point finally is not her intention, but the fact that her novels were received and have functioned in what was then newly exclusionary terms.[20] They were celebrated as "new" because they were not just different but better, and better for what they left out: those "things," as *The Quarterly Review* put it, "that should now be left to ladies' maids and sentimental washerwomen."[21]

But there is a twist to this problem of intention that's only becomes visible when we respond to the "Was Austen a feminist?" dispute with more than a "So what?" Johnson's significant contribution to that debate was to show that Austen's participation in the war of ideas was not to depoliticize but to depolemicize. But polemicization was exactly what happened to the periodicals at the moment when Austen began to write: The 1790s, as Jon Klancher has argued, saw a realignment of periodicals and their audiences according to new "ideological dispositions" and "social distances."[22] Could Austen, in employing a depolemicizing strategy that Johnson cannily identifies as the mark of her feminism, have made publication decisions that have allowed her and her novels to play an unexpected role in the disciplinary exclusion of women and women's writing?

Again, we do not know intentions with certainty, so I pose this scenario of historical indirection as question rather than fact. But, by acknowledging that there were publication options, and that the option taken affected Austen's visibility, we can begin to grasp the complexity of her role in the Great Forgetting—a forgetting that left her both remembered *and* an enigma. An important early boost to visibility and remembrance, for example, was the direct result of her turn to John Murray to publish *Emma*. As Sir Walter Scott's publisher, Murray made it his business to ask Scott to review the novel for the journal he had founded, *The Quarterly Review*. Although unsigned, as David Lodge points out, "the extensive and generally favourable discussion of her work in the *Quarterly* was an important milestone in Jane Austen's literary career, the first significant recognition that she was a novelist of unusual distinction."[23]

Applied to Austen, "unusual" means not only "particular" or "special," but "different" or "strange," for Scott's review helped to institute a tradition of negative appreciation: Austen's virtues came to be habitually articulated in terms of what she lacks—Shakespearean in some ways, but *not* Shakespeare. Scott's recurrent focus is on the "ordinary" nature of her subject matter, the degree to which she attends to the "daily," "common," and "middling." But he compliments the "tact with which she presents characters that the reader cannot fail to recognize" with the telling word "peculiar," setting the negative tone for the praise that follows: "The subjects are not often elegant, and certainly never grand; but they are finished up to nature, and with a precision which delights the reader."[24]

The reputation that emerged from such negativity was, not surprisingly, similarly qualified: "though not destined to be a popular author," writes F. B. Pinion in language that itself, after 150 years, still enacted Scott's structural negativity, "Jane Austen was soon marked for distinction; and such has in the main been the tenor of her success ever since."[25] Austen's success certainly has been qualified, but the binary of "popularity" vs. "distinction" can be misleading. If we assume that "distinction" signals a complexity or high seriousness that makes for difficulty or inaccessibility, as opposed to the simpler pleasures of the "popular," we will have trouble grasping the truly enigmatic tenor of Austen's early reception and its connection to disciplinarity.

On the one hand, Scott does distinguish Austen's novels from the "ephemeral productions which supply the regular demand of watering-places and circulating libraries" (37). On the other hand, however, he stresses as a feature of "some importance" that the reader of *Emma* "may return from his promenade to the ordinary business of life, without any chance of having his head turned" (42). This sense of safety echoes throughout the remarkably repetitive vocabulary of the other initial reviews of the novel:

"amusing, inoffensive" —*British Critic*

"harmless amusement" —*Monthly Review*

"an agreeable relaxation . . . amusing" —*Gentleman's Magazine*

Distinction here—the *Gentleman's Magazine* grants *Emma* a "distinguished degree of eminence" among novels—is the reward for being non-threatening entertainment. Austen's work, that is, was received not only as pleasurable, but as *comfortable*. This was not, let me stress, primarily a matter of patriarchal condescension to domestic subject matter, since Austen's work was being compared to other novels of love and marriage; in fact one point of comparison, according to the *Gentleman's Magazine*, was the "tendency" of Austen's competition "to deteriorate the heart."[26]

To understand this sense of comfort we need to historicize it: What was so disagreeable, so offensive, so harmful that readers equated its absence with literary merit? What was the threat and what was the solution? In her bold speculations on Austen's early writings, Margaret Doody suggests that the published novels were their author's toned-down retreat from the brilliantly "disturbing" comedic power of the earlier works. Chastened, argues Doody, by Cadell's rejection of *First Impressions* and Crosby's refusal to release *Susan*, "Jane Austen in maturity made a choice and went in another direction. At the crossroads, she had to choose, and she then wrote the realistic novel of courtship, closely and apparently even modestly related to the style of novel that had frightened her, stimulated her, and made her laugh. She could not laugh so loudly in the later works."[27] Rather than contrast Austen, as Johnson does, to "her more conspicuously political sister-novelists" (xxiv), Doody's strategy here is to turn Austen back upon herself—to what she had been and might have become. Thus Johnson arrives at depolemicizing as Austen's mature achievement, whereas maturity, for Doody, is the moment Austen compromised what her "genius" had already achieved.

To see the six novels as not only domestic but domesticated—in the terms I have proposed, a "comfortable" solution—is to begin to unravel the enigma of Austen's reception. The problem that invited that solution, however, still needs to be articulated, for Doody's focus, whatever the merits of her valorizing of the Juvenilia,[28] is on what threatens the author, but not the readers. Even the threat of rejection she specifies must be qualified, for Austen herself, as we have seen, also did some rejecting, turning from the periodical option that—with its many variations—might well have accommodated her "laughter." Certainly the readers could not have been threatened by what remained unpublished and thus unread, so the threat must have originated in other writing—in fact, I would argue, in writing itself.[29] Without the proliferation of writing—in quantity and in kinds—that occurred throughout the eighteenth century and accelerated at its close, Austen could not have had choices to make or readers to comfort. Her actions, as well as their reactions, make sense only when we broaden the historical context from a single career to the sphere of activity that enabled it.

A recurring topic of concern as Great Britain was transformed into a print culture was the probable effect of that proliferation: writing's ability not just to reflect or express the real but to change it. The question of writing's constitutive power surfaced throughout the century in a full range of endeavors, from the early political economists, whose "experiments" in writing were efforts not only to discuss productivity but *to be productive*, to Joseph Priestley's strategy of writing a history of electricity to induce scientific progress, to David Hume's efforts to wreak "havoc" on libraries by writing philosophy.[30] Just as today we speculate and moralize about television's influence on attention spans, family values, and even scholarly productivity, so, back then, the new technology of writing gazed self-reflexively on its own unknown potential: a large part of what people wrote and how they wrote had to do with their expectations regarding the productive power of writing. Thus to classify the innumerable eighteenth-century warnings against young women reading novels as simply a manifestation of Augustan conservatism is to miss a crucial historical point—the particular attitude toward change pointed to a more primary issue: writing's capacity to produce that change.[31]

Fiction, in the forms of romance and novel, served as a particularly charged locus of concern about writing's power throughout the century. Early efforts to assuage that concern, led by Richardson and Fielding, focused on the morality of the tale: if writing provided the proper models, then any changes it induced would not be cause for alarm. Such strict propriety, however, as Samuel Johnson's mid-century *Rambler* essay on fiction made quite clear, is not so easily maintained when realism is a priority. Not only is there a greater chance that, "for the sake of following nature," novelists will "mingle good and bad qualities," but "susceptible" readers will be more inclined, argued Johnson, to "follow the current" when the world on the page more closely resembles their own. Thus the more the novel centered on real life, the more suspect a form it became.[32]

The threat, then, was writing, and the solution was (for some reason) Austen's "new" kind of novels. What was so extraordinary about their reception was the lack of suspicion. Reviewers were so relaxed, so unalarmed by Austen's work. They complimented her on realistic characters that come "home to the heart," but, "agreeabl[y]" enough, do not "deteriorate" it (*Gentleman's Magazine*). What reassured them was not a more stringent morality; their admiration for her "accuracy" appears to have displaced rather than aggravated the concern for propriety. In fact, as thematized by Austen in *Northanger Abbey*, that concern was displaced right out of the text; the narrator concludes by "leav[ing] it to be settled by whomsoever it may concern, whether the tendency of this work be altogether to recommend parental tyranny, or reward filial disobedience" (252).

Despite the flippant tone, Austen makes it quite clear that this gesture is not meant to trivialize moral judgments but to mark them as complex—more specifically, as resistant to simplistic cause-and-effect analysis. In fact, the gesture is made in response to an example of such complexity: the cause (the General's "unjust interference" in Catherine and Henry's affairs) does not produce the expected effect ("injur[y]") but rather the opposite—it "improv[es]" their relationship. Only when "convinced" by this turnabout, does the narrator "leave" "recommend[ing]" to others. What is being abandoned, then, is not morality, but the mode of moralizing.

Calling that mode into question, however, is not just a device to end *Northanger*; the cause-and-effect linkage surfaces throughout the novel in Austen's focus on what writing does to those who read it. The threat of writing that the novel enacts is premised on linking, in that manner, behavior on the page to the behavior of readers. The discomforting question is whether we become what we read. Austen's answer—an answer that I would argue signals a change in writing's status from a worrisome new technology to a more trusted tool—is "Yes and no, but don't worry." Catherine Morland does, at times, behave somewhat like the gothic heroines she reads about, but she is neither "born" (13) to be such a heroine or doomed to become one. The linkage is too complex to be predictable, in terms of both what behaviors are enacted and their consequences. As with the General's villainous "interference," even the most threatening experiences contribute, finally, to the "improv[ement]" of "knowledge" (252) that fuels development.

I am not arguing that Austen solved the threat of writing simply by writing it off. This type of overt thematizing certainly played a role in altering perceptions of writing's power—and, to the extent that it did so, exemplified it—but the fate of writing also depended, and depends, both on matters of publication, including access and circulation, and of mode, including kind and institution. Austen's enigmatic "new"ness—and thus her role in the Great Forgetting—derive from her inhabiting a crucial historical intersection of all of these concerns. There, the "taming" of her writing, as Doody describes the changes occurring on the micro-level of the individual career, corresponds with and participates in, the taming, on the macro-level of her society, of writing itself.

I want to be very precise about the kind of claim that I am making here. By linking Austen to such a weighty phenomenon as the taming of writing, I am not trying to repeat, but to explain in a different key, the standard story of her important position within a developing great tradition. The problem, that is, is not whether, in aesthetic or other terms, she deserves to be valorized within the "rise" of the novel and of Literature, but the fact that *she has been* and continues to be. Both the "rise" and the reasons she's in it are matters I am locating within a history of disciplinarity—of the engendering of the modern organization of knowledge. My purpose, then, is not to revalidate established disciplinary knowledge (the category of Literature in which Austen is comfortably remembered) but to put it into history—a history that invites other forms of knowledge and other acts of remembrance. In doing so, I am trying to identify some of the features in Austen—the hooks into a newly forming disciplinarity—that can help explain how she gained and maintained such a privileged position.

The issue of periodical publication, for example, exemplifies the connection between the comfortable and the memorable that served Austen so well. One way to contain writing comfortably is to divide it, valorizing certain kinds and targeting them to specific audiences for specific purposes. In describing the late-century take-off in publication rates, the formation of the two-tier market for fiction, the polemicization of the periodicals, and Austen's refusal to publish in them, I have been attempting to locate her in the marketing changes that made writing more manageable—more like the still titillating and perhaps useful, but ultimately benign amusement thematized in *Northanger*. Staying out of the periodicals and not publishing the early works were exclusionary practices that resonated on both the micro- and the macro-levels: the six novels have, of course, dominated their author's individual oeuvre—a canonical formation Doody is trying to break—and, as markers of the "new" and comfortable, they have helped to enable and sustain the narrowing and hierarchizing that underwrites the discipline we now call Literature.

Austen, in other words, in disciplining the threat of writing, helped to turn writing into a discipline. When writing's threat is subordinated—when it appears to function more as a medium than as an object of attention—other subjects can come into view. Disciplinarity, then, is, historically, the organizational form of comfort with writing: a form in which a narrowing—and thus more easily mastered and monitored—range of inquiry is supposed to ensure a greater depth of understanding. Literature, as the particular discipline that takes writing as its subject, may be said to take this comfort particularly seriously, thus the *Gentleman's Magazine*'s assessment of Austen's novel as an "agreeable relaxation from severer studies."

The price of that comfort was the Great Forgetting. What Austen's "new" narrowing left out were not just those "things" that made writing uncomfortable, but, as we saw in the *Quarterly Review*, the "ladies' maids and sentimental washerwomen" they were "left to."[33] The historical connection was, once again, indirect, for Austen's immediate target was not gender but genre. Those "things" were features of the particular kind of fiction (the sentimental) that was most closely identified with the problem of writing's constitutive power—its capacity, Todd describes the sentimental, to bypass the mimetic and "force" response by linking the "literary" experience with the "living one."[34] But that kind of writing, in turn, was most closely identified with women, so that the taming of writing, through the subsuming of the sentimental within newly comfortable forms, inevitably entailed the disciplinary disappearance of many women writers.

Consistently Austen has been read—Richard Simpson called her the "ironical censurer of her contemporaries" in 1870 [35]—as a source of important models for that subsuming. It's not surprising, then, that the discipline those models enabled has remembered her, while forgetting so many others. Simpson did not intend, nor do I, to suggest that an ambitious and/or mean-spirited Austen deliberately managed to depose her rivals. Rather, I am arguing that her mode of censuring—the ironic containment of inherited features—functioned, like the mode of publication, as another "hook" by which she could be taken up by the very literary histories (Scott, Richard Whately, Simpson, etc.) that left them out.[36]

The abstract-sounding issues of "taming" and "comfort" materialized in those hooks—in matters of where writing appeared and of how familiar features were transformed. As we have just seen, the standard moral didacticism of sentimental fiction was contained in *Northanger Abbey* by Austen's portrayal of the ironic insufficiency of cause and effect. Such maneuvers increasingly differentiated the fiction in the magazines from the fiction in stand-alone volumes, especially as critics valorized those acts as evidence of something new subsuming the old. That subsuming—despite the seemingly substantial gender differences between Austen's "bit[s] . . . of Ivory" and Scott's "Big Bow-wow,"[37]—was what he and other (male) critics could claim to find in, and, to a certain extent, share with, Austen.

What they saw as shared typically followed the two-part pattern of *Northanger*'s conclusion: a narrowing (the refusal to moralize) for the sake of depth (the developmental "improv[ement]" of "knowledge"). Thus Scott argued that Austen's work, "bears the same relation to that of the sentimental and romantic cast, that cornfields and cottages and meadows bear to the highly adorned grounds of a show mansion, or the rugged sublimities of a mountain landscape" (Lodge 42). The sublime is subsumed in Austen, according to Scott, as the turn from the "excitements" of older forms of writing enables a "depth of knowledge" that marks the more comfortable "new" (38). For Scott himself, of course, the subsuming of romance was also crucial, though, in his case, more Romantic features remained, and the newly deep knowledge was less of "ordinary walks of life" than of "national character."[38]

Austen was thus inserted enigmatically into literary history as particularly narrow but thus admirably deep. On one hand, the narrow-but-deep formulation was a crucial disciplinary link to her future in Literature. The concluding gesture of *Northanger*'s narrator—"I leave it to [others]"—is what disciplines do in order to go about their own work. On the other hand, however, the degree of narrowness (domesticity) and the kind of depth (female development) invited the tradition of negative appreciation. Austen was thus a site for the engendering of disciplinarity: Where she published, what she wrote, and the ways in which she has been valued and devalued demonstrate how the new divisions of knowledge were informed by divisions of gender. From its inception, I am arguing, that system of knowledge has functioned to articulate and enact those divisions.[39]

Austen's survivor role in the early-nineteenth-century re-masculinization of writing,[40] then, is not a matter to be adjudicated solely in terms of her individual beliefs—her personal feminism; it is, however, a problem in the historicity of the category of Literature. Current concerns over the stability of that category have helped to generate the "So what?" genre I cited at the start of this essay. The particular "So what?" central to this collection—"Was Austen a feminist?"— is infused at this historical moment with that concern. As a moment troubled by newly disturbing technologies and signs of another re-masculinization,[41] the present invites, even demands, a better understanding of the past—of the forms of comfort secured in Austen's time and of the price.

Notes

1. My thanks to the organizer of this 1993 MLA session, Charles Rzepka.

2. See *The Historicity of Romantic Discourse* (New York: Oxford University Press, 1988), 125-47.

3. Claudia Johnson, *Jane Austen: Women, Politics, and the Novel* (Chicago: University of Chicago Press, 1988).

4. Janet Todd, *The Sign of Angellica: Women, Writing and Fiction, 1660–1800* (New York: Columbia University Press, 1989), 227.

5. Moira Ferguson, ed., *First Feminists: British Women Writers 1578–1799* (Bloomington: Indiana University Press, 1985). Roger Lonsdale, ed., *Eighteenth-Century Women Poets: An Oxford Anthology* (Oxford: Oxford University Press, 1989). Dale Spender and Janet Todd, ed., *British Women Writers: An Anthology from the Fourteenth Century to the Present* (New York: Peter Bedrick Books, 1989).

6. Raymond Williams, *Keywords: A Vocabulary of Culture and Society* (New York: Oxford University Press, 1976, rev. 1983), 183-88. Alvin Kernan, *Samuel Johnson and the Impact of Print* (Princeton: Princeton University Press, 1987).

7. W. Austin Flanders, *Structures of Experience: History, Society, and Personal Life in the Eighteenth-Century British Novel* (Columbia: University of South Carolina Press, 1984), 172, 180.

8. Michael Danahy, *The Feminization of the Novel* (Gainesville: University of Florida Press, 1991), vii, 47.

9. Deborah Ross, *Romance, Realism, and Women's Contribution to the Novel* (Lexington: The University Press of Kentucky, 1991), 3-4.

10. See my argument in "The Rise of Novelism" in Deidre Lynch and William B. Warner, ed., *Cultural Institutions of the Novel* (Durham: Duke University Press, 1996) (forthcoming).

11. See "Eighteenth-Century Periodicals and the Romantic Rise of the Novel," *Studies in the Novel*, 26 (Spring/Summer 1994): 26-42.

12. See James Raven, *Judging New Wealth: Popular Publishing and Responses to Commerce in England 1750–1800* (Oxford: Clarendon Press, 1992), 31-41.

13. See my discussion of Richard Whately in *Historicity*, 138-39.

14. "Eighteenth-Century Periodicals and the Romantic Rise of the Novel," 36.

15. Robert Mayo, *The English Novel in the Magazines 1740–1815 With a Catalogue of 1375 Magazine Novels and Novelettes* (Evanston: Northwestern University Press, 1962), 2, 322.

16. *Angellica*, 220.

17. See Deborah Kaplan's description of this incident in *Jane Austen Among Women* (Baltimore: Johns Hopkins University Press, 1992), 100.

18. Jan Fergus argues persuasively against Jane Austen being the author of a letter signed "Sophia Sentiment" published in *Loiterer* 9 (61).

19. Jane Austen, *Northanger Abbey and Persuasion.* vol. 5 of *The Novels of Jane Austen.*. ed. R. W. Chapman, 5 vols. 3d ed. (London: Oxford University Press, 1932-34), 38.

20. Hierarchization was, of course, already taking place earlier in the century, but could not fully assume its modern form of high and low culture until the instituting of copyright and the take-off in publication at the century's close.

21. Review of *Pride and Prejudice* by William Gifford in *The Quarterly Review*, cited in F. B. Pinion, *A Jane Austen Companion: A Critical Survey and Reference Book* (London: Macmillan, 1973), 181.

22. Jon Klancher, *The Making of English Reading Audiences, 1790–1832* (Madison: The University of Wisconsin Press, 1987), 20.

23. David Lodge, ed., *Jane Austen, Emma: A Casebook* (London: Macmillan, 1968, rev. 1991), 14.

24. Scott's review appeared in the *Quarterly Review* XIV (1815): 188-201. Selections are reprinted in Lodge, 36-43.

25. Pinion, *Jane Austen Companion*, 180.

26. These reviews, all published in 1816, are conveniently collected in Lodge, *Jane Austen*, 43-45.

27. Introduction in Jane Austen, *Catharine and Other Writings*, ed. Margaret Anne Doody and Douglas Murray (Oxford: Oxford University Press, 1993), xxxviii.

28. I use "disturbing" and "comfortable" not as aesthetic, but as historical, categories— categories that can help me describe the naturalization of writing in the eighteenth century.

29. I am following Raymond Williams here in using "writing" as shorthand for the entire configuration of "writing, print, and silent reading." See Raymond Williams, *Writing in Society* (London: Verso, 1983), 6.

30. On political economy, see David McNally, *Political Economy and the Rise of Capitalism: A Reinterpretation* (Berkeley: University of California Press, 1988), 1. On Joseph Priestley, see Charles Bazerman, "How Natural Philosophers Can Cooperate: The Literary Technology of Coordinated Investigation in Joseph Priestley's *History and Present State of Electricity* (1767) in *Textual Dynamics of the Professions: Historical and Contemporary Studies of Writing in Professional Communities*, Charles Bazerman and James

Paradis, ed., (Madison: University of Wisconsin Press, 1991), 16. David Hume's argument regarding "havoc" concludes *An Enquiry Concerning Human Understanding*.

31. I am focusing here on the ways in which the British came to terms with—"natural-ized," to use Raymond Williams's word—the "new" technology of writing. Evidence for that naturalization exists not only in explicit comments on the power of writing, but also in the ways different kinds of writing are produced, mixed, circulated, reviewed, and reproduced. For a discussion of the explicit attitudes toward writing during the eighteenth century, focusing particularly on the oral/written binary, see Nicholas Hudson, *Writing and European Thought, 1600–1830* (Cambridge: Cambridge University Press, 1994).

32. Samuel Johnson, *The Rambler*, 4, Saturday, 31 March 1750, reprinted in Samuel Johnson, *Selected Writings*, ed. Patrick Cruttwell (London: Penguin Books, 1968, rpt. 1988), 149-53.

33. The hierarchizing, in ways I do not have the space to explore here, transposed socioeconomic difference into aesthetic value.

34. Janet Todd, *Sensibility: An Introduction* (London: Methuen, 1986), 4, 6. Todd points out that, "at the same time" readers are "forced to respond to the emotion conveyed," the "devices" of sentiment—"asterisks, dashes, meandering narrative and fragmen-tation"—indicate "the inadequacy of the medium (language) in which, despite their intrusive presence, most of the business of the work is still transacted." In regard to the history of writing, then, the sentimental can be seen as transitional: both enacting (acting out?) writing's power and, by articulating it as inadequate, partic-ipating in the "taming" I am describing (4).

35. Richard Simpson, "Jane Austen," *North British Review*, LII (1870), 129-32, reprinted in Lodge, *Jane Austen*, 53-57. Lodge cites this essay as "one of the finest studies of Jane Austen ever written" (16).

36. None of these hooks is necessarily unique to Austen, and no single one of them can alone account for her disciplinary fate. Other hooks, as well as the ways they combine, need to be identified and studied.

37. The reference to "Ivory" is in *Jane Austen's Letters: To Her Sister Cassandra and Others*, ed. R. W. Chapman, 2d ed. (London: Oxford University Press, 1952), 468-69. "Bow-wow" is reprinted in *Jane Austen: The Critical Heritage*, ed. B. C. Southam (London: Routledge & Kegan Paul, 1968), 106. Claudia Johnson notes an increasingly "rigid distinction" by 1815 between "male" and "female" novels (xiv).

38. Scott uses this formula of "more Romantic incident" and "national character" to help to distinguish Maria Edgeworth from Austen, but it certainly applies to his differ-ences with Austen as well. See Ian Duncan's enlightening discussion of Scott's efforts to subsume romance in *Modern Romance and Transformations of the Novel: The Gothic, Scott, Dickens* (Cambridge: Cambridge University Press, 1992).

39. See my argument about engendering disciplinarity in "Gender, Sublimity, Culture: Retheorizing Disciplinary Desire," *Eighteenth-Century Studies*, 28 (Fall 1994): 37-50.

40. See, for example, Todd's description of Wollstonecraft's fate in *Angellica*, 214-15. Gary Kelly describes the "re-masculinization" in *Revolutionary Feminism: The Mind and Career of Mary Wollstonecraft* (London: Macmillan, 1992), 227.
41. See, for example, Susan Faludi, *Backlash: The Undeclared War Against American Women* (New York: Crown Publishers, 1991). Also, Susan Jeffords, *The Remasculinization of America: Gender and the Vietnam War* (Bloomington: Indiana University Press, 1989).

II

Critical Reexaminations

4

Jane Austen and the Marriage Plot: Questions of Persistence

Laura Mooneyham White

Feminist dissatisfaction with the marriage plot has been stewing for a great deal longer than this century's roiling boil of complaint might suggest. Long before Virginia Woolf protested in *A Room of One's Own* against the stories told "when love was the only possible interpreter"[1] of a woman's life, George Eliot closed *Middlemarch* by reminding her readers that "Marriage, which has been the bourne of so many narratives, is still a great beginning, as it was to Adam and Eve, who kept their honeymoon in Eden, but had their first little one among the thorns and thistles of the wilderness."[2] But it has been the portion of feminists in the latter half of this century to make a comprehensive critique of the oppressiveness of the marriage plot, this ancient narrative structure that creates closure by pairing off female and male protagonists. There is indeed much to complain about if all plots that are to end happily must do so by providing mates for our heroes or heroines, given that such a requirement implies that marriage closes plots (and thus people's lives) "naturally" and that marriage is the only desirable end for female protagonists. Such critical dissatisfaction collects even around authors like Jane Austen, who provides much for feminists to praise. Unalterable, after all, is the fact that each of Austen's novels relies on the marriage plot as its central structuring device, and this reliance on her part has inevitably led many critics to express a wide range of demurrals with Austen's cultural values as they seem to be expressed by her novels. My purpose is to show some of the limits of this critical perspective and come, by way of Jane Austen, to a partial defense of the marriage plot.

A preliminary danger with critiques of the marriage plot lies in their sometimes overreaching into the realm of the prescriptive, a problem Annette Kolodny and others have addressed. When one form of narrative is deemed unwholesome, the natural impulse is not only to identify narratives that conform more thoroughly with the critic's normative values but also to call for, even to endorse, only those narratives that do as the critic wishes. As Kolodny observes about the feminist search for common denominators among women writers of style or subject matter, "if the anthologies of feminist writings offer us repeated outcries against those men who would claim to speak authoritatively for and about women, it follows that any handy group of current women writers ought not to be granted the privilege of speaking for and about all women altogether . . . what [one] must avoid . . . is the tendency to become prescriptive, suggesting what women ought to write."[3] But this fault does not characterize the fairest and most insightful of feminist criticism, so I do not wish to do more than draw cursory attention to it.

More common, however, and linked to the fault of prescriptiveness, is the problem of overly programmatic revisionings of narrative. Calling for other narrative ends to substitute for the marriage plot, as do Rachel DuPlessis and other committed reimaginers of narrative structure, can sometimes lead to programmatic practice and analysis. DuPlessis's justified dissatisfaction with the marriage plot, for instance, leads her to call for variant narrative ends that rely on human relationships other than those between heterosexual adults: "reparenting, female bonding, including lesbian ties, mother-child dyads, brother-sister pairs, familial transpositions, the multiple individual, and the transpersonal protagonist."[4] These different patterns of human connection do, of course, satisfy the narrative desires of many contemporary readers, but these categories primarily describe what DuPlessis *wants* to be written—and if followed, could lead to new forms of potentially restrictive convention. These narratives are to substitute for the conventions of nineteenth-century fiction, which DuPlessis wishes to delegitimate: "the subordination of quest to love, the death of the questing female, the insertion into family life."[5] We infer that legitimate plots *must* subordinate love to quest, show the triumph of the questing female, and reject family life, an inference that may straitjacket narrative practice. Furthermore, it doesn't take long for a reenvisioned sort of narrative closure itself to turn into a cliché; one might cite the novelty-grown-demodé that Julian Barnes attacks in his recent *Flaubert's Parrot* with a decalogue of narrative types he would prohibit. Prohibition #6a reads: "no novels in which carnal connection takes place between a human being and an animal. The woman and the porpoise, for instance, whose tender coupling symbolizes a wider mending of those gossamer threads which formerly bounds the world together in peaceable companionship. No, none of that."[6] One might puzzle—briefly—why the marriage plot becomes stale only in the many thousandth year of its existence while it only takes three or four novels about people and porpoises conjoining before the impulse arises to say "stop."

EMMA, WAYNE BOOTH, AND THE MARRIAGE PLOT

Even the best and most thoughtful of criticisms of the marriage plot can be flawed by faults beyond that of implicit or explicit prescriptiveness: sometimes by too-easily accepted premises about the reading experience, sometimes about assumptions of a limited function for marriage in a narrative, and sometimes about how the contemporary normative interpretation of marriage constitutes an uncritically accepted ideal. Wayne Booth's careful reassessment of Austen's *Emma* in *The Company We Keep* (1988) exemplifies some of the difficulties faced by even the most skilled critics of the marriage plot. In his 1967 *The Rhetoric of Fiction*, Booth had praised and defended the happy ending of *Emma*; as he explains in his 1988 essay, *Emma* was a novel that "for years seemed to [him] ideologically flawless."[7] Booth's later essay is itself a reevaluation of feminist complaints about *Emma*'s end and ultimately a defense of that end. The complaints are serious ones:

> The most obvious objection that might raise to this work, taking it seriously as the educational force it cannot fail to be, is that Emma's ultimate happiness is identified with learning to see the world as Knightley sees it; with acceding to his judgment on all important matters; and finally with bowing to that man in loving but inevitably submissive vows of matrimony. . . . It would not be hard to conclude . . . that this wonderful story, one of the greatest of novels, one that on its surface seems least guilty of anything that could be called sexism, is in fact a dangerous work to put into the hands of the young. It will miseducate its female readers by confirming their sense of dependence on and inferiority to men; it will miseducate its male readers by confirming their egotism and their cheerful willingness to assume the role of lord and master.[8]

The heart of Booth's strategy is to show that Austen's ironic perspective on the marriage plot legitimates its use because the superior irony of the narrator instructs us toward a right reading. Booth claims that Austen uses the marriage plot preeminently because novels in her day required them— they were "*simply* required formally."[9] And against these external require-

ments readers should set their understanding of Austen's subversive acknowl-
edgment that happy endings are fantasies: "Though all *is* finally well for
Emma and George Knightley, in their fairy-tale world, we have been taught,
unrelentingly, that *all is far from well in the real world implied by the book.*"[10] Here
Booth accepts the basic logic of what K. K. Ruthven has termed the
"contradictionist" mode of criticism, one articulated by Marxists such as
Althusser and Adorno and appropriated by feminists, in which the "business
of a critic . . . is to examine a literary work for traces of the ideologies which
shape it, whether its author was aware of them or not, and to point to
discrepancies between what the work purports to tell and what a careful
reading of it shows. In this type of enquiry a good book is one that questions
the ideologies it articulates, like *Tess of the d'Urbervilles* or *Jude the Obscure*, whose
heroines are not constrained by contemporary ideologies of female virtue
and bourgeois marriage."[11] *Emma* may then be a "good book" if Booth can
show Austen's subversive development of the limitations of the marriage plot,
a project Booth shares with most feminist critics of Austen.[12] One problem
with such "contradictionist" logic is an inevitable one: It can, as Ruthven
explains, "recoil upon the user."[13] Thus, any method that demonstrates the
contradictions of bourgeois marriage plots can be used to demonstrate
equally well the contradictions of feminism.[14] Surely current social conditions—even among committed feminists—demonstrate the contradictions
between the ideals of feminism and its practice.

Furthermore, Booth, like most feminist critics, assumes that our present
values about marriage are on their face far superior to those of Austen and
that the current value we place on equality between marriage partners is an
unquestioned ideal. One may share these values, as I most emphatically do,
without assuming their universal ideality, centrality, or permanence. An
unexamined belief in the rightness of one's own values can, after all, lead to
even further critical distortions, such as those attacked by Alistair Duckworth
at the end of his "Jane Austen and the Construction of a Progressive Author."
Disturbed by one critic's disappointment in Austen's deathbed piety, he asks:
"In pursuit of an autonomous and progressive author do we fail to see those
aspects of a deeply pious woman for whom manners, ideally, were the living
embodiment of religious principle? In our desire to restore a Nietzschean
sense of the body to Austen's fiction do we fail to credit her belief—whatever
our own might be—in the existence of a soul?"[15] We should be careful to
avoid the assumption that current values, however deeply held and seemingly
just, may not be the absolute last word—nor the only meter by which we
may judge an author like Austen whose worldview differed from contemporary values in significant measure.

Booth goes on to suggest that a reading which does not see Austen's marriage plot as an externally required fantasy is indeed potentially injurious to present-day readers: "Unless we can somehow incorporate something like an ironic vision of the ending—even while pretending not to, even while enjoying the fairy tale to the full—we are indeed confirming its capacity to implant a harmful vision of the sexes."[16] This premise—the *prima facie* injuriousness of romance plots, within a society or for a reader—needs to be argued, not accepted forthwith. And yet arguing this premise sometimes leads to further—and equally problematic—unargued premises, as in Mary Poovey's "*Persuasion* and the Promises of Love." Poovey discusses the split between public and private spheres in Austen and shows with force and clarity the central contradiction between the idea, one Austen endorses, that romantic love exerts moral authority, particularly beyond the private sphere, and the realities of bourgeois society. She claims that "the notion that romantic relationships actually have the kind of social power this emotional prominence [given to the 'premises and promises of romantic love'] suggests is actually an illusion: in the absence of institutions that actually link the private and public spheres, romantic relationships, by their very nature, cannot materially affect society." Here, of course, is another unargued premise, restated by Poovey on the same page in this manner: "In Jane Austen's society, of course, romantic love did not alter the institutions of marriage or property or female dependence."[17] I would at the very least suggest that there is nothing in such a claim to merit that offhand "of course," for to show that romantic love commonly failed to remake the institutions of marriage, property, or female dependence to match the expectations of its own ideology is far short from showing that romantic love exerted *no* influence upon the social systems of the nineteenth century.

These unargued premises are accompanied in Booth's defense of *Emma* by a too-ready acceptance of some common criticisms of the marriage plot, particularly by Booth's taking as a given the deleterious effect of *Emma*'s marriage plot upon readers, as if the question of the adequacy of the moral or social modeling of a text were the central question at issue when we consider a novel's value. As a beginning defense of Austen—if not of the marriage plot—one should note that *Emma* would not be the only book one reads. Booth criticizes *Emma* for endorsing a narrative close in which a flawed heroine finds her "perfect happiness" with a wiser husband who instructs her, but he neglects Austen's flexibility with the marriage plot—that is, her willingness to close narratives with relatively equal partners (e.g., *Pride and Prejudice*) or with a wiser woman finding happiness after she has educated her flawed husband into a recognition of her superior deserts (e.g., *Mansfield Park* or *Persuasion*). But one's defense of *Emma* should not rest solely on the properties of Austen's other novels. More important, if readers are damaged by reading texts whose central values are in any or in some degree at odds with the central values of their own culture, then the truth of narrative and cultural history will declare that *all* texts of the past are in some way at odds with the central values of today's culture—even if we were all in agreement about what those values are—and that the damage done by reading is pervasive and inescapable. In some ways, we *do* read *The Iliad* to learn how to hack at each other and to risk being infected by the bloodthirsty values of Achilles and Hector, yet usually the lessons are mediated and overpassed by our own cultural standards.[18] We may be able to read plots such as *Emma*'s as we do Wallace Stevens's "The Ordinary Women," who read of marriage but who stay unmarried. The women in this poem study books from their window sills, "And there they read of marriage-bed. . . . /And they read all night long.[19]

I am well aware, however, that arguing for readerly immunity or at least resistance to marriage plots does not constitute the best defense of marriage plots themselves, given that such a position seems to admit that marriage plots menace readers unless they are ignored or undermined by a strong ironic reading. Rather, a defense of the marriage plot should be set along lines that allow for a larger understanding of marriage's role in narrative closure. It is not enough to say, as did Booth, that marriage as narrative resolution is "simply required formally," or to argue, as does Jean Kennard in her *Victims of Convention* (1978), that the independence and verve of heroines such as Dorothea Brooke or Emma Woodhouse are "sacrificed to structural neatness"[20] when the plots end with the heroines' marriages. Rather, it persists in the fictive imagination for some compelling reasons, and while the attack on the marriage plot as indicative of repressive social conditions and ideologies is well justified, feminist critics might benefit from seeing beyond the historical and cultural dimension of marriage.

Structuralist critics on the one hand and psychoanalytic critics on the other offer supplementary analyses of marriage's role in narrative. The structuralist Northrop Frye aligns with the psychoanalytic critic Peter Brooks to tell us that the movement to a wedding in fiction represents the achievement of psychic identity and that this psychodrama's logic persists even when (as always) particular cultural and historical expressions of the relationships between men and women fall into question. If the goal of every fictive event is identity, the quest for which is acted out by the protagonist and felt by the reader, then the marriage of protagonists represents the accomplishment of that identity. For *Emma*, marriage takes its meaning from the heroine's psychic growth; her marriage is "most significant as a social ritual which metaphorically ratifies a transformation in Emma herself."[21] That accomplishment is thus signaled, *represented*, by the act of comic closure—by the wedding bells of *Emma* and by those of every other marriage plot. As D. A. Miller argues in *Narrative and Its Discontents*, narrative closure always necessitates the working out of a structure of readerly identity.[22] Peter Brooks's psychodynamic model of narrative, a model explicated in his 1984 *Reading for the Plot*, likewise describes closure as the psychical equivalent of readerly identity—and plot as the history of the quest for that identity: "The deviance and error of plot may necessarily result from the interplay of desire in its history with the narrative insistence on explanatory form: the desire to wrest beginnings and ends from the uninterrupted flow of middles, from temporality itself; the search for that significant closure that would illuminate the sense of an existence, the meaning of life. The desire for meaning is ultimately the reader's."[23] This orientation toward the end is impelled then by the desire for identity. What Northrop Frye claims about this quest for identity in romance applies with equal force to the comic romances of Jane Austen: "Identity means a good many things, but all its meanings in romance have some connection with a state of existence in which there is nothing to write about. It is existence before 'once upon a time' and subsequent to 'and they lived happily ever after."[24] In the comic romance, identity is the state before and after plot, the realm of non-narratibility, where "there is nothing to write about." Marriage plots are games played within the context of the unstable self and are fueled by that energy which desires integration, union, closure. In comedy, we achieve— or feel that we have achieved—psychic integration through the power of wedding bells at a narrative's close.

SENSE AND SENSIBILITY AND THE
FAILURE OF THE MARRIAGE PLOT

As I argued in *Romance, Language and Education in Jane Austen's Novels* (1988), the persistence of the eros quest in narrative means that a novel such as *Sense and Sensibility*, which lacks an eros quest, can sometimes fail.[25] Such a failure will take place, however, only if the values of the novel's world imply that marriage is *the* symbol by which integration between protagonists becomes possible. It is Austen's own reliance on marriage as the trope by which conflicts are resolved that makes for structural problems when the central conflict in the novel lies between two sisters. Austen's imagination—and the conditions of her art—require that education be linked to a sexual conflict—

literally heterosexual, between male and female. In all of Austen's novels except *Sense and Sensibility*, education and then marriage are the integral products of the relationship between hero and heroine. In these novels, education is romance, and vice versa, and Austen's values hold that marriage be the natural result of education and love. Whether the hero educates the heroine, as in *Emma* and *Northanger Abbey*, or the heroine educates the hero, as in *Mansfield Park*, or each educates the other, as in *Pride and Prejudice*, the clashes and conjoining between lovers constitutes the royal road to the only acceptable closure for Austen's imaginative world: marriage.

There is, however, only a very limited educative relationship between hero and heroine in *Sense and Sensibility*. Marianne and Brandon do not educate each other; how can they when they do not even have one instance of reported dialogue in all of the novel? Brandon only flanks Elinor as a representative of sense. Nor do Edward and Elinor have any educative give-and-take until after their engagement is a settled thing and we are in no further suspense about their romantic resolution. The double bow of moral and sexual conflict has never been tautened between hero and heroine, so there can be no important relaxing of tension. For this reason, the marriages have failed to engage the interest of many readers, not merely because they wish Brandon and Edward were more handsome and interesting, though surely this must be the case, but also because the sisters' unions with these heroes fail to enrich our understanding of the novel's chief thematic conflicts. In the end, the conflict that shapes the novel is a sexless, and therefore a sterile, one. I do not mean, of course, to imply that a narrative end reliant upon either the connections between sisters or between two women, *vide* DuPlessis's formulations, lacks the constituent psychic dimensions necessary for a successful plot; far to the contrary. But in Austen's fiction, the quest for identity through sororial love is out of bounds. Marriage cannot resolve the central clash of ideology represented by Marianne and Elinor, and thus Marianne's capitulation to Elinor's values at the novel's close cannot satisfy. A novel that lives by the marriage plot must bring its marriage plot to life.

PERSUASION AND THE REIMAGINED MARRIAGE PLOT

Austen's insistence upon happy unions at the close of each of the novels was generally far more successful and far less programmatic than in *Sense and Sensibility*. Her last successful marriage plot, *Persuasion*, may even suggest a reconfiguration of certain crucial elements of this form of narrative that foreshadows some of this century's experiments with the marriage plot. Stanley Cavell offers us a useful model for reconditioning the marriage plot by suggesting in his analysis of Hollywood films in *The Pursuit of Happiness* (1981) that this century's abandonment of the belief in the "perfect happiness" promised by novels such as *Emma* does not spell the end of marriage plots. Rather, Cavell argues, the plot of remarriage emerges, in which after the first romantic resolution, things fall apart. Only after the disruption represented by separation or divorce may a wiser and more seasoned romantic resolution be devised for the protagonists. Taking as his exempla such films as *The Lady Eve* (1941) and *Bringing Up Baby* (1938), Cavell explains: "what I am calling the comedy of remarriage. . . cast[s] as its heroine a married woman, and the drive of its plot is not to get the central pair together, but to get them back together, together again. Hence the fact of marriage in it is subjected to the fact of the threat of divorce."[26] Cavell believes that the preeminence of such a reinterpreted marriage plot in twentieth-century narratives has been caused by the rise of feminism and by the serious questioning of marriage as a legitimate cultural entity.

What may give pause is the curious existence of an earlier sort of plot of remarriage in *Persuasion*, written, in 1816, over 100 years before the Hollywood screwball films developed and refined the comedy of remarriage. Austen's *Persuasion* may anticipate this modern strain of marriage plot in that it concerns a single woman past her prime ("past her prime" in Austen's day means that the heroine is 27); the novel begins eight years after a serious relationship with the hero that almost carried through to marriage. The plot concerns the attempt to "get them back together, together again" which characterizes the plots of remarriage Cavell is describing, so that Anne and Wentworth, "once so much to each other, now nothing," can be something to each other again.[27]

Such a narrative is a thoroughgoing novelty in Austen's work, because never before had the period of courtship that leads to love and its declaration been left out of her novels. The narrative interest only begins at the point of "retentive feelings" that must find expression even at the cost of prudence or of reliving old hurts (*P*, 60). Cavell points out that the plot of remarriage commonly insists with Shakespearean force upon the necessity of "foolishness" for happy love stories (e.g., the final achievement of being a "mug" in *The Lady Eve*),[28] and *Persuasion* may show Austen's closest rendering of the folly of love in its portrayal of Wentworth's and Anne's reeducation into feeling. Wentworth at the novel's start speaks of his foolishness with no self-awareness; planning to marry whatever good-looking girl comes his way, he brags, "If I am a fool, I shall be a fool indeed, for I have thought on the subject more than most men" (P, 62). To be truly a fool, however, Wentworth must lose his pride, and Anne must surrender some of her prudence. This novel may have this more modern cast and employ this variant of the marriage plot exactly because the older, wiser and more independently minded heroine Austen chose could not develop in a plot that involved the awakenings of first love and because Austen's mature assessment of the risks and injustices of the courtship system led her to seek a plot that would show, in a sense, the "threat of divorce."[29] Even the happy ending of *Persuasion* is precarious; we are assured of Anne and Wentworth's happiness only in the context of the threat Napoleon and war in general pose to sailors and their wives. *Persuasion* demonstrates, at any rate, Austen's surety that the achievement of the marriage plot is an act of faith, in the future and in the achievements of narrative.

SANDITON AND THE UNDOING OF THE MARRIAGE PLOT

Does the persistence—even if reconfigured—of the marriage plot mean that marriage plots have a necessary ubiquity? If we reject a position that echoes Hamlet's cry, "I say we will have no more marriages" (III.ii.154-5), must we exchange it for a position that claims that narratives *without* marriages are flawed? I believe not—for to be bound by even as important a human structure as marriage would fail to represent the multidimensionality of human experience. How could one suggest that the movement to heterosexual pairing is *the* central narrative experience when heterosexual pairing is so clearly not a part of so many people's lives?

One last example from Austen may demonstrate that the persistence of the marriage plot—and its importance—is not the same as its inevitability. *Sanditon*, Austen's last and unfinished novel, may represent a narrative in which the central female character is meant to remain unmarried, unaffected by the romance plot set for more minor characters. This novel, which Jane Austen left unfinished at her death in 1816, is a remarkable work— remarkable in and of itself and remarkable as a work of Austen's. A reader familiar with the completed novels enters *Sanditon* with the feeling of breathing a new air. An attempt to understand the subject and design of *Sanditon* in terms of Austen's previous novels is perhaps best undertaken in a spirit that relishes difference and contrast. After all, as I have said, Austen's completed novels uniformly take for their subject a heroine's progress toward maturity and matrimony, progress in which the latter stands as reward for the former. But when we reach *Sanditon*, the old subject seems discarded. Here the subject is neither the education of the heroine nor her eventual romantic fate, but rather the condition of society. Society is the protagonist, as it is in such Victorian novels as *Barchester Towers* and *Middlemarch*. *Sanditon* records a new place, a seaside resort eager for the tourist trade, and a new, more openly commercial age, exposing both the flaws and energy of an emerging era.

Charlotte Heywood is the heroine of *Sanditon*. But Charlotte is not a typical Austen heroine. Though her steady good sense and her status as an observer rather than a participant in the action might tempt one to group Charlotte with such virtuous and perceptive heroines as Elinor Dashwood, Fanny Price, and Anne Elliot, closer examination of her character reveals significant differences. What Charlotte lacks are these heroines' traumatic situations. Charlotte is not disinherited, unhappy, disregarded, or oppressed; she is no Cinderella figure destined for a radical reversal of fortune. She bears her unmarried status with equanimity. What then can Austen do—or care to do—for Charlotte?

Uncharacteristically, the sexual plot that in any other Austen narrative would lead heroine to hero seems here to hold at best a subordinate position. In fact, there does not seem to be a discernible plot of romance for the heroine by the end of chapter 12, the end of the fragment—a point at which, as John Lauber has noted, Darcy is thoroughly interested in Elizabeth in *Pride and Prejudice* and at which comparable development of the romance plot has already occurred in every one of the novels.[30] We are so conditioned by the pattern of Austen's novels that we come to *Sanditon* predisposed to find the heroine a mate, since the hero as reward has been for Austen *the* essential element of narrative design and closure. But who is he in *Sanditon*? Critics who not unreasonably assume a continuation of the marriage plot's preeminence (such as Tony Tanner, John Halperin, and Joseph Kestner) generally conclude that in *Sanditon* Mr. Sidney Parker is the man destined to marry Charlotte.[31] As Halperin points out, since *Sanditon* does include the claim that "young Ladies that have no Money are very much to be pitied,"[32] we very well may assume that "husbands must be found for them."[33] And a novelistic continuation of *Sanditon* (by "Jane Austen and Another Lady," the lady being one Anne Telscombe) sails unhesitatingly into a final love scene between Charlotte and Sidney ("It was the first time he had used her name. Like the touch of his hand in the tea rooms, it made her heart begin to pound with a happiness so heady, so immediate, and so violent that she could not have spoken a word") without any doubt that such an ending was what Austen intended.[34] As Telscombe explains in the afterword, "why depart from such a well-worn and ready-to-hand formula? Why should anyone feel Jane Austen herself intended to do so in her seventh novel if it had already taken her so triumphantly through six?"[35]

Why indeed? We do not meet this marital possibility for Charlotte until the penultimate page of the novel-as-fragment, in chapter 12: "Sidney Parker was about seven or eight-and-twenty, very good-looking, with a decided air of ease and fashion, and a lively countenance." (S, 425). His age seems appropriate, and his looks are promising, though perhaps too good. But the "decided air of ease and fashion" sounds far more like a description of one of Austen's cads, say, of Frank Churchill or of Willoughby, than it does of an Austen hero. Halperin has pointed out that the cad proper of this novel, Sir Edward, is pitifully inept at the business of seduction;[36] posing no threat, Sir Edward leaves a structural hole in the usual pattern of Austen's characterization. At any rate, Sidney Parker's character may have been intended to fill the cad position so poorly and shabbily occupied by Sir Edward. John Lauber believes that Sidney Parker is probably not meant to be a complete cad like Willoughby, Wickham, or Mr. Elliot but that he may be not far from the more appealing cad of Emma: "That Sidney Parker would have become the antihero is unlikely, but it is easy to imagine him playing an ambiguous role, in the manner of Frank Churchill."[37] And the earliest mention of Sidney Parker, from his hypochondriacal brother, raises further objections to Sidney as hero: "He lives too much in the world to be settled: that is his only fault.—He is here and there and everywhere" (S, 382). To be here, there, and everywhere could not more firmly disqualify one from being a proper hero in Austen's world, even in the flux of Sanditon; such butterfly habits, we remember, are chief black marks against Frank Churchill and Henry Crawford. When Sidney shows up in chapter 12, he is not coming to stay with his family but is passing through from one resort to the next: "He was just come from Eastbourne, proposing to spend two or three days, as it might happen, at Sanditon—but the Hotel must be his Quarters—He was expecting to be joined there by a friend or two" (S, 425). As Irene Taylor points out, "For Austen, the disease of activity is a disease of the social spirit. . . . Clearly if Sidney Parker is to deserve Charlotte, he will have to employ his energies more worthily, have to build for himself a solid place in life, probably by settling into a profession."[38]

This disturbingly discordant characterization raises a refreshing possibility: What if Austen never meant Charlotte to marry? Both Lauber and D. A. Miller feel that such a narrative close would be in keeping with the fragment's values.[39] Lauber remarks, "Charlotte Heywood, if not to be matched with the skeptical Sidney Parker, might simply have returned thankfully to the peace and stability of her family's home and traditional way of life."[40] Miller goes further: His assurance that the marriage plot in Sanditon is dismantled rests on his reading—not merely of the disruptions and flux of the society of the novel's world but of what he terms the "culture of morbidity" in the novel, a culture of hypochondria, bodily dislocation, and sickness: "if the socialization of hypochondria at Sanditon changes [the middle class's] status, the resultant culture of morbidity in turn transfigures the elements and operation of social space, whose ethos can no longer be epitomized, indeed may not even be at all tenable, by the marriage plot that in Austen's other novels never relaxes the rigor of its grip on every episode." Miller's analysis extends to describing the world of *Sanditon* as "postconjugal."[41]

If marriage symbolizes the growth of the self, then Charlotte, a fully mature personality, might not require it; on her deathbed, the unmarried Austen may have recognized the limitations of her marriage plots and devised a plot that allows self-sufficiency to an unheroed heroine. Austen's earlier works all emphasize that through marriage one becomes part of a social and economic entity. Marriage allows the heroine to join the wholeness of society even as she joins the unity of male and female. But the social and psychological integration marriage has represented may never have been a narrative goal in this last Austen narrative. In the flux of *Sanditon*, marriage's utility as a symbol of this all-encompassing integration is seriously marred. There is no stable society left in which to place oneself, either singly or two by two. When the Parkers' meandering carriage breaks down near the Heywood home, one knows that Austen meant this moment to symbolize one in a series of assaults on English tradition: those on the move causing upheaval for those content to stay still. Here Austen bravely faces a new world in which the endings are open, in which marriage and its attendant securities are no longer guaranteed. *Sanditon* may represent the undoing of Austen's earlier sexual determinism. As a text in which the erotic seems to be unmoored from its earlier position as social anchor, *Sanditon* allows the reader of Austen to experience that surprise, emptiness, and excitement appropriate to a new form of fictional understanding.

But new forms of fictional understanding do not undo others; *Sanditon*'s fragmentary example is of interest exactly because it goes against the grain of the marriage plots that comprise Austen's completed works. Marriage plots persist, particularly in popular culture, where their preeminence in the last decade of the twentieth century, given our culture's well-founded suspicions of marriage, may seem very odd indeed. We must, I think, acknowledge the persistence of a plot that currently offends and offer room for explanations of that plot's persistence that go beyond the most-traveled ground of critique, that of dissatisfaction with particular historical and social practice, toward some elementals of human experience.

Notes

1. Virginia Woolf, *A Room of One's Own* (New York: Harcourt Brace Jovanovich, 1929), 87.
2. George Eliot, *Middlemarch*, ed. David Carroll (Oxford: Oxford University Press, 1988), 676.
3. Annette Kolodny, "Some Notes on Defining a Feminist Literary Criticism," *Critical Inquiry* 2 (1975): 87.
4. Rachel DuPlessis, *Writing Beyond the Ending* (Bloomington: Indiana University Press, 1985), 35.
5. DuPlessis, *Writing Beyond the Ending*, 34-35.
6. Julian Barnes, *Flaubert's Parrot* (New York: Vintage, 1984), 99.
7. Wayne Booth, *The Company We Keep: An Ethics of Fiction* (Berkeley: University of California Press, 1988), 423.
8. Booth, *The Company We Keep*, 427, 430.
9. Booth, *The Company We Keep*, 431 (my emphasis).
10. Booth, *The Company We Keep*, 435 (Booth's emphasis).
11. K. K. Ruthven, *Feminist Literary Studies: An Introduction* (Cambridge: Oxford University Press, 1984), 32.
12. A representative example of this sort of reading of *Emma* may be found in Zimmerman's explicitly titled "The Proud Princess Gets Her Comeuppance: Structures of Patriarchal Order," *Canadian Review of Comparative Literature* 3 (1976): 253-68, in which Emma is seen as a "proud princess transformed into Griselda" whose final placement at Hartfield creates "an uneasy synthesis of patriarchal and matriarchal elements" (255). A less simplistic and more recent (and cogent work) that answers Booth, among others, on *Emma* may be found in Wendy Moffat's "Identifying with Emma: Some Problems for the Feminist Reader," *College English* 53, no. 1 (1991): 45-76.
13. Ruthven, *Feminist Literary Studies*, 33.
14. Ruthven, *Feminist Literary Studies*, 33.
15. Alistair Duckworth, "Jane Austen and the Construction of a Progressive Author," *College English* 53, no. 1 (1991): 89.
16. Booth, *The Company We Keep*, 435.
17. Mary Poovey, "*Persuasion* and the Promises of Love," in *The Representation of Women in Fiction*, ed. Carolyn Heilbrun and Margaret R. Higonnet (Baltimore: Johns Hopkins University Press, 1983), 173-74.
18. As a teacher in one of the required core-curriculum course at Columbia warned his students: "The women in the *Iliad* are honor gifts. They're war booty, like tripods. Less than tripods. If any male reading this poem treated women on campus as

chattel, it would be very strange. I also trust you to read this and not go out and hack someone to pieces" (David Denby, "Does Homer Have Legs?" *New Yorker* [6 September 1993], 54). David Denby's review of Homer's value and by extension the value of core-curriculum courses also includes another jocular warning against the dangerous effects of reading, especially the texts in great books courses, this from Carolyn Heilbrun: "Great-books courses teach young men to be warriors the first semester, priests the second; an exaggeration, but a small one" (54). We may infer that young women are taught that they may be neither warriors nor priests but booty.

19. Wallace Stevens, "The Ordinary Women," in *The Palm at the End of the Mind* (New York: Random House, 1974), 76-77.

20. Jean R. Kennard, *Victims of Convention* (Hamden, CT: Archon, 1978), 14.

21. Ruth Yeazell, "Fictional Heroines and Feminist Critics," *Novel* 8 (1974): 35.

22. D. A. Miller, *Narrative and Its Discontents: Problems of Closure in the Traditional Novel* (Princeton, NJ: Princeton University Press, 1981).

23. Peter Brooks, *Reading for the Plot: Design and Intention in Narrative* (New York: Knopf, 1984), 140.

24. Northrop Frye, *The Secular Scripture: A Study of the Structure of Romance* (Cambridge, MA: Harvard University Press, 1976), 54.

25. Laura Mooneyham, *Romance, Language and Education in Jane Austen's Novels* (London: Macmillan, 1988).

26. Stanley Cavell, *Pursuits of Happiness: The Hollywood Comedy of Remarriage* (Cambridge, MA: Harvard University Press, 1981), 1-2.

27. Jane Austen, *Northanger Abbey and Persuasion.* vol. 5 of *The Novels of Jane Austen*, ed. R. W. Chapman, 5 vols, 3d ed. (London: Oxford University Press, 1932-34), 78. Subsequent references are cited parenthetically in the text as *P*.

28. Cavell, *Pursuits of Happiness*, 58-60.

29. Cavell, *Pursuits of Happiness*, 2.

30. John Lauber, *Jane Austen*, (New York: Twayne, 1993), 114.

31. See John Halperin, "Jane Austen's Anti-Romantic Fragment: Some Notes on Sanditon," *Tulsa Studies in Women's Literature* 3 (1983): 183-91; Tony Tanner, "In Between—Anne Elliot Marries a Sailor and Charlotte Heywood Goes to the Seaside," in *Jane Austen in a Social Context*, ed. David Monaghan (Totowa, NJ: Barnes & Noble, 1981), 180-94; and Joseph Kestner, *Jane Austen: Spatial Structure of Thematic Variations* (Salzburg: Institut für Englische Sprache und Literatur, 1974).

32. Jane Austen, *Sanditon*, in *Minor Works*, vol. 6 of *The Novels of Jane Austen*, ed. R. W. Chapman (London: Oxford University Press, 1954). Subsequent references are cited parenthetically in the text as *S*.

33. Halperin, "Jane Austen's Anti-Romantic Fragment," 190.

34. [Anne Telscombe], *Sanditon* (Boston: Houghton Mifflin Co., 1975), 319.

35. [Telscombe], *Sanditon*, 328.
36. Halperin, "Jane Austen's Anti-Romantic Fragment," 189.
37. Lauber, *Jane Austen*, 115-16.
38. Irene Taylor, "Afterword: Jane Austen Looks Ahead," in *Fetter'd or Free: British Women Novelists, 1670-1815*, ed. Mary Anne Schofield and Cecilia Macheski (Athens: Ohio University Press, 1986), 423.
39. Lauber, *Jane Austen*; and D. A. Miller, "The Late Jane Austen," *Raritan* 10 (1990): 55-79.
40. Lauber, *Jane Austen*, 116.
41. Miller, "Late Jane Austen," 75, 77.

5

Jane Austen and the Burden of the (Male) Past: The Case Reexamined

Jocelyn Harris

In their lively and influential book, *The Madwoman in the Attic: The Woman Writer and the Nineteenth-Century Literary Imagination*,[1] Sandra M. Gilbert and Susan Gubar apply Harold Bloom's Freudian paradigm about the male artist's "anxiety of influence" to women writers.[2] If men resent the burden of their belatedness, find their oedipal relationship to powerful predecessors crippling, and struggle heroically with their poetic fathers in order to invalidate them, Gilbert and Gubar argue that the situation is far worse for women, who must rage at the weight of the male-dominated past both in subversive commentary and in characters acting as their own furious doubles. "A nineteenth-century woman," write Gilbert and Gubar, was "constricted and restricted by the Palaces of Art and Houses of Fiction male writers authored" (*MA*, xi). They believe that the male poet's anxiety of influence transmutes in the female poet into "an even more primary 'anxiety of authorship,'" that is, "a radical fear that she cannot create" (*MA*, 48-49). They speak of "the loneliness of the female artist, her feelings of alienation from male predecessors coupled with her need for sisterly precursors and successors, her urgent sense of her need for a female audience together with her fear of the antagonism of male readers, her culturally conditioned timidity about self-dramatization, her dread of the patriarchal authority of art, and her anxiety about the impropriety of female invention" (*MA*, 50). These phenomena of "inferiorization," they argue, inevitably result in an anger that enables women to rise from "the glass coffin of the male-authored text" into a "dance of triumph, a dance into speech, a dance of authority" (*MA*, 44).

Gilbert and Gubar call upon Jane Austen as the first proof of their argument that women overcame their anxiety of authorship by covert means, and imply that she is one of those women writers who revised male genres, "using them to record their own dreams and their own stories *in disguise.*" Thus, they suggest, women writers "achieved true female literary authority by simultaneously conforming to and subverting patriarchal literary standards" (*MA,* 73). Such a "swerve," they say, empowers men, but in women it is "a strategy born of fear and dis-ease." Since they are "[l]ocked into structures created by and for men, eighteenth- and nineteenth-century women writers did not so much rebel against the prevailing aesthetic as feel guilty about their inability to conform to it." Fearful of speaking directly, women authors prefer oblique ways of speaking that reveal hidden meanings and veiled intentions by means of ingenuity and indirection (*MA,* 74-75). Jane Austen for one, say Gilbert and Gubar, "concealed her own truth behind a decorous and ladylike facade, scattering her real wishes to the winds or translating them into incomprehensible hieroglyphics" (*MA,* 101). Austen, they claim, "admits the limits and discomforts of the paternal roof, but learns to live beneath it," making "a virtue of her own confinement," and discovering like other women writers "an effective subterfuge for a severe critique of her culture" (*MA,* 121) in duplicity and parody (*MA,* 80). Developing their hypothesis that women's parodies and ironies unconsciously exhibit angry revulsion from their predecessors' stories, they decide that Jane Austen's "furious females," Lady Susan, Mrs. Norris, Mrs. Ferrars, Lady Catherine de Bourgh, and Mrs. Churchill, are her own angry doubles and her surrogates (*MA,* 169-74).[3]

Is this really true of Jane Austen? Is she indeed a victim responding even more anxiously and savagely than men to her predecessors? Does she represent her own self in this collection of dreadful harridans? I shall suggest that the evidence from her novels suggests otherwise; indeed, that the very origins of Jane Austen's creativity lie in her allusiveness, her confident, even cheerful intertextuality with other authors. Austen certainly remembered women predecessors such as Jane West and Frances Burney, but I want to argue here that she was not a bit afraid of the men. Male authors as well as female provide origins for her work when she makes a deliberate, powerful, and I believe mostly conscious choice to revisit and remake these earlier authors, out of respect, companionship, and even love. Michael Worton and Judith Still describe intertextuality as both erotic and violent: I suggest that for Jane Austen we can dispense with the violence and concentrate on the eroticism.[4] That is, I shall appropriate Nancy Chodorow's gendered model of human development[5] in order to argue that while men writers may indeed inevitably play out their oedipal role of separation and murderous competition, Jane Austen's womanly bonds with her predecessors, male as well as female, provide rich and productive origins for her fictions.

To return to Gilbert and Gubar. Tracing the anguish of women writers to what Virginia Woolf cryptically called "Milton's bogey," they interpret her to mean his misogyny, his "story of woman's secondness, her otherness, and how that otherness leads inexorably to her demonic anger, her sin, her fall, and her exclusion from that garden of the gods which is also, for her, the garden of poetry." In this way, they write, Milton's founding myth of creative and patriarchal origins has come to dominate the tradition of literature in which women attempt vainly to be heard: "to the female imagination Milton and the inhibiting Father—the Patriarch of patriarchs—are one" (*MA*, 188-192). Like Blake, however, they also read Milton against the grain, and reveal a "titanic Eve . . . akin to Satan the Romantic outlaw," who, they claim, inspired the Brontës to invert Milton's hierarchy of power (*MA*, 201). But as if admitting that she does not fit their schema, Gilbert and Gubar silently omit Austen from the list of authors who tackle "Milton's bogey." It is therefore revealing to realize, first, that Jane Austen openly works from Milton in at least two of her books, and, second, that her reading of him is neither subversive nor antagonistic, as Gilbert and Gubar suggest.[6] One would not expect it to be so, given the timing of her career in the early rather than the late days of Romanticism and remembering also her orthodox religious beliefs.

In *Sense and Sensibility*, for instance, Austen calmly and confidently appropriates Milton's ideas for her own purposes.[7] Like *Paradise Lost*, her work involves a prohibited correspondence with a tempter, disobedience, lying, moral fall, the knowledge of death, punishment, mutual recrimination, the impulse to self-destruction, and finally new life in the daily, fallen world. Here Willoughby plays the parts of both Satan and Adam in an exploration of false constructions of manliness, especially those which figure it as handsome, strong, poetic, and impulsive. The exclusively solipsistic love between the beautiful Marianne, her hair tumbling like Eve's down her back (*SS*, 60), and the manly Willoughby, who carries her artless and blushing into the house as Adam led Eve into the paradisal bower, ends with a fall into experience, when Willoughby's deceptions teach her to know both evil and her own vulnerability to death. Her fall is actual when they meet on an "important hill" whose details recall Eden's (*SS*, 344), a scene prefiguring her fall like Eve's into carnal love and pain, and the recognition that Willoughby's "ardent love" is "not even innocent to indulge" (*SS*, 333).

Sense and Sensibility connects explicitly to Milton's fallen paradisal enclosure when again like Eve, Marianne wanders willful in the ruined garden at

Cleveland in the "prohibited" county of Somerset, where plants are nipped by frosts and the long grass is wet with rain. Here, "assisted by the still greater imprudence of sitting in her wet shoes and stockings," she learns the reality of death (SS, 303-6). Once recovered, however, she will echo the last lines of Paradise Lost, "thou to mee/Art all things under Heav'n, all places thou" (Book 12, 617-18) when she promises "I shall now live solely for my family. You, my mother, and Margaret must henceforth be all the world to me" (SS, 347). But it is Colonel Brandon who becomes a new Adam to her when in pointed echo of the last line of Paradise Lost he takes "his solitary way to Delaford" and to Marianne (SS, 341). Austen, then, uses the story of Genesis to much the same purpose as Milton did, to warn women against the quick sensual impressions that could prove so dangerous to them. She seems to regard his warnings as helpful to women when she shows Marianne as inflamed by literature, by secondhand experience such as Cowper's melancholic poetry or indeed by the romantic images of Paradise Lost itself, and she adapts Eve's farewell to the place topos (SS, 27) to indicate that in the fallen world we must inhabit, the selfishly narcissistic absorption of a Marianne and a Willoughby will not realistically do. Other bonds, other ties and duties call women to a life beyond the solipsism of love, to the public world rather than the private. Where Eve had resigned herself to the loss of Paradise by promising to obey, depend on Providence, and be worldly wise by simply being meek (Book 12, 561-69), Marianne also looks to a time when her "spirit is humbled, my heart amended, and that I can practise the civilities, the lesser duties of life, with gentleness, and forbearance" (SS, 347). Like Eve, she weeps to leave Barton, but not as she had done once before at Norland when in echo of Eve farewelling Paradise (Book 11, 269-85) she had burst out extravagantly, "when shall cease to regret you!—when learn to feel a home elsewhere!—Oh! happy house, could you know what now I suffer in viewing you from this spot, from whence perhaps I may view you no more!—And you, ye well-known trees! . . . No; you will continue the same . . . insensible of any change in those who walk under your shade!" (SS, 27). By drawing upon Milton, Jane Austen can set romantic love against the steady loyalty of a Colonel Brandon, a man offering the companionate marriage that Milton called a happier Paradise within.

In Mansfield Park, too, the garden at Sotherton is resonant with Miltonic implication. Austen's lawn, high wall, green, apparently locked door, wilderness, and knoll all echo features of Milton's garden, but the difference is that where his garden is prelapsarian, hers alludes to the Fall. Details read with Milton in mind become newly important when Mary and Edmund speak of the labyrinth as an emblem of deception, or when Mary's mind is led astray and bewildered. Miltonic vocabulary fills the scene where the company at Sotherton, tempted by "all the sweets of pleasure-grounds" (*SS*, 90), find the door to the wilderness unlocked, and passes through. Mary and Edmund take "a very serpentine course" that leads them away from "the first great path" (*SS*, 94-95); Mary leans Eve-like on Edmund's arm, and in her "feminine lawlessness" defies his rational arguments (*SS*, 95). This theme of disobedience and fall is repeated by Maria, who when confronted with the iron gate cries out, "Prohibited! nonsense! I certainly can get out that way, and I will." Rushworth posts away for the key "as if upon life and death" (*SS*, 101), but she disobeys and pushes by the gate. Once again, Austen deepens the significance of her novel by appropriating Milton, by making her characters reenact the Fall. Far from being blocked by her powerful predecessor as the Bloomian model suggests, Austen's writing of *Paradise Lost* into *Mansfield Park* invites her readers to recollect. Through intertextual allusion, she gestures swiftly to a knowledge they shared.

The evidence from Jane Austen suggests that applying the oedipal model to all writers from all ages is anachronistic and unhelpful.[8] In short, the "anxiety of influence" is a dangerously universalizing discourse, for Freud's ideas do not necessarily apply to the eighteenth century from which Jane Austen derived the bulk of her critical ideas. Like Freud himself, we all see through Romantic spectacles now (that is our own special burden of belatedness) but it was only the Romantics who placed a definitive premium on originality and uniqueness.[9] One of the major tropes of the eighteenth century speaks of writers as *dwarves* standing on the shoulders of giants or as dwarves standing on the shoulders of *giants*. In either case, most critics thought it legitimate so to stand, even unthinkable not to avail oneself of the wisdom and bold expression of the past. It is logical to believe that Jane Austen herself, steeped in the literature and beliefs of the eighteenth century, understood its widely accepted perceptions about the necessary relations between texts, which earlier critics called imitation, paraphrase, and translation. The classical writer Longinus, for instance, whose treatise on the sublime had become famous early in the century, argued in his chapter 13 that imitation and emulation of great writers of the past was inspiring, while in his 1755 *Dictionary*, Johnson had called imitation "a method of translating looser than paraphrase, in which modern examples and illustrations are used for ancient, or domestick, for foreign." As Howard Weinbrot further explains it, recognition of the poem imitated was thought necessary for the reader's pleasure, or to point out new poetic directions.[10] Jane Austen could expect her readers to read her documents as palimpsests and to appreciate the way she had thickened up her meanings.

Gilbert and Gubar single out Milton from the pantheon, but Milton is by no means the only male author from whom Jane Austen chose to work. Most especially, we know from family records that her knowledge of Samuel Richardson was "such as no one is likely again to acquire," that she appreciated his consistency of characterization, and was as familiar with the wedding days of his heroines "as if they were living friends."[11] Richardson's long rich novels provided Austen with a cornucopia of ideas to plunder, and her cheeky parodies of him in the Juvenilia[12] were the way to learn her trade, by imitating, copying, mastering his style, and moving beyond it. Typically she tests Richardson by transposing events, characters, and speeches from his context to her own; she misapplies his tones and registers, she inverts his priorities, and she wildly exaggerates his scenes. By so doing she opens up gaps to dislocate the reader and make her burst out laughing. And since these early works were written for a family who knew Richardson almost as well as she, she developed the habit of counting on reader responsiveness as she would later depend upon a more general audience to recognize Milton.

At first, and as a young woman, Austen's literary-critical imperative makes her want to improve on Richardson, especially her favorite History of Sir Charles Grandison. For instance, if Sir Charles had been offered Harriet Byron's hand, meals, and money before he could even propose, Jane Austen's Mr. and Mrs. Webb greet the totally unknown Mr. Gower by pressing on him a ludicrous abundance of objects including their house and grounds and their eldest daughter, for they are overwhelmed with the task of endeavoring to make a return for his beneficence in accepting them. That is, she tests Richardson by pushing him to absurd extremes, but she is not essentially hostile to him as the Bloomian model insists. Like an adolescent to a parent, such fooling is learning with Austen.

In Northanger Abbey she can still parody Richardson when she conflates Richardson's Rambler 97, which advises women not to be the first declare their love, with the opening of Pope's Rape of the Lock in her remark "it must be very improper that a young lady should dream of a gentleman before the gentleman is first known to have dreamt of her" (ch. 3). And a lovely interrogation of Clarissa rings in her final sentence: "I leave it to be settled by whomsoever it may concern, whether the tendency of this work be altogether to recommend paternal tyranny, or reward filial disobedience." Because her affectionate reference is recognizable to all her contemporaries, she rounds off the novel with a laugh. But soon afterward, as I have suggested in Jane Austen's Art of Memory, she read Mrs. Barbauld's appreciative introduction to Richardson's correspondence in 1804 and learned to take him very seriously indeed. Pride and Prejudice and Mansfield Park especially play off the issues, characters, and episodes of *Grandison*, one in a sprightly and one in a somber key, but with little sign of Bloomian hostility or anger.

Jane Austen draws most of the characters in *Pride and Prejudice* from the early letters of *Grandison*, and her plot for Jane Bennet follows along the lines of Richardson's for Harriet Byron. Elizabeth Bennet combines the satiric tongue of Charlotte Grandison with the inner seriousness of Harriet, Lydia borrows details of her adventures from the abduction of Richardson's heroine, and both Mr. Collins and Mr. Darcy, himself a second Sir Charles, draw on the proposal scenes of Richardson's rake, Sir Hargrave Pollexfen. In *Mansfield Park* she plays *Grandison* another way, exploring its themes of education, friendship, and marriage through a new variety of characters. As for *Clarissa*, she appropriates its main plot directly for the two Elizas and for Marianne in *Sense and Sensibility*,[13] with Willoughby playing a Lovelace no less dangerous for being reincarnated as a Regency rather than a Restoration rake. Austen "swerves" however when she reworks the ball scene between Lovelace and Anna into one between Willoughby and Elinor. She "swerves" again to give Marianne the second chance that Richardson, hardening his heart against demands from readers, had denied Clarissa. In her metatextual reading of Richardson, she saves Marianne-Eliza-Clarissa from rape, lets her live, marries her to a sort of Hickman, and makes her happy. Here allusion and divergence become not a Bloomian dismemberment of an earlier text but the remaking of an author she found worthy of the closest and most attentive admiration. As Ruth Perry has recently revealed, many women authors had already reacted to *Clarissa* in just this way, paying it the same homage of rewriting and re-presentation.[14]

Jane Austen's third significant male predecessor is Shakespeare: As a hint in the first chapter about true love never running smoothly reveals, *Emma* draws all its main elements from *Midsummer Night's Dream*. Her novel shows its Derridean "différance" only by its contemporaneity and by the way it compresses Shakespeare's cast. She makes her characters double, triple, and quadruple the parts they play, each shift showing a new side to the character (Emma "plays" Titania, Hippolyta, Hermia, and Puck, for instance). *A Midsummer Night's Dream* is a play about the imagination, in all its creative and confusing aspects: so too is *Emma*, whose very heroine is called an "imaginist" (*E*, 335). The vocabulary, characters, and scenes of Austen's midsummer world closely follow Shakespeare's, with a similar movement toward tolerance, forbearance, and generosity at the end. Here Austen simply turns Shakespeare into her contemporary, without irony, without parody, and certainly without expressing anger toward him. Women writers may have felt shame at their lack of access to those male codes, Latin and Greek, but the whole of English literature has always been open to them and to women and other uneducated readers.

In *Persuasion*, Austen calls up a fourth important male writer, Chaucer, as her quotation from him about men's privileged education clearly signals (*P*, 234). Like the Wife of Bath's Loathly Lady, Anne Elliot blooms again, with the Wife's weatherbeaten appearance being transferred to Mrs. Croft. Other elements of the Wife's Tale, such as her fall and Jankyn's self-blame, recur at the Cobb, while Chaucer's concern with power in marriage and his definition of gentilesse as merit rather than outward beauty, rank, or wealth inspire all the major characters, events, and ideas of the novel, as I explain in *Jane Austen's Art of Memory*.

In fact, in *Persuasion* Jane Austen calls up a vast range of works from the very beginnings of literature in English to the latest publications of her day. She takes whatever she likes from anywhere, from Chaucer, Shakespeare, Richardson, Thomson, Byron, and Scott to Coleridge's "Kubla Khan," published the summer she finished her first draft in August 1816—she alludes to it when she describes the "green chasms between romantic rocks" at Pinny (*P*, 95). This last reference deftly communicates Anne's exuberant breaking out of the limitations of female education, poverty, and psychological inferiority, since against the assumption that women are physically weak Austen sets Mrs. Croft, a model of female health, strength, and adaptability who shares the reins of power with her husband. And in defiance of the doctrine of feminine passivity, Austen lets Anne propose to Wentworth by means of the constancy debate. Anne's life becomes a powerful example when Austen, granting her literary and actual agency, endows her with a voice after a lifetime of silencing. Like Cordelia, Anne's gestures of true love to her father were unappreciated; unlike Cordelia, however, she learns to speak, and she takes her fate into own hands. Anne's poverty and powerlessness resulted from the illogical cruelty of male primogeniture that Austen deconstructs so thoroughly from the first page on: from this too Anne gladly escapes. Remembering Chaucer, Austen redefines heroism as Anne's steadfastness, sensibility, and intelligence, together with Wentworth's martial, romantic, and domestic skills. In *Persuasion*, she presents a brave new world of meritocracy rather than one of privilege. And in the final chapters of the book, Jane Austen definitively rejects Harville's collection of misogynist texts (*P*, 234), so like that of Chaucer's Jankyn, in favor of her own authorities, most notably the example of Anne Elliot.

Milton, Richardson, Shakespeare, and Chaucer are the four predecessors from whom Jane Austen mainly works, and they all happen to be men. Others include John Locke on education and the workings of the mind, for she draws extensively on his *Treatise* and his *Essay on Understanding* for *Northanger Abbey* in which a young woman educated (or rather uneducated) on Lockeian principles learns to think by following the epistemological prescriptions of Locke. Cowper provides her with a paradigm of sensibility in *Sense and Sensibility*, Fielding helps her rush confidently to an ending in *Northanger Abbey*, and Thomson offers an image of hope for the unwitting Anne when spring promises to return and winter is overlooked. Anne supplies herself with various examples of constancy and inconstancy from Shakespeare's plays to meditate upon, and a reference to his sonnets promises that a love truly told, like Anne Elliot's, will outlive time and death, though only black marks on a white page.

Jane Austen finds many different ways to work intertextually. The mode of the Juvenilia, intertextuality as parody, can surface as late as *Persuasion*, where she writes a swift and accurate spoof of *King Lear* for Sir Walter: "What! Every comfort of life knocked off! Journeys, London, servants, horses, table,—contractions and restrictions every where. To live no longer with the decencies even of a private gentleman! No, he would sooner quit Kellynch-hall at once, than remain in it on such disgraceful terms" (*P*, 13). When he stalks off not to the hearth but to rainy Bath, Austen uses *Lear* to place Sir Walter as a tyrannical old patriarch unwilling to relinquish power in old age. But parody serves to reveal his divergence from Lear, when, stripped of money and power, he fail to understand human frailty and never learns (as Anne compassionately sees) that he is a poor forked creature like other men. The "swerve" of the allusion diminishes Sir Walter Scott rather than Shakespeare, who remains the original ideal.

Literature derives from culture as well as books, and especially in that late work *Persuasion*, we see Jane Austen appropriate not just Romantic works but a remarkable constellation of Romantic ideas. Since *Persuasion* has often and casually been called Romantic, it is useful to tick it off against the definitions that every student knows, those of W. H. Abrams.[15] If Wordsworth had called for scenes from common life, Austen tells the story of an ordinary, dispossessed woman, Anne Elliot; if the transcendent meanings of symbolism appealed to the Romantics, Austen's symbolic use of the hazelnut (*P*, 88) and the turning of the seasons (*P*, 85) shows her using the same kinds of resonances; if great poetry derives from the spontaneous overflow of powerful feelings and its subject is the poet's own feelings, "emotions recollected in tranquillity" through deep reflection, second thoughts, and revisions, Austen's deft deployment of the limited omniscient point of view enables events to be shown through the reflective, remembering, revising mind of Anne Elliot; if external nature arouses the poet to "feelingful meditation"

concerned with central human problems, tawny leaves prompt Anne to muse
on the passing of time and beauty (P, 84); if Romanticism concerns itself with
solitary figures engaged in an elusive quest, with social nonconformists and
outlaws, Anne decisively rejects the patriarchal society that marginalized and
ignored her because she was a powerless woman; and if Romanticism promises new beginnings and high possibilities, Anne's marriage to Wentworth
brings about just such a new start and the chance of unbounded happiness.
Romantic characters, says Abrams, follow unquenchable aspirations beyond
their assigned limits: Anne's quixotic constancy for Captain Wentworth
results in "quick alarm" mixed with the glory of being a sailor's wife, in the
imperfect ending beloved of the Romantics (P, 252). Her mixed feelings,
Romantically "exquisite" in their mingled pain and pleasure, are matched by
the mixed qualities of Captain Wentworth, chivalric over the child (P, 80)
and the carriage (P, 91), but ungenerous to the older Anne and unthinkingly
rigid in his attitude to women on ships (P, 68-69). Martial hero he may be,
but he flounced off in suicidal pride when Anne accepted Lady Russell's
persuasions (P, 66) and only at the last knows himself to have been weak,
jealous, and resentful (P, 237).

Jane Austen, then, deploys a cluster of Romantic ideas in *Persuasion*, but
she also "regenders" them, to use Anne K. Mellor's word,[16] when she makes
the central, reflecting figure a woman rather than a man, redefines heroism
as that divine virtue constancy, and transfers the whole debate from the
public to the private world. She criticizes the cult of Romantic melancholy
as debilitating and immoral when Benwick feeds his griefs (P, 100) or when
Anne laughs herself out of indulgence in hers (P, 85). In fact, Austen revisions
the entire history of western culture when she denies its traditional assumptions that women are vain, inconstant, necessarily mute, ignorant, and
unequal. *Persuasion* especially challenges two millennia of misogynistic slurs:
For instance, she quotes pointedly from *The Rape of the Lock* (P, 144) to suggest
that Sir Walter's narcissistic admiration of himself is equally as reprehensible
as Belinda's (it is his clock that strikes "eleven with its silver sounds"). As to
constancy, she fills the revised ending with quotations from Shakespeare and
Richardson to "prove" that it is men who are fickle rather than women, for
example when in echo of the song in *Much Ado About Nothing* about men being
deceivers ever, one foot on sea and one on shore, to one thing constant never,
Anne excuses Benwick's inconstancy by his business at sea, and Captain
Harville replies that the peace has in fact turned him on shore (P, 232-33).
When Anne takes charge at the Cobb, she shows that indeed she is "more
equal to act, more justified in acting" (P, 241), while in that last, rich scene,
Anne protests against men's domination of knowledge, claims the authority

of experience, and proves, like Desdemona, half the wooer when she reveals her true feelings to Harville. Now it is Wentworth who is silenced. Forced womanlike to express his desire in a letter, he defers to Anne's judgment and choice at the end (*P*, 237).

Important questions are raised by Jane Austen's deliberate intertextuality. I believe that all writers have to read widely and intensely before they can create, and that far from being a victim of the past, Austen places herself proudly within a great tradition of literature written by both men and women. She takes her rightful place among her friends, her lifelong literary companions, working consciously and dynamically, always alert to the inevitably intertextual nature of the writer's craft. In deliberate dialogue with the past, she assimilates and absorbs the strong male voices of her author-friends. And if Mikhail Bakhtin is right to say that dialogism has always been the characteristic mark of the novel, Austen is only doing what comes naturally to writers of fiction.[17] Never the cringing and angry victim described by Gilbert and Gubar, Austen is confident both of her powers, and of her affiliative relation to a loved literary past.

My argument also recuperates Jane Austen's authority as an author. Our focus on the material conditions of female authorship may seem oddly to coincide with humanist agendas privileging the artist, though where humanists seize upon intention as the only arbiter of meaning, feminist critics foreground the woman author to insist on her agency and power in the face of historically constructed gender. Jane Austen might satisfy everyone, for while she defies the double doctrines of the author's death and of the reader's triumph (she is vigorously alive in her text, and we ignore her signaled meanings at our peril), she also deconstructs most thoroughly, in *Persuasion*, our modern "triple bogey" of gender, class, and power.

The evidence from Jane Austen might also challenge theories about the power of genre to shape a work, for she draws on poems and plays as well as on novels. She works not only from that exclusively women's tradition for which some have sought, and not only from that woman-dominated genre, the novel. Nor do texts force themselves on the author or her characters as J. Hillis Miller believes: when he writes of a literary text being "inhabited . . . by a long chain of parasitical presences, echoes, allusions, guests, ghosts of previous texts,"[18] he seems to envisage authors as helplessly passive, Aeolian harps vibrating to the winds of influence. But Austen actively *chooses* what texts she will draw upon. In similar fashion Anne Elliot indulges in, then rejects, the autumnal messages of Shakespeare's sonnets and advises Benwick not to give way to the Romantic melancholy he manufactures out of his reading. It is with the utmost deliberation that Austen inserts all those quotations and references about constancy into the second version of the proposal scene (we know so, because they were nonexistent in the first), for she is a selective artist setting up signposts for her readers. We are entitled now to resist them, but there can be no doubt what she intends her intertextual reference to convey: significance. And since she could expect readers to have read the same texts as she, starting with her beloved sister Cassandra, reader response theory is everywhere an assumption in her work. She incites reactions that she knows will match her own.

I use the word "deliberation" deliberately, for her reputation has been much damaged by Henry James's vicious remark that she was "enviably unconscious" as all women writers, in his opinion, are.[19] Against his view of the author as an empty receptacle, therefore, I set a selective, willed, and aware Jane Austen; against Gilbert and Gubar, I describe an empowered and deliberately intertextual artist who enjoys her sense of entitlement to the past, rather than an angry author doubly victimized for being belated and a woman. Recent feminist commentary has modified their representation of Jane Austen in *The Madwoman in the Attic*: for instance, Deborah Kaplan provides evidence of a supportive female community, and Claudia Johnson paints a cool and controlled Jane Austen who is perfectly capable of analyzing the patriarchal society she inhabits.[20] Johnson's work implicitly dispels any idea that Austen has to work covertly, or that she needs to express her "true" feelings through furious doubles like Mrs. Norris. Gilbert and Gubar may represent the woman artist as lonely, alienated from the male past, looking for sister writers, writing primarily for women, dreading the response of men, timid about performance, dreading the artistic patriarchy, and anxious about female creativity. But in my reading of her, she is never alone, for her literary companions, male as well as female, are legion. She draws on the women's tradition but by no means uniquely, for she turns to men and women writers simultaneously. And far from being ashamed of her lack of education, she proclaims in her letter to the Regent's Librarian that she is smarter than classically educated pedants such as he, though most readers, including the Regent's Librarian, have missed the irony and point (I believe that all Jane Austen's apparent self-deprecations should be read thus slantwise). She seeks not only a female audience but a male one, for she appeals to men to reject the book of stereotypes, to examine the experience and condition of women, and to rewrite their old definitions of masculinity and power—oblivious and selfish patriarchs come off badly throughout her works, as Claudia Johnson shows. And finally, far from being anxious about the propriety of female invention, Jane Austen actually boasts of it in *Northanger Abbey* when she praises the largely female genre of novels as being superior in genius, wit, and taste to history itself (*NA*, 37). Therefore, while the murderous oedipal image of writers angrily confronting their predecessors may well apply to men, it simply does not work for this particular woman author, and perhaps not for others as well. And if Nancy Chodorow is right to observe that Western women pay for their loving quality relatedness by their low self-esteem, Jane Austen breaks the mold. Empathic and yet self-confident in her very female connections with other authors, Austen regenders Romanticism, defies the misogynistic myths, and shows herself even more congenial to feminists than we knew.

Notes

1. Sandra M. Gilbert and Susan Gubar, *Madwoman in the Attic: The Woman Writer and the Nineteenth-Century Literary Imagination.* (New Haven, CT: Yale University Press, 1979). Subsequent references cited parenthetically in the text as *MA*.

2. Harold Bloom's *The Anxiety of Influence: A Theory of Poetry* (New York: Oxford University Press, 1973).

3. Alison G. Sulloway also sees Austen's satire as a legitimate response to attacks on women's dignity, but discovers in her a gallant, transcending, compensating joy. See *Jane Austen and the Province of Womanhood* (Philadelphia: University of Pennsylvania Press, 1989).

4. Introduction to *Intertextuality: Theories and Practices.* ed. Michael Worton and Judith Still (Manchester: Manchester University Press, 1990), 2.

5. Nancy J. Chodorow, "Family Structure and Feminine Personality," in *Woman, Culture & Society* (Stanford, CA: Stanford University Press, 1974), 43-66. See also Carol Gilligan, *In a Different Voice: Psychological Theory and Women's Development* (Cambridge, MA: Harvard University Press, 1982).

6. Further details may be found in my *Jane Austen's Art of Memory* (Cambridge: Cambridge University Press, 1989).

7. All references to Jane Austen's novels are from *The Novels of Jane Austen*, ed. R. W. Chapman, 5 vols. 3d ed. (London: Oxford University Press, 1932-34). Subsequent references to *Sense and Sensibility* (vol. 1) are noted parenthetically in the text as *SS*. Subsequent references to *Emma* (vol. 4) are noted parenthetically in the text as *E*. Subsequent references to *Persuasion* (vol. 5) are noted parenthetically in the text as *P*.

8. Janet Todd also remarks that Gilbert and Gubar's reading, though "immensely helpful for feminist criticism," was "a largely ahistorical and ungeneric one, removing Austen from her contemporary context." She provides a useful summary of the debate about Austen's politics before swerving to a different argument, that Austen's

"opposition to sensibility in all its forms" was her "main motivator . . . beyond party political purpose." See her "Jane Austen, Politics and Sensibility," in *Feminist Criticism*, ed. Susan Sellers (Toronto: University of Toronto Press, 1991), 71-87.

9. In *Intertextuality*, Worton and Still remark that "[a]lthough the term *intertextuality* dates from the 1960s, the phenomenon, in some form, is at least as old as recorded human history," and they begin with Plato (2). "Imitation is thus not repetition, but the completion of an act of interpretation," they write (6). See also my "Learning and Genius in *Sir Charles Grandison*," in *Studies in the Eighteenth Century*, vol. 4, ed. R. F. Brissenden and J. C. Eade (Canberra: Australian National University Press, 1979), 167-91, and "Richardson: Original or Learned Genius?" in *Samuel Richardson: Tercentenary Essays*, ed. Margaret Anne Doody and Peter Sabor (Cambridge: Cambridge University Press, 1989), 188-202.

10. Howard Weinbrot, *The Formal Strain: Studies in Augustan Imitation and Satire* (Chicago: University of Chicago Press, 1969), 14-15.

11. See chapter 3 of *Jane Austen's Art of Memory* for the various references to Richardson.

12. See appendix I to *Jane Austen's Art of Memory*.

13. Gilbert and Gubar, *Madwoman in the Attic*, note briefly that Richardsonian plots exist within her novels (119).

14. Ruth Perry, "Clarissa's Daughters, or the History of Innocence Betrayed: How Women Writers Rewrote Richardson," *Women's Writing* 1, no. 1 (1994): 5-24.

15. W. H. Abrams, *A Glossary of Literary Terms*, 5th ed. (New York: Holt, Rinehart and Winston, 1988).

16. Anne K. Mellor, *Romanticism and Gender* (New York: Routledge, 1993). Mellor traces Austen's "hostility to the romantic imagination and to romantic love" to Mary Wollstonecraft: see "Why Women Didn't Like Romanticism: The Views of Jane Austen and Mary Shelley," in *The Romantics and Us: Essays on Literature and Culture*, ed. Gene W. Ruoff (New Brunswick, NJ: Rutgers University Press, 1992), 274-87. As I explained earlier, however, Milton gave Austen—and perhaps Wollstonecraft—a similar message.

17. Worton and Stills, ed., *Intertextuality*, 15.

18. J. Hillis Miller, "The Limits of Pluralism III: The Critic as Host," *Critical Inquiry* 3 (Spring 1977): 446.

19. Henry James, "The Lesson of Balzac," reprinted in *The House of Fiction: Essays on the Novel*, ed. Leon Edel, Wesport, CT: Greenwood Press, 1973.

20. Deborah Kaplan, *Jane Austen Among Women* (Baltimore: Johns Hopkins University Press, 1992); and Claudia Johnson, *Jane Austen: Women, Politics, and the Novel* (Chicago: University of Chicago Press, 1988).

6

Consolidated Communities:
Masculine and Feminine Values in Jane Austen's Fiction

Glenda A. Hudson

Three of Jane Austen's novels end with marriages that have incestuous overtones. In *Mansfield Park*, Fanny and Edmund are first cousins; moreover, they have been brought up as brother and sister in the same household. In *Emma*, the heroine marries her brother-in-law, Mr. Knightley, who throughout much of the novel shares a fraternal relationship with her. In *Sense and Sensibility*, Elinor, like Emma, marries her brother-in-law, Edward Ferrars. And in the same novel, Colonel Brandon tells Elinor the story of his desire to marry Eliza Williams, a sister-in-law brought up as his sister. Such relationships serve a singular purpose in Austen's work. With these in-family marriages, she challenges the traditional dynamics of power and system of values in male/female relations. Instead of creating marriages in which power is associated with sex, Austen offers siblinglike unions that highlight moral and spiritual values. These unions profoundly alter the balance of power between men and women in her novels.

I have already called attention to Austen's in-family marriages in a previous study.[1] In this essay, I wish to highlight and expand my earlier arguments in light of my recent research on the works of other women writers of Austen's period. In particular, I wish to focus on Austen's subtle handling of gender politics in her presentation of ideal egalitarian relationships based on fraternal qualities, an issue I deal with only briefly in my earlier work.

In reassessing my own argument, I have found Anne Mellor's *Romanticism and Gender* (1993) most helpful. She argues that the idea of community in the

writings of Wollstonecraft, Austen, Edgeworth, Dorothy Wordsworth, and
Mary Shelley is based on "a cooperative rather than possessive interaction
with a Nature troped as a female friend or sister, and promoted a politics of
gradual rather than violent social change, a social change that extends the
values of domesticity into the public realm."[2] For Mellor, Austen espouses a
value system grounded in a belief in "women's capacity for intellectual and
moral growth, in the desirability of egalitarian marriages based on rational
love and mutual esteem, and in the prototype of domestic affection and
responsibility as the paradigm for national and international political relations."[3] I wish to elaborate on Mellor's argument by demonstrating the ways
in which Austen's siblinglike unions promote a new concept of a relatively
coequal and gender-free community in which the sterling attributes of both
men and women predominate, and where women are valued as much as men.
In this way, I contend, she reveals herself as a meritocrat, who is committed
to the well-being and advancement of estimable women and men.

In "When We Dead Awaken: Writing as Re-vision," Adrienne Rich
comments, "We know more than Jane Austen or Shakespeare knew: more
than Jane Austen because our lives are more complex, more than Shakespeare
because we know more about the lives of women—Jane Austen and Virginia
Woolf included."[4] In some senses, of course, Rich would seem to be right.
But she fails to consider that we have lost the deep awareness of collateral
ties of family and kinship evident in Austen's time period. To ignore these
dynamics, which have now become so attenuated that we are barely capable
of appreciating them at all, is to elide the possibility that in many ways we
know far less than Austen did. In any event, some historical context may
prove helpful.

In Austen's day, the incest taboo applied as much to familial members
related by marriage as to blood relatives. Forbidden degrees of marriage were
rooted in the laws of Chapters 18 and 20 in the Old Testament Book of
Leviticus. During the Reformation, the secular courts reduced the number of
previous incest taboos from cousins in the sixteenth degree to close blood
relatives according to the Levitical degrees (which excluded first cousins).
But, at the same time, the courts added the prohibition (believed to be implied
by Leviticus) that a man could not marry his deceased wife's sister. To
complicate matters, in 1603 the Church of England adopted a Table of
Kindred and Affinity that extended the incest taboo to relatives connected
by marriage.[5] The scope and detail of such laws suggest that the network of
kinship and affinity was much broader in the eighteenth century than it is
today, since affines were treated like consanguineal relatives. And so it was
that, at a time when sexual relations between affinal relatives were often

regarded to be as incestuous as intercourse between blood relations, incest presented itself as a major and intricate concern in the lives of people living in close contingency with blood relatives and in-laws. The incest theme prevailed in literature of the period precisely because this ultimate taboo affected an entire constellation of relatives. The fearful but alluring subject of forbidden degrees of marriage between affinal relations (who was permitted to have sex and who was not) therefore held a perennial fascination and impressed itself consciously or otherwise in people's minds.

In presenting endogamous relationships, Austen was following a pattern well established in English novels of the eighteenth century. The literary legacy passed down to Austen was laden with undercurrents and instances of brother/sister incest—incest evaded, suggested, or committed. Moreover, the obsession with such forbidden love was not limited to particular subgenres of the novel or to specific ideologies; it crossed boundaries, emerging in reactionary and radical works, in gothic, sentimental, parodic, conventional, and innovative novels. Indeed, the incest motif crops up in so much of the literature of Austen's period that it becomes almost a formula or a code, adding a *frisson* of horror to provoke the reading public.[6]

Margaret Doody argues in her biography of Frances Burney that "the incest-fixated eighteenth century found in incest a complex symbolism for sexuality outside conventional social structures, and free of the hierarchies and estrangements of customary heterosexuality."[7] Since manners and customs regarding heterosexual love and courtship were so rigid, so clearly defined and demarcated in the eighteenth century, it is not astonishing that contemporary writers sublimated their deepest feelings in the description of sibling love. The rapture of sibling love could be expressed without fear of repercussions, sexual guilt, or social stigma (unless, of course, the siblings overstepped boundaries and actually indulged in a physical relationship). Moreover, the patriarchal order of love conventions, which was delimiting for the female, meant that sibling love was a way for the female to manifest love without the fear of being viewed as forward or unladylike. It was also a way for her to assert relative equality with a male, by setting forth her individual worth intellectually and morally without having to submit to the status of mere sexual object. Fraternal love gave both participants a type of freedom, especially the female; it also put them on equal footing and allowed them great indulgence in that there was no need for the female to be chaperoned, to display false modesty or coyness in order to attract the male, or for the male to put on a show of artificial gallantry. The attachment of the siblings was ideally one of spontaneity, confidence, and warmth without reserve or inhibition. They saw each other in all of their varying moods and built up a spiritual or mystical communion in which they were able to anticipate and comprehend each other's thoughts and feelings as if they were their own. Since siblings had fewer restrictions socially and emotionally, writers found it easy to dream about the erotic possibilities of such propinquity and such intimacy.

Over the last 20 years, numerous critics have endeavored to prove that Austen was involved in the literary debates of her time, that she was exposed to contemporary currents which she then responded to and disseminated in her own fiction.[8] Several have convincingly argued that Austen took particular interest in the works of contemporary female novelists.[9] Austen had access, for instance, to the novels of Charlotte Smith, Charlotte Lennox, Sophia Lee, Mary Robinson, and Agnes Maria Bennett. In Smith's *Emmeline* (1788), Delamere's passion for his cousin and father's ward, Emmeline, smacks of incest. The narrator's hints that Emmeline and Delamere may be siblings are underscored by the uncanny resemblance of Emmeline and Delamere's sister Augusta and by Lord Montreville's implacable opposition to the marriage of the cousins. Even though Delamere relentlessly pursues Emmeline, she refuses to marry him on the grounds that such an alliance would cause disruption in his family. While Austen certainly follows the pattern of Smith's *Emmeline* in her depiction of the successful union of two cousins brought up as brother and sister in *Mansfield Park,* she ridicules the absurd contrivances of the incest motif in the fiction of Lennox, Lee, Robinson, and Bennett. In Lennox's *Henrietta* (1758), for instance, the heroine meets her brother, Courteney, after being separated from him for many years. Without realizing who she is, Courteney unsuccessfully attempts to seduce Henrietta (who is also entirely ignorant of his connection to her). After he discovers identity, Courteney is contrite. In Lee's *The Recess* (1783-85), the illegitimate Mrs. Marlow retires to a secret place because she married a man whom she shortly after discovered to be her brother. And in Robinson's *Vancenza* (1792), Elvira discovers from a secret document that the father of her fiancé is also her own parent. As a result of this revelation, Elvira sickens and dies. Similarly, in Bennett's *Agnes De-Courci* (1789), Edward Harley marries his beloved Agnes only to discover soon after the wedding that they are siblings. As a result of this discovery, Edward commits suicide, and the heroine goes into a terrible fit.

Austen clearly wanted to write what is nowadays termed a best-seller.[10] In an attempt to accomplish this goal, she drew on and modified such popular works as those of Smith, Lennox, Lee, Robinson, and Bennett. And part of the successful formula of these late eighteenth-century novels involved the integration of the incest or quasi-incest issue. That is to say, Austen's pointed interest in endogamous unions or domestic passion was by no means idiosyncratic. In *Mansfield Park,* for example, Austen draws on the formula of the "orphan" girl (who lives in the same household with and either loves, or is loved by, a male relative) found in the sentimental and gothic fiction of Charlotte Smith and Ann Radcliffe.[11] But Austen transfigures the sentimental scenes and rhetoric of Smith and Radcliffe by stressing male and female commensurability instead of divergence. She also adapts other formulae for her own purposes. The two-brother, two-sister prescription in *Emma* was a familiar plot in novels of education in the late eighteenth century.[12] In the gothic novel, such a plot had potential for creating incestuous configurations. For example, Charles Brockden Brown's *Wieland* (1798) is the story of incestuous impulses activated in the relationships of Theodore and his sister Clara and Theodore's wife Catherine and her brother Henry.[13] But while Austen's fiction employs typical incest-generating frameworks, her handling of incestuous relationships is unique. Her treatment not only satirizes the handling of the issue of in-family marriage in other eighteenth- and early nineteenth-century works but also turns it into a foremost component of her aesthetic and moral vision and offers a means of creating balance in the relations of the sexes.

Although Austen's novels of domestic realism differ vastly from the works of her literary predecessors and contemporaries, the fantasy of incest is still present in her fiction, as it was in the drawing rooms of her time. However, the type of incest introduced by Austen did not involve blood siblings, but rather foster siblings, first cousins, and in-laws—individuals bound by strong familial obligations, whose affections have been formed within the domestic circle, and whose relationships are viewed by other members of society as fraternal. In Austen's works, shared experiences and familial associations are as important as mutual parentage; the relations between foster siblings raised as siblings, or a man and woman who treat each other as siblings, hold the same obligations and ramifications as those between blood siblings. It is important to note, however, that the sexual aspect of the incestuous unions is consistently downplayed. In contrast to contemporary novelists, she eschewed any overt appeals to titillation or prurience in her presentation of sibling attraction. Instead she meditates on the salutary effects of such relationships, in particular, the ideal balance of power between equals.

In Austen's novels, incest between cousins and between in-laws who act toward each other like blood brother and sister seems to be purposive, and it is promoted as a way of fortifying the family. Unlike other literary works of the time, where incest increases horror or creates moral confusion and violence, Austen's novels present incestuous alliances that preserve order and reestablish domestic harmony. In this way, Austen does not appear to be breaking any taboo or taking a scandalous stand in her depiction of endogamous unions; rather, she seems to be concerned with desensationalizing the fixation with incest and forging her ideal conceptualization of an egalitarian domestic arrangement based on fairness and integrity. Moreover, her handling of endogamous unions forms a revolutionary chapter in the fictional depiction of male/female relations. And while Austen is certainly concerned with the economics of authority and control in her work, her portrayal of the dynamics of male/female power concentrates on ethical and emotional rather than sexual and political matters.

The uniqueness of Austen's conception becomes clear when her handling of the incest motif is contrasted with that of her contemporaries. Unlike most eighteenth-century authors, Austen offers these endogamous relations as microcosmic paradigms of her aesthetic and moral vision. The in-family marriages of Fanny and Edmund, Emma and Mr. Knightley, and Elinor and Edward are rooted in a profound and abiding domestic love, which merges spiritual, intellectual, and physical affinities. These qualities have been largely overlooked by feminist critics, who tend to focus their attention on political and economic realities. Maaja Stewart notes, for example, that women are affiliated in Austen's texts with younger brothers because they are both displaced by primogeniture. Such an association "can sentimentalize the power structures created [by younger brothers], power structures characterized not by display but by concealment of their own historical and economic bases." She goes on to argue that the concealment "depends on women who have internalized and idealized patriarchal power while simultaneously denying its status as power by translating 'power' into 'love.'"[14] Such arguments fail to take into account Austen's visionary quality in her depiction of unions between women and younger brothers, such as Fanny and Edmund and Emma and Mr. Knightley. Her novels unquestionably reflect her justified frustration with women's economic dependence, the neglect of their education, and the unfair inheritance laws of her day. But at the same time they present an ideal conception of how families should interact. In other words, in Austen's fiction, economic grounds for rivalry or jealousy between virtuous relatives are virtually eliminated, allowing for an unadulterated focus on moral growth and puissant emotional ties. Thus, Austen's in-family unions are relatively free of the traditional pattern of male dominance and female passivity in eighteenth-century fiction, since her couples are cast in the same mold and are placed on the same par with each other.

To be sure, Austen's balance of power in relationships tends to apply to certain socioeconomic groups more than others. Austen's version of the family is progressive for members of the middle class, which in her time incorporated the landed gentry and the urban capitalist class.[15] Moreover, her bias is very clearly with individuals who make their money and earn a living. She refers specifically to the order and domestic harmony of the landed gentry being preserved and reestablished, but it is important to realize that Austen portrays a mobile society. Members of the lower-middle class reinvigorate the gentry, as in the case of Fanny and William in *Mansfield Park*. Above all, Austen's ideal community is a meritocracy, founded on the values of competency, charity, sense, reason, and usefulness. Individuals from the gentry and the professional classes (such as the navy) may gain admission to this group, providing that they have the kind of qualities designated by the author as desirable. Austen's community is therefore available to some and not all; but she discriminates more on moral than social grounds. For Austen, "equality" is a historically specific term. In the absence of any political equality for women and a limited franchise for men, she posits a system of relations between individuals based on a hierarchy of moral qualities. For Austen, the ideal relations between men and women are relatively equal in terms of the available options. In short, these relations are the best that can be attained in her day, and they project a vision of a progressive utopian society.

In Austen's portrayal of siblinglike marriages, conventions of likeness and symmetry are substituted for the established patterns of dissimilarity and authority. At the close of her novels, a new type of domestic configuration is presented that places paramount importance on cooperation and communal responsibility. For her part, Austen downplays the significance of sexual difference in her fiction and sets forth a type of gender equality that counteracts the notions of dissimilarity and disproportion. She dramatizes this alternative through her focus on symbiotic coalitions of close siblings and siblinglike lovers in the domestic sphere.

Amalgamating both masculine and feminine values, the organizations of brothers and sisters at the end of her novels illuminate and reappraise the traditional criteria for "marriage." And although home and family are her chosen arenas, Austen's complex manipulation of the domestic scene throws light on much broader social and cultural contexts. While many passages seem to suggest that male values embrace stewardship and responsibility and that female values encompass fidelity, gratitude, and compliance, Austen implies that men and women need to possess all of these qualities. In Austen's novels, males are not the sole keepers of male values, nor are women of women's. From a late twentieth-century viewpoint, one may see that for Austen, there is not a historically specific descriptor of the sex-segregation of values.

Based on mutual respect, individual worth, and shared beliefs, her sibships herald a new dimension in the English novel to the extent that they are relatively egalitarian communities. In this sense, her celebration of sibling relationships represents a literary *and* a social innovation. It redefines the nature of power by turning away from the patriarchal hegemony evident in texts by most of her contemporaries. Instead of this hegemony, Austen offers a metamorphosed community of brothers and sisters, epitomizing the values the author would have us affirm: consolidated feminine *and* masculine values applied to achieve progress in the future. In this respect, it may be argued that Austen creates an harmonious synthesis of roles and values as a solution to problematic gender politics. Moreover, her depiction of symmetrical, concordant sibling relations may be viewed as a means to restore the vitality of the home or the estate during a time of transition and moral chaos. The sibships modify and surpass the traditional narrative closure and proffer a vision of social restitution.

By way of examining how Austen manifests these ideals, we may like to focus on her handling of incestuous relations in a specific novel. While the issue of incest is certainly relevant in *Emma* and *Sense and Sensibility*, the most clear-cut example of a siblinglike marriage in Austen's fiction occurs in *Mansfield Park*. Not only are Fanny and Edmund first cousins attached by matrilineal, consanguineal ties (which Mary Crawford emphasizes in her reference to their similarity in appearance), but they have been raised as brother and sister under the same roof. Despite contemporary criticism of marriage between close consanguineal relations (even though it was legal) and the prohibition of marriage between close affines,[16] Austen approves of the marriage of cousins Fanny and Edmund. Indeed, there is every reason to believe at the end of the novel that the siblinglike cousins will live happily and prosperously together. The endogamous union preserves the inviolability of Mansfield and excludes the risks attendant on marriage outside the family—to the Crawfords, for example. The marriage is more than just a conventional happy ending; it is symbolic of Austen's anxiety about moral transvaluations and radical change.

Claudia L. Johnson declares that "the concluding assertion of familiality [in *Mansfield Park*] . . . is really only a retrenchment, not an alternative."[17] And Johanna H. Smith attempts to demonstrate the "crippling effects" of the relationship of Fanny and Edmund in *Mansfield Park*.[18] The tendency on the part of otherwise astute critics to view these incestuous marriages as static and debilitating is rather curious. Johnson feels that the close of the novel is "unsettling" and does not offer the satisfaction usually provided by a happy ending. Smith's argument is that the marriage of Fanny and Edmund symbolizes "a paralyzed retreat within the family" and anticipates "the nineteenth-century inescapable family."[19] But Austen's works reveal nothing of the sort.

On the contrary, for Austen, the incestuous marriage of Fanny and Edmund is healing and curative. Faced with the loss of spiritual values and the turmoil of public life during her time, Austen suggests that a retreat to family life is appropriate and necessary to solidify moral standards.

Mansfield Park concludes optimistically with the expulsion or removal of menacing intruders and with the preservation and revivification of the home and family. Incest in Austen's novels creates a loving and enclosed family circle; by drawing in the bonds of the family tighter and tighter, the household is strengthened and reconsecrated. But Austen's vision is far from being ethereal. She makes a case for balance in male/female relationships and does so in a practical and critical way. In her presentation of in-family alliances, Austen focuses on the cultivation of virtue and sense rather than sexual power. In this respect, she differs vastly from her contemporaries who capitalized on sexual fantasies in their depictions of incestuous or quasi-incestuous relations.

From the beginning of *Mansfield Park*, Edmund acknowledges Fanny's good sense, sweet temper, and grateful heart. "I do not know any better qualifications for a friend and companion,"[20] he comments. Moreover, he is uncomfortable without his cousin's approbation of his actions. This need for approval works both ways, as tends to be the case in most ideal brother/sister relationships. As Fanny's champion and comforter, the narrator tells us, Edmund "had supported her cause, or explained her meaning, he had told her not to cry, or had given her some proof of affection which made her tears delightful" (152). In return, Fanny's feelings about Edmund "were compounded of all that was respectful, grateful, confiding, and tender" (*MP*, 37). The mutual support and affection of Fanny and Edmund suggest an abiding, deeply sympathetic relationship between siblings. On this showing, we can see that Austen seeks equality for her characters through their ability to cooperate with each other and their willingness to balance the needs of the self and of others. Her concern is clearly with spiritual and moral growth, not with sexual and political mastery. Far from being a separatist, Austen highlights qualities such as esteem, respect, appreciation, and accommodation, all of which should be shared by men and women.[21]

In *Mansfield Park*, Fanny and Edmund's love is stimulated by their shared childhood experience and associations. And yet it would be wrong to discount the effect of their more mature roles and duties as brother and sister. When Fanny and Edmund are both engaged in sending a letter to her beloved brother William, Fanny becomes an "interesting object" (16) in her cousin's eyes. Furthermore, Edmund helps to educate Fanny, encouraging her taste and correcting her judgment. Such relations require an emotional investment. It is hardly surprising then that these fraternal obligations should encourage, in some cases, an affection that goes well beyond what is merely expected of brothers and sisters. And so, in the course of *Mansfield Park*, Fanny's love becomes more passionate than sororal. She grows jealous of the unworthy Mary Crawford and is enraptured by Edmund's compliments on her own face and figure, as well as his expressions of regard for her. Her love deepens throughout the novel. After reading the letter in which Edmund expresses doubts about his relationship with Mary, Fanny cries distractedly, "Oh! Write, write. Finish it at once. Let there be an end of this suspense. Fix, commit, condemn yourself" (*MP*, 424).

For his part, Edmund attempts to differentiate between his fraternal love for Fanny and his conjugal love for Mary. These two, he claims, are "the . . . dearest objects I have on this earth" (*MP*, 264). He seems to regard Fanny as his "sister," his "friend and companion" (*MP*, 26), whereas Mary is his lover and intended wife. But even early on in the novel, Austen provides hints that his unconscious feelings for his cousin rival and even exceed those for his intended spouse. In his letter to Fanny, he proclaims that he cannot give up Mary because "she is the only woman in the world whom I could ever think of as a wife." But shortly afterward he tells Fanny that "I miss you more than I can express" (*MP*, 421-3). It is perhaps his social conscience, governed by the unconscious taboo of incest, that makes his thoughts inexpressible. To articulate them would raise them to the preconscious or conscious level. Nevertheless, we learn that Edmund believes Fanny was born to be "the perfect model of a woman" (*MP*, 347), and Mary reminds Henry that "[Fanny's] cousin Edmund never forgets her" (*MP*, 297). Before the Mansfield ball, Edmund shows his "grateful affection" (*MP*, 270) for his cousin with his gift of a gold chain for William's cross, "a token of the love of one of your oldest friends" (*MP*, 261). And during a conversation with Fanny at the ball, Edmund presses his cousin's hand to his lips "with almost as much warmth as if it had been Miss Crawford's" (*MP*, 269).

That Austen stresses Edmund's brotherly affection until the end of the novel is of special import. When Fanny decks herself out in her finery to go to dinner at the Grants, Edmund looks at her "with the kind smile of an affectionate brother" (*MP*, 222). Likewise, as Fanny leaves for Portsmouth, her cousin gives her "the affectionate farewell of a brother" (*MP*, 374). Apparently unaware of Fanny's love for him, Edmund tries to be of service to his cousin by his encouragement of Henry Crawford's suit, despite Fanny's vehement protest, "Oh! never, never, never; he will never succeed with me" (*MP*, 347). After attempting to persuade Fanny to marry Henry, Edmund adds insult to injury by ushering his cousin "with the kind authority of a privileged guardian into the house" (*MP*, 355). Following the scandal involving Maria Rushworth and Henry Crawford in London, Edmund arrives in Portsmouth to claim his cousin; pressing her to his heart, he barely articulates, "My Fanny—my only sister—my only comfort now" (*MP*, 444). In light of the disappointment and suffering in Edmund's relationship with Mary, "Fanny's friendship was all that he had to cling to" (*MP*, 460).

Edmund's love for Fanny seems to be of a different quality from hers for him. She is in love with him throughout most of the novel, whereas Edmund's conjugal love for her is not apparent until the end of *Mansfield Park*. He has to see first that an "outsider" is *not* for him after all. In Fanny's case, she has been deeply attached to her cousin since she was a child. Her tender feelings toward Edmund intensify as she matures; her love has always been more than sisterly or cousinly regard. But Edmund's brotherly affection changes to conjugal love only when his relationship with Mary fails; it dawns on him that his beloved "sister" would make an excellent wife and that going outside the home has moral risks. In other words, Edmund learns that marriage to Fanny will be the best alliance of all because their relationship has been strengthened by their early associations and instinctive understanding, his guiding and protection of her, and their mutual love and esteem for one another's uprightness and rectitude. Austen's emphasis, as always, is not on the physical but on the fraternal, spiritual quality of their relationship. In this respect, the union of the cousins is consecrated and serves to verify and reinforce Austen's view of the sacredness of the home, which remains untainted in this "world of changes" (*MP*, 374). For Austen, this type of egalitarian relationship between quasi-siblings suggests that only the family, not the state or public sphere, can solve the problems experienced by men and women.

In a sense, Austen's idea that only the family can solve such problems inadvertently contributed to Victorian formulations of separate spheres and the "angel in the house," in which many have identified a lack of freedom for women. These relations were certainly not in effect in Austen's day, but it is both compelling and poignant to note that her novels proffer a vision of social redemption that ironically paved the way for Victorian domestic constrictions and constructions. Unlike Victorian successors, Austen argues that private virtues such as sympathy, tolerance, and magnanimity should lead all public action. Victorian literature may be seen as a regression from Austen's more enlightened stance. As Mellor notes, it was "a backlash in which female intelligence, activity and power was once again *restricted* to the arena of the domestic household."[22] In viewing writers of the Victorian period in this way, Austen's forging of a new utopian community based on fraternal qualities seems even more revolutionary from the point of view of late twentieth-century feminism.

Some critics have claimed that the overall mood of *Mansfield Park* is pessimistic and regressive. For instance, Julia Prewitt Brown remarks that in *Mansfield Park* and *Emma* "time and history are arrested. The sense of stasis . . . is partially explained by the incestuous marriages with which they end . . . This is the darker side of cooperation in Jane Austen. In *Mansfield Park*, cooperation is a kind of inertia."[23] But such a reading becomes difficult to sustain at the conclusion of the novel, where the mood is obviously one of optimism and satisfaction; far from being regressive, the incestuous marriage not only proves to be reenergizing but also carries with it distinct moral and social benefits. Indeed, the cooperation between the siblinglike lovers forms the crux of Austen's moral vision in *Mansfield Park*. The union of Edmund and Fanny is a perfect marriage because of their spiritual affinities and their similarities of taste and temper: "the happiness of the married cousins must appear as secure as earthly happiness can be.—Equally formed for domestic life, and attached to country pleasures, their home was the home of affection and comfort" (*MP*, 473). For Austen, such a union is the only domestic establishment worth having, and in this case it is only attainable *inside* the private sphere of the home rather than the public domain. Such marriages, based on siblinglike solidarity and equality, form a foundation for social redemption.

In her portrayal of in-family marriages, Austen presents a momentous innovation that should be considered in feminist reappraisals. Specifically, she makes a commitment to a masculine and a feminine point of view in her construction of marriages based on the foundation of sibling ties. The incestuous themes of *Mansfield Park*, *Emma*, and *Sense and Sensibility* offer a progressive development in the treatment of what had become a standard novel formula. Moreover, the in-family marriages provide a frame of reference in which to view contemporary events; they manifest Austen's desire to preserve the vitality of the home or the estate and to vindicate family order and values. These, then, are the types of alliances that Austen most favors and approves. The marriages of Edmund and Fanny, Mr. Knightley and Emma, and Edward and Elinor, far from seeming illicit unions, become more nearly moral imperatives.

Notes

1. Glenda A. Hudson, *Sibling Love and Incest in Jane Austen's Fiction* (London: Macmillan, 1992).

2. Anne K. Mellor, *Romanticism and Gender* (New York: Routledge, 1993), 3.

3. Mellor, *Romanticism*, 52.

4. Adrienne Rich, *On Lies, Secrets, and Silence: Selected Prose, 1966–1978* (New York: W. W. Norton, 1979), 176.

5. On Reformation changes in prohibited degrees of marriage, see Sybil Wolfram, *In-laws and Outlaws: Kinship and Marriage in England* (New York: St. Martin's Press, 1987), 23-30.

6. For a list of eighteenth-century novels dealing with the subject of brother/sister incest, see J. M. S. Tompkins, *The Popular Novel in England, 1770–1800* (Lincoln: University of Nebraska Press, 1961), 66. See also Montague Summers, *The Gothic Quest: A History of the Gothic Novel* (London: Fortune Press, 1938), 391-92 for more commentary on incest in gothic novels.

7. Margaret Doody, *Frances Burney: The Life in the Works* (New Brunswick, NJ: Rutgers University Press, 1988), 161.

8. On this subject, see Marilyn Butler, *Jane Austen and the War of Ideas* (Oxford: Clarendon Press, 1975); Mary Poovey, *The Proper Lady and the Woman Writer: Ideology as Style in the Works of Mary Wollstonecraft, Mary Shelley, and Jane Austen* (Chicago: University of Chicago Press, 1984); Mary Evans, *Jane Austen and the State* (London: Tavistock, 1987); Claudia Johnson, *Jane Austen: Women, Politics, and the Novel* (Chicago: University of Chicago Press, 1988); and Alison Sulloway, *Jane Austen and the Province of Womanhood* (Philadelphia: University of Pennsylvania Press, 1989).

9. See, for example, Margaret Doody, "Jane Austen's Reading" in *The Jane Austen Companion*, ed. J. David Grey (London: Macmillan, 1986), 360-61.

10. In *Partings Welded Together: Politics and Desire in the Nineteenth-Century English Novel* (London: Methuen, 1987), David Musselwhite argues that the hard-headed Austen was obsessed with making money from her fiction and that *Mansfield Park* was written to appeal to a much broader audience by using the sensationalist formula of *Lovers' Vows* (16-31). I am more struck by how Austen incorporates the best-selling formula of sensationalism in the shape of incest in her work and how she undermines it.

11. In Radcliffe's *The Romance of the Forest* (1791), for example, Adeline is pursued by her uncle and surrogate father, the Marquis of Montalt.

12. See Gary Kelly, *English Fiction of the Romantic Period, 1789–1830* (London: Longman, 1989), 115.

13. See William Patrick Day's commentary on siblings in American gothic novels in *In the Circles of Fear and Desire: A Study of Gothic Fantasy* (Chicago: University of Chicago Press, 1985), 125-29.

14. Maaja Stewart, *Domestic Realities and Imperial Fictions: Jane Austen's Novels in Eighteenth-Century Contexts* (Athens: University of Georgia Press, 1993), 74.

15. See Terry Lovell, "Jane Austen and the Gentry: A Study in Literature and Ideology" in *The Sociology of Literature: Applied Studies*, ed. Diana Laurenson (Keele: University of Keele, 1978), 15-37.

16. See Nancy Fix Anderson, "Cousin Marriage in Victorian England," *Journal of Family History* 11 (1986): 286-87.

17. Johnson, *Jane Austen,* 119.

18. Johanna H. Smith, "'My Only Sister Now': Incest in *Mansfield Park,*" *Studies in the Novel* 19 (Spring 1987): 1-15.

19. See Johnson, *Jane Austen,* 115; Smith, "My Only Sister," 2.

20. Jane Austen, *Mansfield Park,* vol. 2 of *The Novels of Jane Austen.,* ed. R. W. Chapman, 5 vols. 3d ed. (London: Oxford University Press, 1932-34), 26. Subsequent references are cited parenthetically in the text as *MP.*

21. On Austen as a separatist, see, for example, Maaja Stewart's argument in *Domestic Realities and Imperial Fictions* that moral terms have "gender-specific connotations" (36) and that Austen's women make the country home a maternal space that masks male belligerence with new models of "female domesticity and virtue" (106). See also Mary Poovey on the redefinition of "feminine" character and increase in male authority in *The Proper Lady and the Woman Writer,* 15-30, 212-24.

22. Mellor, *Romanticism,* 212.

23. Julia Prewitt Brown, *Jane Austen's Novels: Social Change and Literary Form* (Cambridge, MA: Harvard University Press, 1979), 99.

III

Feminist Discourses in Dialogue

7

Vindicating Northanger Abbey:
Mary Wollstonecraft, Jane Austen, and Gothic Feminism

Diane Hoeveler

> The world is the book of women.
> —Jean-Jacques Rousseau

> This desire of being always women,
> is the very consciousness that degrades the sex.
> —Mary Wollstonecraft

Dracula has long been recognized as the epitome of the nineteenth-century male gothic genre. Its climax—the apocalyptic battle of good against evil—is reached when the male warriors are led into the struggle by the intuitions and sensitivities of the infected and clairvoyant Madame Mina. When Van Helsing and Mina are on the outskirts of Dracula's castle and evening falls, Van Helsing draws a circle around Mina and places her in front of a fire and away from the three seductive female vampires who are luring her to join them. At that point we know ourselves to be witnessing a scene that redounds with archetypal significance. Mina is being protected here not simply from women who represent flamboyantly fatal femininity, but from vampiresses who themselves embody the most repellent male fantasy about women—that they are diseased and that that disease exudes sexuality, lust, and a form of cannibalism. It is crucial that Mina be kept from contact with such pollutants, for Mina embodies within *Dracula* the idealized feminine construct as represented by the male gothic tradition. We are told over and over again that

Mina is a perfect specimen of womanhood because she possesses, alone of all her sex, "a man's brain and a woman's heart."

When we are told that the highest praise that can be meted out to a woman in the gothic universe is that she should think like a man and emote like a woman, then we know that we are once again within the parameters of the most prevalent ideology circulating in England during the late eighteenth and nineteenth century, the androgynous compulsion. But androgyny as presented by a male gothic author is significantly different when depicted by a female gothic writer. When women present the most praiseworthy heroine they can imagine, such a woman looks very different from Mina Harker. The gendered constructions of femininity that we have from the major British female writers working in the same gothic tradition—at least from Wollstonecraft to the Brontës—look substantially more victimized, less sexually interested or aware, and more self-consciously manipulative of men and the society in which they are battling for their very existences. And yet there is an uncanny similarity between the women in the female gothic canon and Stoker's Mina, and that similarity seems to reside in the need to be or at least to pretend to be a "manly woman." To "think like a man" was an ideal that Wollstonecraft not only embraced as her own; she invented it. Her novelistic heroines and the pathetic women she depicts in A Vindication of the Rights of Woman (1792) are all struggling to escape the same dilemma— consciousness of their femininity coded and internalized as difference and weakness.

To tell a woman that she thinks like a man is the highest praise that can be given to a woman in a patriarchal society. But where and when exactly did such an attitude originate among women? It is my contention that the valorization of the masculine woman first assumed widespread circulation in the writings of Mary Wollstonecraft. To read Wollstonecraft's two quasi-sentimental novels—Mary, A Fiction (1788) and The Wrongs of Woman, or Maria (published in 1798)—is to realize that the female gothic ideology originated in the hyperbolic gestures and the frenzied poses of victimage that tip these novels over the edge from sentimentality into gothicism. In writing these two novels—the latter unfinished and stalled, as if the author was paralyzed and compelled to imagine only various scenarios of disaster for her heroine— Wollstonecraft exposed the tyranny of sentimental literary formulae for women. She revealed that for women of all classes, life really was the way it was depicted in sentimental and melodramatic fiction—a series of insults, humiliations, deprivations, and fatal or near-fatal disasters. The female gothic novelistic tradition is generally considered to have originated in the gothic novels of Ann Radcliffe, four major novels (1790-98) that provided the subject matter, techniques, and literary conventions of popular melodrama, first on the stage in England, then in France, and later in the Hollywood films that have continued to promulgate what I would call the ideology of "gothic feminism," or the notion that women earn their superior rights over the corrupt patriarchy through their special status as innocent victims.[1]

Gothic feminism is not about being equal to men; it's about being morally superior to men. It's about being a victim. My contention is that a dangerous species of thought for women developed at this time and in concert with the sentimentality of Richardson and the hyperbolic gothic and melodramatic stage productions of the era. This ideology taught its audience the lessons of victimage well. According to this powerful and socially coded formula, victims earn their special status and rights through no act of their own but through their sufferings and persecutions at the hands of a patriarchal oppressor and tyrant. One would be rewarded not for anything one actively did but for what one passively suffered. Women developed in this formula a type of behavior that we would recognize as passive-aggression; they appear to be almost willing victims, not because they were masochists but because they expected a substantial reward on their investment in suffering. Whereas Richardson's Clarissa found herself earning a crown in heaven for suffering the advances of Lovelace, the women in female gothic texts are interested in more earthly rewards. The lesson that gothic feminism teaches is that the meek shall inherit the gothic earth; the female gothic heroine always triumphs in the end because melodramas are constructed that way. Justice always intervenes and justice always rectifies, validates, and rewards suffering. Terrible events can occur, but the day of reckoning invariably arrives for gothic villains. The message that this ideology peddled actually fostered a form of passivity in women, a psychic fatalism recently labeled "victim feminism" by Naomi Wolf.[2] But whereas Wolf thinks this sort of behavior is of recent origin, we know, however, that it originated in Wollstonecraft, a writer whose bifurcated vision spawned a contradictory "feminist" heritage that women are still struggling to understand.

But how did a variety of eighteenth-century discourse systems converge to construct the ideology of gothic feminism? It would appear that the sentimental novel tradition, the hyperbolic and melodramatic gothic, and the educational treatises by "Sophia" and other eighteenth-century women all combined to produce an ambience rife with anxiety about gender, gender roles, and appropriate gender markings. Codifying what it meant to be "feminine" and "masculine" in this newly rigid bourgeois civilization consumed vast amounts of many people's energies. And central to the dispute about how the "feminine" woman could protect herself were the writings of

Mary Wollstonecraft, *agent provocateur* of the notion that women are the innocent victims of a patriarchal system designed to oppress and disfigure their talents and desires. If the patriarchy did not exist, Wollstonecraft would have had to invent it to make her case for women. But fortunately for her, Jean-Jacques Rousseau was writing books that intrigued and infuriated her in almost equal measures. The major problematics and issues in the construction of what we recognize as "femininity" and "feminism" can be found in the strange shadow-boxing Wollstonecraft engaged in with her strawman Rousseau in *A Vindication of the Rights of Woman* . If we have revised history to codify the *Vindication* as the first "feminist" manifesto, Wollstonecraft herself saw the work in a rather different light. She was writing in the context of both the sentimental novel and the hyperbolic sentimental—the gothic novel and melodrama. Indeed, her own two attempts at novel writing show her constructing the sentimental heroine as the blameless victim of a male-created system of oppression. What we recognize as "feminist" rage at systemic injustice in Wollstonecraft's oeuvre can be understood only if it is set in its full gothic and melodramatic contexts.[2] If gothic husbands can chain their wives to stone walls in caves, then what sort of action is required by women to protect and defend themselves against such evil tyranny? Batting one's eyes and demure, docile behavior is hardly adequate protection against the lustful, ravening patriarch. "Gothic feminism" was born when women realized that they had a formidable external enemy in addition to their own worst internal enemy, their consciousness of difference perceived as weakness.

In 1798 Jane Austen sat down to write the novel that was published posthumously as *Northanger Abbey*.[3] More topical than any of her other works, *Northanger Abbey* reads as a critique of both the gothic and the sentimental sensibilities that were being foisted on women readers at the time. If Catherine Morland, coded as "gothic," is victimized and rather foolish, then so is Isabella Thorpe, coded as "sentimental." In many ways, *Northanger Abbey* fictionalizes the major points in Wollstonecraft's treatise, showing that women who are given inadequate educations will be victims of their own folly as well as of masculine hubris, lust, and greed. Taught from birth to fetishize their physical appearance as their only means of survival, women can only become as foolish as Mrs. Allen or as cunning as Isabella. Like lapdogs coddled and petted, such women are physically weak and mentally vacuous, living only for the attentions occasionally doled out to them by their masters. Into such a world of slaves steps the gothic tyrant, the ultimate male master with a whip. But in true Hegelian fashion, the master is as obsessed with the slave as the slave is with the master. If the slave were to write a novel, it would be about the master, and thus we have the Radcliffe oeuvre. If masters were to write novels they would be about slaves, and thus we have the Rousseau and Richardson corpus. In *Northanger Abbey* Austen attempts to rise above both postures and see both master and slave simultaneously. Her Catherine Morland is as sympathetic (or unsympathetic) as Henry Tilney. But Mrs. Tilney is dead and the patriarchal General, her tyrannical husband, is very much still alive, still haunting the dreams of young women who would like very much to live in the sentimental landscapes of their own literary musings. Wollstonecraft hovers over *Northanger Abbey* as blatantly as do Radcliffe, Burney, and Rousseau. In writing this most literarily dense work, Austen sought to reshape and redefine the central historical, social, and intellectual debates of her era. She sought finally to suggest that playing at and profiting from the role of innocent victim was as close as many women would ever get to being "feminists" in a society that polarized the genders as thoroughly as hers did.

By 1803, the year Jane Austen sold the manuscript of *Northanger Abbey*, the gothic heroine was a highly codified ideological figure, complete with stock physical traits, predictable parentage, and reliable class indicators. Clearly, this heroine was ripe as a subject for parody, and such, presumably, was Austen's motive when she created her gothic heroine-in-training, Catherine Morland. Trying to determine exactly what *Northanger Abbey* is or is not as a work of fiction and who Catherine Morland is or is not as a heroine has occupied Austen critics since the book was published in 1817. But there is no clear consensus on the novel, on Catherine, or on Austen's motives in writing a novel so seemingly dissimilar from her first two works, *Pride and Prejudice* and *Sense and Sensibility*.[4]

We can, I think, safely postulate that Austen was dealing in all her novels with structured moral dichotomies, and that on some level the dichotomy permeating this particular world would appear to be place, or the notion of place as made manifest in moral and gendered values and as embodied in the supposed split between Bath and the Abbey. But there is no real juxtaposition here. The "feminine" world of Bath—social artifice, hypocrisy, surface show contradicting reality, a species of "imprisonment" (*NA*, 22)—does not actually contrast with the "masculine" world of Northanger Abbey—psychic artifice, self-haunting and haunted, the lies that conceal the mercenary motives for marriage in a vacuous society. Both worlds are equally unreal, rejected by and rejecting of the heroine. Both worlds are essentially the same, Bath being only what we might recognize as the tamer, "cooked" daytime version of the "raw" Northanger, while the Abbey at night, as constructed by Catherine's gothic imaginings, is the nightmare version of Bath. The parody or lack of parody in Austen's work stems from the ambiguity or confusion about this notion of gendered place: either the entire external network that we know as society for women is a gothic monstrosity—or there is no gothic realm at all—only faulty education and the over active imaginations of female gothic novelists feeding false fantasies to adolescent females. We are in the realm here of Berkeley, Locke, and other empiricist philosophers who would tell their readers that all ontological reality is ultimately a mental construct and subject to one's own psychic control and manipulation. If we conceive of Catherine Morland as a proverbial tabula rasa, then we can begin to appreciate what Austen was trying to accomplish with this most misunderstood of her novels.

Individual women in Austen's novels are the raw material on which Wollstonecraft's theories about female education and socialization can be tested and proved. *Northanger Abbey*, as I have already noted, reads as a sort of fictionalized *Vindication*, personifying in its various female characters the lived results of stunted and pernicious educations. To be schooled in the arts of femininity as effectively as Isabella Thorpe has been is to be fitted for nothing but deception, cunning, and misery. All of the female characters in the novel are pawns, powerless, or fearful of male prerogatives. All, that is, except Catherine. She is the heroine of the novel because she is too dense to understand clearly at any time what is going on around her. She bungles her way to a good marriage, not through any merit of her own, but through the author's conscious manipulations of our (and Henry's) sympathies. When Catherine is victimized by General Tilney and shown the door in very uncivil terms, she earns her special melodramatic status as a "victim" of oppression, malice, and fraud. And once she has earned such status, the heroine is worthy of her man. According to Wollstonecraft's formula, a victim is always rewarded because such is the case in the melodramatic scheme of things. Her suffering is reified as value and stands as lucre to be exchanged for a husband.

But all this is to get ahead of ourselves. Let's begin at the beginning and examine exactly how Austen constructed and at the same time deconstructed gothic feminism. We could begin by examining Catherine's surname, suggesting that like all gothic heroines she exists to accrue "more land." Her social and financial status are the crucial issues throughout the text, as, indeed, they are throughout all sentimental and gothic texts. But Austen passes lightly over this point and begins her novel with the more self-consciously literary statement: "No one who had ever seen Catherine Morland in her infancy would have supposed her born to be an heroine" (*NA*, 13). If we read this sentence and conclude only that Catherine does not fulfill the physical characteristics of a heroine, as she clearly does not, we miss the larger allegorical implication that Austen intends here. All women, she hints, are born the heroines of their own rather inconspicuous lives, whether they look the part or not. All women, whether they live in the south of Italy or France or the middle of England, have the desire for exciting, fulfilling, meaningful lives, and all are engaged in quests for such lives whether the conditions are propitious or not. Catherine is Austen's Everywoman heroine—plain, ordinary, insufficiently educated, nothing special—but she still manages to become a heroine by following her instincts, waiting passively, and suffering injustices from the hands of a misguided patriarch.

In addition to her physical plainness—her "thin awkward figure, a sallow skin without colour, dark lank hair, and strong features" (*NA*, 13)—Catherine has quite ordinary and shockingly healthy parents. Her father, a clergyman · named Richard, has no taste whatever for "locking up his daughters" (*NA*, 13), and the mother manages to produce ten children and remain in the best of health. No hidden vaults here, no foundlings in the neighborhood, but never fear, in short, "[S]omething must and will happen to throw a hero in her way" (*NA*, 17). The implication is clear: a heroine needs finally one item to be a heroine, a hero. Appearance, parentage, social trappings and complications, all of these are mere excess baggage. A woman needs a man to test her spirit and define her character, and Catherine is introduced to two: the false suitor John Thorpe and the true suitor Henry Tilney. The double plot, so typical of allegorical poems such as *The Faerie Queene* and Austen's more immediate satiric target, Charlotte Smith's *Emmeline, The Orphan of the Castle* (1788), reminds us once again that Austen is manipulating the fairy-tale conventions of the double-suitor plot to suggest the entire artifice of the mating customs that prevail in her supposedly enlightened society. Substitute parents are quickly provided for in the guise of Mr. and Mrs. Allen, who actually take on the qualities of fairy godfather and godmother in that their supposed dowry for Catherine propels all of the subsequent plot complications. In innocently presenting herself as the ward or heir of the Allens, Catherine participates rather unwittingly in the Bath game of social deception. Her first catch is John Thorpe, but ironically Thorpe snares bigger prey for her by spreading the unfounded rumor of Catherine's wealth to General Tilney, who bites. There is, Austen suggests, no fool like an old fool.

So Catherine sets off for "all the difficulties and dangers of a six weeks' residence in Bath," "her mind about as ignorant and uninformed as the female mind at seventeen usually is" (*NA*, 18). We chuckle at the uneventfulness of Catherine's separation from her mother. With so many children at home she is, one can only surmise, grateful to have one taken off her hands. But the contrast to the gothic world is made explicit when Mrs. Morland cautions

Catherine about the dangers she may face in the outside world. Does she warn her daughter against "the violence of such noblemen and baronets as delight in forcing young ladies away to some remote farmhouse"? No, her concerns are more practical: "'I beg, Catherine, you will always wrap yourself up very warm about the throat, when you come from the rooms at night; and I wish you would try to keep some account of the money you spend; I will give you this little book on purpose'" (*NA*, 18-19). This is the first time we have seen a gothic heroine handle the books, so to speak. In all of Radcliffe's novels the heroine never handles her own money. In fact, money appears in Radcliffe's works only as a landed estate or an inheritance, not as something that can be freely spent and accounted for by the heroine. The change is significant, for with Catherine, whose pseudo inheritance is so central to the plot, we have the figure of a woman who represents empty cash value and yet who spends her own money. The opposite had been true with Radcliffe's heroines. The change represents a subtle shift in how the middle class represented and thought about itself. Once merely potentiality, they have become embodied. They can spend, whereas before they merely embodied the potential to spend.

But if Catherine is not the typical gothic heroine, neither is Mrs. Allen the typical gothic duenna figure. Austen alludes to the older woman who conspires against the innocent young heroine and contrasts this figure to the slow-witted Mrs. Allen. The narrator asks us to wonder whether this woman will "by her imprudence, vulgarity, or jealousy—whether by intercepting her letters, ruining her character, or turning her out of doors"—victimize the gothic heroine (*NA*, 20). In fact, it is not fashion-crazed Mrs. Allen who will commit any of these untoward deeds to poor Catherine; she will be too busy trying on dresses to pay much attention at all to her young ward. But these outrages will occur and they will be committed by Catherine's "dear friends," the Thorpes and General Tilney. This instance of foreshowing, used throughout the text, suggests the ironic distance and narrative control Austen employs over both her authorial sympathies and her readers'. By laughing at the stock gothic tortures that assail the typical gothic heroine before they occur, Austen preemptively defuses their power when they actually do happen in the text.

No, the greatest tragedy to confront our heroine Catherine is not to be asked to dance her first night out in Bath. Totally ignored, Catherine spends her first night as an empty signifier: "Not one, however, started with rapturous wonder on beholding her, no whisper of eager inquiry ran round the room, nor was she once called a divinity by anybody" (*NA*, 23). The gothic novel, in elevating to a ridiculous level a young woman's sense of herself as the object of the obsessive male gaze, can only fail to set up a disappointment for Everywoman. Not to be noticed and praised by a room full of strange men is for Catherine almost as ignominious a fate as an attempted kidnapping and rape in the gothic arsenal of shock and abuse techniques. In fact, later in the week, when the same sad situation occurs again and Catherine finds herself without a dancing partner, she muses that her lot is identical to the fate of an abused and harassed gothic heroine: "To be disgraced in the eye of the world, to wear the appearance of infamy while her heart is all purity, her actions all innocence, and the misconduct of another the true source of her debasement, is one of those circumstances which peculiarly belong to the heroine's life, and her fortitude under it particularly dignifies her character" (*NA*, 53). A more succinct and self-conscious description of the female gothic heroine could hardly be found. One just laughs at the "disgrace" and feels that Austen has trivialized not simply Catherine, but Adeline and Ellena and Emily and all the other gothic heroines whose "disgraces" perhaps were not so immense after all.

It is not long, however, before our hero is introduced and the real education of Catherine begins. The first conversation between the two lovers is instructive, for it reveals the artificial play-acting that passes for polite discourse between the sexes. Although Henry Tilney is aware that they are acting, Catherine is not, and the humor in the situation arises from her complete naïveté about social conventions. When Henry presses her on the contents of her journal, she is flustered because she does not keep a journal. A journal, after all, would suggest a level of self-consciousness that Catherine at this stage of her life simply does not possess. But it is significant that for the first time in the novel the act of writing appears as a metaphor for defining and inscribing one's femininity. Indeed, Henry goes so far as to state: "My dear madam, I am not so ignorant of young ladies' ways as you wish to believe me; it is this delightful habit of journalizing which largely contributes to form the easy style of writing for which ladies are so generally celebrated. Everybody allows that the talent of writing agreeable letters is peculiarly female" (*NA*, 27). If keeping a journal is supposed to hone a woman's skill for letter writing, then some sort of not very veiled panegyric on the epistolary sentimental novel tradition appears to be the real subject here. But consider that it was not women who wrote the letters that formed *Clarissa* and *Pamela*, but a man ventriloquizing a woman's sensibility and subjectivity. Henry seems to suggest that both sexes have come to a new level of understanding and rapprochement through the acts of writing and reading each others' works. If Richardson can depict a woman's situation as sensitively as he does in *Clarissa*, then a female author should be able to understand a man's mind as thoroughly and present that vision to the world through her writing. Needless to say, all this passes right by our Catherine.

Henry, in fact, acts out this female ventriloquizing when he next engages in a conversation with Mrs. Allen about the price of muslin. If she can haggle over muslin by the yard, so can he. Henry wins Mrs. Allen's total devotion by confessing that he managed to buy "a true Indian muslin" for just five shillings a yard. He impresses her even further by worrying aloud about how Catherine's muslin will hold up to washing. By this time, even Catherine begins to suspect that the two of them have been the objects of his ever-so-solicitous mockery: "Catherine feared, as she listened to their discourse, that he indulged himself a little too much with the foibles of others" (NA, 29). But Austen is making a point here about education and about who is best qualified to instruct young women in the arts of "femininity." That is, Henry implies to Mrs. Allen that she has failed miserably in her duties to Catherine and that he, a mere man, is forced to step in and complete her educational process. As a credential he brandishes his superior skills in bargaining for fabric. But the more serious intent is to suggest that women's education is too serious a subject to be left to female amateurs. Only men have the sufficient backgrounds and knowledge to educate women, and until they do so women will suffer in their ignorance.

Henry also parodies in these two exchanges the "man of feeling," the effeminate man who is acceptable to women because he has been effectively castrated by the social conventions of sensibility and civility. Catherine finds him "strange" (NA, 28), suggesting that his female ventriloquism is not to her more primitive tastes. She is going to insist on playing the gothic game, and as such she needs a strong abusive father figure before she can appreciate and accept the castrated son figure. Enter Henry's father General Tilney, benighted enough to put credence in the rumors spread by the oafish John Thorpe. The General's villainy, as several critics have noted, is not particularly on the grand gothic scale, but merely a matter of simple mercenary greed and insensitivity to Catherine once he learns that she is not the heiress he had assumed she was. Although compared several times to Radcliffe's "Montoni," the General is only a common garden-variety father: boorish, self-important, overbearing.

But the issue that has gone largely unnoticed in this confusion about Catherine's supposed inheritance is the importance that the role of rumor and gossip play in shaping people's perception. Both forms of unofficial and unsanctioned "feminine" discourse constitute the crux of a suppressed female oral tradition that preserves the stories that male tyrants want long forgotten. Largely employed by female servants, the rumors and gossip that circulate about the Marquis de Villeroi's role in the murder of his wife (in *Mysteries of Udolpho*) and Schedoni's murder of his brother (in *The Italian*) take the entire text to be spelled out. But the power of accumulated rumor finally forces the truth out into the open, thereby saving the heroines from the mystifications that happen when one is dealing only with false surmises and conjectures based on partial narratives. Power structures exist by mystifying their own edifices and methods. Rumor and gossip force those methods out into the light of day for examination. It is no coincidence that gossip as a negative term is generally associated with women, servants, and other marginalized and easily scapegoated groups. They have, after all, nothing to lose and everything to gain by circulating stories about tyrants and the abuse of power.

So what does it mean that John Thorpe is the source for the majority of gossip and rumor throughout this text? Does dealing in rumor and gossip "feminize" him? In fact, quite the contrary. The anthropological studies we have on gossip show that the right to gossip is generally viewed as the province of those who have earned their membership in the inner circle of the tribe or clan. Gossip is condemned only when it is engaged in by those who do not have full membership status in this inner circle. (Thus, at that point, women and servants are condemned for dealing in gossip, because they are not recognized as full members of the power community.) But research consistently demonstrates that the more powerful a man is, the more he deals in gossip as a source for information about the community—all of its dealings and events.[5] It makes perfect sense that John Thorpe and General Tilney would be gossiping about Catherine Morland, a new source of income on the market. Discussing her supposed financial status would be little different in their minds from discussing the value of stocks and bonds and any other projected or potential investment. The fact that neither had the slightest idea of her real worth forms the core of the humorous irony. When John Thorpe thinks he has a chance to acquire Catherine, then she is immensely rich and desirable. When he learns that she has decisively rejected him, then he constructs her as a pauper. Neither version is an accurate depiction of her financial standing. And yet both versions of Catherine reveal the woman as blank slate. For the Thorpes and Generals of this world, woman is only what the more powerful man says she is; she has no ontological reality in herself, only as much or as little as he assigns to her.

The stage is further set for the pedagogical project when Catherine meets her false female mentor, Isabella Thorpe, John's hopelessly mercenary and manipulative sister. Isabella shrewdly decides that novel reading will be the basis of their alliance, and once again the subject of writing emerges in the text as an indicator of gender acculturation. The discussion about novels, particularly women's novels, reveals a defensiveness that is both amusing and painful to read. Catherine loves to read novels because, as the narrator shrewdly observes, she is in a novel herself: "Alas! If the heroine of one novel be not patronized by the heroine of another, from whom can she expect protection and regard?" (NA, 37). The narrator's very self-conscious ficti-tiousness here is strikingly original, as is the narrator's dismay that women are embarrassed to be seen reading the novels of, say, Fanny Burney when they would be praised instead for reading some dull volume of the *Spectator*. But why does Isabella want Catherine to read gothic novels with her? The answer would appear to lie in Isabella's desire to find someone who will share her novelistically induced fantasies about life. In Isabella's mind she is a heroine in a sentimental novel, penniless but deserving, the object of love and adoration from countless men who will be only too willing to lavish riches for the privilege of purchasing her. Unfortunately, she has read too many novels and imbibed from them the false belief that women can manipulate and control men in life as easily as they do in sentimental novels.

Isabella as false confidante is doubled by Henry's sister Eleanor, the true confidante who is shown at the end of the novel to have more power over her father than anyone. Eleanor's power stems from her rather sudden marriage to a titled aristocrat, which gives her leverage over the General. But throughout the text Eleanor acts as a foil to the showy, empty Isabella, who is supposedly engaged twice and comes up with nothing. The subplot we would rather see would concern the courtship of Eleanor and Lord Longtown, the adventures of the Lord's maid and her laundry list, and the identity of "Alice." When Eleanor asks Catherine to write to her at Lord Longtown's residence "under cover to Alice" (NA, 228), we sense that the more interesting gothic plot was occurring elsewhere all the time.

When Catherine picks up *The Mysteries of Udolpho*, she knows that she is reading a book that, as she admits, she could spend her whole life reading with pleasure. The conspiracies that Catherine is compelled to spin out about the General murdering his wife, or perhaps just burying her alive in a deserted wing of the Abbey—these imaginings are more obviously cribbed from *The Sicilian Romance*. Later John Thorpe names *The Monk* as his favorite novel, perhaps unaware that its tale of matricide and incestuous rape of a sister reveals more than he might like about his own interests. We know the moral fiber of these characters by knowing the moral visions of the novels they prefer. This is a world of mirrors where blatantly self-consciously fictional characters define themselves by their allegiance to other blatantly self-conscious fictional cre-ations. In a hall of mirrors there is no reality, only constructions and construc-tions of constructions. One senses that Catherine's challenge as a literary character is to emerge from the gothic universe of Radcliffe and situate herself instead as a character in a Burney novel. It is a particularly propitious sign that John Thorpe does not like Burney's work, "such unnatural stuff" (*NA*, 49), suggesting that if he does not understand it it must be profound.

With the major characters and conflict established, let us examine the three major gothic incidents in the text as keys to understanding Austen's manipulation of the conventions of gothic feminism. The first episode concerns the General's character and the Abbey as a ruin, the second Catherine's discovery of ordinary domesticities in the dead mother's cabinets and bedroom, and the final incident involves Catherine's expulsion and flight from the Abbey. These are familiar scenes and have been discussed at length before, but I intend to argue that Austen was hopelessly ambivalent about her attitude toward what I would label "gothic feminism" and that this ambivalence causes the alternate hyperbole and deflation in these episodes. Almost like melodramatic setpieces in a period drama, Austen inserts the gothic incidents as virtual *tableaux-vivants*, designed on the surface to garner our amusement and cause us to chuckle. But the net effect of mingling the gothic with the domestic and sentimental romance produces instead a strange hybrid—the awareness that the domestic is gothic or that we cannot think any more about the domestic without at the same time recognizing its gothic underpinnings, its propensities for violence, abuse, and exploitation of women.

The first time Catherine sees the General she is struck by his physical attractiveness. Later when she visits the Tilney residence she finds the General infinitely more attractive than Henry. In fact, she muses to herself that the General was "perfectly agreeable and good-natured, and altogether a very charming man, . . . for he was tall and handsome, and Henry's father" (*NA*, 129). That last phrase, tacked on as if as a reminder to herself, suggests that Catherine's initial attraction is less to the son than to the father. All this changes, however, almost as soon as she sets off for Northanger Abbey. Catherine is convinced that it is the General who changes once he is within his own domicile. But clearly his character—imperious, demanding, manipulative, and dominating—is simply revealed more starkly. Suddenly Catherine sees that the General "seemed always a check upon his children's spirits, and scarcely anything was said but by himself" (*NA*, 156). He is a veritable master of the dining room, pacing up and down with a watch in his hand, pulling the dinner bell "with violence," and ordering everyone to the table immediately (*NA*, 165). Only in his presence does Catherine feel fatigue. The strain from answering his boorishly probing questions about the size of Mr. Allen's estate has begun to wear on our poor heroine.

The General, living in his Abbey, is a patriarch and usurper, similar to the patriarch and usurper inhabiting Walpole's *Castle of Otranto*. Northanger Abbey, we are told, was "a richly endowed convent at the time of the Reformation" (*NA*, 142), but it fell, as did all property belonging to the Roman Catholic church, like spoils into the hands of Protestant warlords. General Tilney, whose military mien is no accident, continues the war on convents, so to speak, by preying on the prospects both of his daughter and the supposed inheritance of Catherine. The female gothic, suggests Austen, concerns itself with just this sort of tale of female disinheritance and suppression. Catherine thinks that in living in an abbey she will wander around "long, damp passages," explore "its narrow cells and ruined chapel," and thrill to "some traditional legends, some awful memorials of an injured and ill-fated nun" (*NA*, 141). It is the buried nun, the rightful owner of the usurped Abbey, who haunts the female gothic. But within the domesticated landscape that Austen and her heroine inhabit, the nun becomes first the murdered wife and then the murdered wife becomes simply an ordinary woman beaten down and defeated by the demands of life with three children and an ill-tempered husband. The idea of the Abbey as a female community of nuns, living in seclusion from men and escaping the demands of marriage and childbirth—this is what the General and his ancestors have usurped. There is no longer in England any form of communal escape for women. There is only the reality of women as property, sources of income, breeders of heirs—the sad and oft told tale of female disinheritance, "buried nuns."

And yet *Northanger Abbey* has managed to elide its gothic past almost totally. The General, we learn, is an energetic remodeler, even transforming the ruined section of the Abbey into a suite of offices for himself. Instead of dark and dank, Catherine finds light and airy. Instead of old and moldering, she finds new and absolutely up-to-date furnishings. She does succeed, however, in locating two old chests, and we know ourselves suddenly to be in *The Romance of the Forest*. One chest in that text contained the father's skeleton and the other the manuscript he left behind recounting his final hours awaiting murder. Catherine has been primed by Henry to play the gothic game with the chests, and she is only too willing. Both, however, disappoint. The first contains only linen and the second the famous laundry list left by Lord Longstown's maid. Hoping to have found a broken lute, perhaps a dagger (preferably blood stained), instruments of torture, a hoard of diamonds, or the "memoirs of the wretched Matilda" (*NA*, 158-60), the domesticities can only be a bitter disappointment to the overly imaginative Catherine: "She felt humbled to the dust. Could not the adventure of the chest have taught her wisdom? A corner of it, catching her eye as she lay, seemed to rise up in judgment against her. Nothing could now be clearer than the absurdity of her recent fancies. To suppose that a manuscript of many generations back could have remained undiscovered in a room such as that, so modern, so habitable!—or that she should be the first to possess the skill of unlocking a cabinet, the key of which was open to all!" (*NA*, 173). The self-chastisement that occurs here is predicated on the belief that other women have gone before Catherine and that they have had the same compulsions to ferret out the truth that lies buried within the patriarchal family. The large and imposing cabinet with the visible key tropes the family's apparent transparent status as an institution that is open to complete scrutiny and understanding by all. A deeper examination of this episode suggests that in fact women have not explored or analyzed the structure of the family. They have accepted its bulk and its power to contain and define them. They have, in very real senses, allowed themselves to be buried alive within all of the separate cabinets that dot the landscape of England. The linen and the laundry list are the visible residue of women's lost and unpaid labor for the family. The domesticities, rather than reassuring Catherine, should have horrified her.

We are next presented with Catherine's growing obsession with the dead Mrs. Tilney. She is figured first through her daughter's memories of her mother's favorite walk, a path that the General studiously avoids. Next we learn that the General is so insensitive as not to want to hang his dead wife's portrait in a prominent place in the Abbey. From these two facts Catherine spins out her murder plot and finally admits to herself that she truly hates the General: "His cruelty to such a charming woman made him odious to her. She had often read of such characters" (*NA*, 181). But why such an investment of emotion in the General? Why does he elicit such strong feelings in Catherine? Protesting too much, we already are aware of her attraction to him, an attraction that she could only repress and deny by inventing such a horrible crime that he would have to be truly unworthy of her regard and admiration. Yes, the General must have killed his wife; therefore, I cannot be attracted more to him than to his son.

Further playing the oedipal detective, Catherine decides to snoop next into the circumstances of Mrs. Tilney's death, learning that it was caused by a fever that came on suddenly when her daughter was not at home. Catherine leaps to the conclusion that Mrs. Tilney, like the Marchioness de Villeroi in *Udolpho*, has been poisoned by her husband and that the General has been suffering from guilt ever since. No wonder he stays up late at night: "There must be some deeper cause: something was to be done which could be done only while the household slept; and the probability that Mrs. Tilney yet lived, shut up for causes unknown, and receiving from the pitiless hands of her husband a nightly supply of coarse food, was the conclusion which necessarily followed. . . . all favoured the supposition of her imprisonment. Its origin—jealousy perhaps, or wanton cruelty—was yet to be unravelled" (NA, 187-88). Can the search for a gothic stone cave be far behind? The psychic transition here from imagining murder to revising it to imprisonment simply—all this suggests childhood and adolescent anxieties about adult sexuality. The fixation on "something" that is "done which could be done only while the household slept"—all this is too familiar. We're dealing here with a child's imaginings about what her parents do at night when they are no longer under her watchful gaze. The notion that the mother is secretly imprisoned, "shut up for causes unknown," and fed only at night by the father—this is a crude version of a child's sense of sex as a violation and a physical assault. We need not ponder too long to realize that Catherine fears marriage as much as she claims to desire it.

Now, Catherine has no knowledge of life except as it has been presented to her in novels, mostly female gothic novels. She chooses to read the General as a character in a novel, mixing Montoni and Mazzini with a dash of Montalt and Schedoni. Yes, she muses, she knows his type all too well. She has, after all, read dozens of novels: "She could remember dozens who had persevered in every possible vice, going on from crime to crime, murdering whomsoever they chose, without any feeling of humanity or remorse; till a violent death or a religious retirement closed their black career" (NA, 190). But whether the General literally murdered his wife or merely made her life so miserable that she found her own way to the grave is irrelevant. The result in either case is the same: the mother is dead and the General is alive.

Let the scene shift to Catherine's greatest gothic adventure: the perilous journey down galleries and deserted wings of the abbey to the dead mother's bedroom. The room itself is bright and ordinary and empty; there is absolutely no mystery or intrigue or wax figure or prisoner at all. Death is as real as the female gothic tries to make it unreal. The empty room stands as a simple reminder that in real life death cannot be wished away, cannot be denied, cannot be covered over with fantasies of a mother who comes back as if from the dead. The female gothic novel, in dealing with the territory of wish-fulfillment, attempted to convince its readers that evil and mortality can be denied by the resourceful female gothic heroine. Catherine receives here instead the slap of life across her face. And Henry's rebuke does not make the realization any easier to accept: "Remember that we are English, that we are Christians. Consult your own understanding, your own sense of the probable, your own observation of what is passing around you. Does our education prepare us for such atrocities? Do our laws connive at them? Could they be perpetuated without being known, in a country like this, where social and literary intercourse is on such a footing, where every man is surrounded by a neighbourhood of voluntary spies, and where roads and newspapers lay everything open?" (*NA*, 197-98). This statement, generally considered to be the high point of anti-gothic sensibility in the text, has been analyzed exhaustively by a number of critics, most of whom read it straight. But it is a highly coded ideological statement that positions masculine-controlled "newspapers" as discourse systems superior to female gothic novels as sources for the truth. It suggests that in the perfect state that is England, literacy and "education" have eradicated evil, and yet there is no universal educational system for women or the lower classes. It smugly asserts that "neighbourhood spies" will report all wrongdoing, as if such a system of veritable espionage were a selling point for the area. And what about our "laws"? Surely they do not protect the lives or estates of married women and children. In short, Henry seeks to persuade Catherine that she has all the advantages that he, as an upper-class, educated, and employed male, possesses. The logic here seems to run something like this: As a male I consider the visions proffered by female gothic novels to be foolish and untenable, and if you were as wise as I am you would agree with me. In valorizing Henry's smug enlightenment attitude, it would appear that Austen shares or at least would like to share Henry's outlook and privileges; it would appear that Austen wants to be one of the boys.

The novel's final gothic episode is almost anticlimactic. Catherine is expelled from the abbey at 7:00 in the morning with no escort and even less money. This incident is frightening and embarrassing for Catherine, largely because it is so inexplicable. Catherine has been unable to understand the General's motivations throughout the novel, and this final episode merely reverses the General's blunt and self-seeking behavior. Whereas before he had been laboring under the mistaken notion that Catherine was a wealthy heiress, now he embraces the mistaken notion that she is a pauper. The General as evil gothic villain is just perpetually and perceptually confused and mistaken, and such, apparently, is the extent of evil in Austen's novelistic universe. The rejection Catherine suffers, however, is smoothed over as effortlessly and hastily as an antigothic novelist can manage. Eleanor appears as *deus ex machina*, Henry proposes offstage, and the newlyweds begin their life together surrounded by "smiles."

The gothic, it would appear, has finally been buried, and all is right with the world. But the gothic has functioned throughout this text as a continually disruptive and undercutting presence, and the conventions of romance cannot bury the atavistic presence of Radcliffe and her imitators. The dead mother, the stolen convent, the incestuous and adulterous impulses that seethe just beneath the surface of this highly polished veneer of a novel—all suggest that Austen was as attracted to the potential for evil in life as she was compelled to finally deny its power and allure. Voicing Henry's enlightenment pieties gives her a feeling of safety and power, a sense that she is immune to the decay and death inherent in marriage and childbearing, that they are indelicacies that affect other women, not her heroines, not her. Austen's Catherine will find out what is behind the black veil only on her wedding night, and by then the novel will be safely concluded. But gothic feminism, playing at and profiting from the role of innocent victim of the patriarchy, will continue and thrive as a potent female-created ideology. Enter Jane Eyre.

Notes

1. My use of the term "gothic melodrama" is indebted to the discussion in Peter Brooks, particularly his observation that melodrama, like the gothic, deals in "hyperbolic figures, lurid and grandiose events, masked relationships and disguised identities, abductions, slow-acting poisons, secret societies, mysterious parentage" (3). See Brooks, *The Melodramatic Imagination: Balzac, Henry James, Melodrama, and the Mode of Excess* (New Haven, CT: Yale University Press, 1976). The evolution of the ideology I have dubbed "gothic feminism" is developed more fully in my forthcoming book "Gothic Feminism: The Melodrama of Gender and Ideology from Wollstonecraft to the Brontës."

2. See Naomi Wolf, *Fire With Fire: The New Female Power and How It Will Change the 21st Century* (New York: Random House, 1993).

3. My discussion of Wollstonecraft is largely based on Poston's very useful second edition of the *Vindication* (Mary Wollstonecraft, *A Vindication of the Rights of Woman.*, ed. Carol H. Poston, 2d ed. [New York: W. W. Norton, 1988]). "Feminism" in Austen is best understood, to my mind, by reading side by side the studies by Butler and Kirkham. See Marilyn Butler, *Jane Austen and The War of Ideas* (Oxford: Clarendon, 1987), and Margaret Kirkham, *Jane Austen, Feminism and Fiction* (Totowa, NJ: Barnes and Noble, 1983).

4. Jane Austen, *Northanger Abbey and Persuasion*, vol. 5 of *The Novels of Jane Austen.*, ed. R. W. Chapman, 5 vols, 3d ed. (London: Oxford University Press, 1932-34). Subsequent references are cited parenthetically in the text as *NA*.

5. The critical commentary on *Northanger Abbey* is, like much of the work on Austen as a whole, contradictory and highly speculative. Among the dozens of secondary

studies, I have found the most suggestive work on Austen's treatment of the gothic to be found in the writings of Howells, Wilt, and Morrison. See Coral Ann Howells, *Love, Mystery, and Misery: Feeling in Gothic Fiction* (London: Athlone, 1978); Judith Wilt, *Ghosts of the Gothic: Austen, Eliot and Lawrence* (Princeton, NJ: Princeton University Press, 1980); and Paul Morrison, "Enclosed in Openness: *Northanger Abbey* and the Domestic Carceral," *Texas Studies in Language and Literature* 33 (1991): 1-23.

6.   Some of the most influential anthropological studies done on gossip were conducted by Max Gluckman and Robert Paine, who concludes that "a man gossips to control others and accordingly fears gossip as it threatens to control him. Hence, a man tries to manage the information that exists about others and himself by gossiping about others (and drawing others into gossip-laden conversations), on the one hand, and by trying to limit gossip about himself." See Paine, "What is Gossip About? An Alternative Hypothesis," *Man* 2 (1967): 283; and Max Gluckman, "Gossip and Scandal," *Current Anthropology* 4 (1963): 307-16. For a more literary treatment of much of the same material, see Patricia Meyer Spacks, *Gossip* (Chicago: University of Chicago Press, 1986).

8
—

In Defense of the Gothic:
Rereading Northanger Abbey

Maria Jerinic

Late last year I received a new selection from my favorite paperback book club—an eagerly anticipated addition to nineteenth-century trivia. But the title bothered me: *What Jane Austen Ate and Charles Dickens Knew: From Fox Hunting to Whist—the Facts of Daily Life in 19th-Century England*. On the cover are two elongated spheres, one of which contains a woman holding a dessert platter and the other a bearded, suited man delivering what seems to be an academic reading or lecture. The Dickens image may be appropriate, but I never imagined Austen concerned with the presentation of dessert. Rather I prefer to picture her hunched over a rickety writing table dashing off manuscripts. Why not "what Jane Austen wrote with"? Why does Dickens get to "know" and Austen only get to "eat"? The juxtaposition of these two images implies that women in the domestic realm cannot "know." Their activities, like baking, do not demand the vigorous rational activity required by the work of a public figure such as Dickens. Because women do not know, they then cannot make decisions and must have them made for them.

A reading of Jane Austen's *Northanger Abbey*[1] as a mere parody of the gothic novel (a popular critical impulse)[2] replicates a similar set of assumptions. It asks the reader to focus on Austen's text primarily as a warning of the negative effects gothic romances can have on young female readers while considering Catherine Morland a victim of *Udolpho's* influence and thus a lesser Austen heroine, not to be compared to an Elizabeth Bennet or an Emma Woodhouse. However, I would argue that such an interpretation ignores the importance

Austen assigns to women *reading*, regardless of genre. While I would disagree with critical opinions that label *Northanger Abbey* a parody of the gothic, I do not, for a moment, deny Austen a strong social critique. The object of Austen's parody and the real threat to women, however, is not the gothic novel but it is men, particularly men who wish to dictate to women what they should and should not read. Austen does not want to reshape or reform men, but her text does insist that women be allowed the same opportunities as men to choose what they read.

Consequently, I will argue that Catherine Morland is not manipulated by her reading experience, rather she is validated by it.[3] In fact, the importance of her reading becomes increasingly clear when she is contrasted with those who do not read, Mrs. Allen, Isabella Thorpe, and John Thorpe. My argument will also encourage a rethinking of the relationship between *Northanger Abbey* and the gothic novel.[4] I would like to consider *Northanger Abbey*, as Judith Wilt does[5], an imitation, and not a complete rejection, of Ann Radcliffe's *The Mysteries of Udolpho* (1794).[6]

Northanger Abbey and *The Mysteries of Udolpho* both contribute to an eighteenth-century conversation revolving around reading, textual influence, and women. It is important to stress, however, that this conversation is dependent on the explosion of print technology. Although the printing press was invented in the fifteenth century, it was not until 1700 that printing began "to affect the structure of social life at every level."[7]

This "transformation to print culture" could not help but affect drastically the social world, which witnessed it as England (or even Europe) changed from an "oral-scribal to a print society." Writers sought to redefine themselves while a system of patronage became increasingly less important and the roles of "critics, editors, bibliographers, and literary historians" more so. The "literary audience" was also transformed "from a small group of manuscript readers or listeners" to a new "public audience of readers" with an accompanying rise in literacy.[8]

Writing as a new technology was regarded warily. Just as our contemporary culture is concerned with the effects of electronic technology (e.g., the possible influence of television on its viewers), eighteenth-century society was uncomfortable with the effect of print on its readers. In the earlier part of the century, many writer/critics, both men and women, found themselves in the interesting position of discussing *their* discomfort with writing, which they believed might induce moral corruption in both sexes. If the reader were to peruse a text describing the actions of an immoral character, the argument went, she or he would repeat this behavior. But because this concern with writing was discussed through the medium of writing itself, writers were hard-pressed to condemn wholeheartedly print technology. As the century progressed, however, the fear of textually induced moral corruption became increasingly gendered. As people became more comfortable with print technology, women were considered the primary potential victims. Society, no longer so afraid of men's textual corruption, allowed writing to become uncomfortable with issues other than itself.

Austen wrote at a time when novel production was skyrocketing[9] and women "to a degree unprecedented in western Europe [became] visible as readers and writers."[10] The late eighteenth-century readership—encouraged by the establishment of lending libraries—was composed largely of "upper- and middle-class women who preferred to read Literature, and especially novels, written by women."[11] Women as readers then became a subject of writing itself. Ros Ballaster reminds us of the numerous literary representations of young female romance readers "who are unable to separate fact from fiction"[12] while Beth Lau advocates that in the second half of the eighteenth century, the female romance reader who spent her days in circulating libraries reading sentimental novels was disparaged.[13] Austen's novel, however, while decentering print as a culprit, does not blame the woman reader. Rather *Northanger Abbey* celebrates the figure of the reading woman, exhibiting instead a discomfort with men and conversations about reading with them. This discomfort concerns not only bad men, Montonis and General Tilneys, but boorish men who don't really read, such as John Thorpe, and good men who do read, future husbands such as Henry Tilney.

Austen presents Catherine as an everywoman, "'extraordinary only because she is ordinary.'"[14] She was always a plain little girl who eventually begins to look "almost pretty" (*NA*, 3). Neither is she unusually bright for "[s]he could never learn anything before she was taught; and sometimes not even then, for she was often inattentive, and occasionally stupid" (*NA*, 2). She is, at the commencement of this story, the average young woman, "her person pleasing. . . . —and her mind about as ignorant and uninformed as the female mind at seventeen usually is" (*NA*, 5). By stressing her prosaicness, Austen allows Catherine to be any middle-class woman. Because she does not stand out from her peers, what happens to her could equally happen to other women readers. Catherine's reading material is also not extraordinary; rather she prefers books that are "all story and no reflection" (*NA*, 3), although she does branch out to read the fare of heroines-in-training: Pope, Gray, Thompson, Shakespeare, and especially, Radcliffe. Austen often rails Catherine for her ignorance, but at least Catherine is an avid reader. She wakes up in the morning to immediately begin reading and is often reluctantly torn away from the text. When not reading, she is preoccupied with what she had been reading and is constantly on the watch for someone who will discuss *Udolpho* with her.

But Catherine's reading, while temporarily leaving her with what Austen calls the "luxury of a raised, restless, and frightened imagination" (*NA*, 34), does not encourage her to conjure up "visions of romance" (*NA*, 159). In fact, prior to Henry's story of what she might expect at the Abbey, Catherine does not succumb to fanciful speculations even while she is entranced in *Udolpho's* plots, or, prior to that novel, any other supposedly unedifying material. When Eleanor Tilney appears at a Bath ball leaning on Henry's arm, Catherine does not for a moment assume the worst and

> thus unthinkingly throwing away a fair opportunity of considering him lost to her for ever, by being married already. But guided only by what was simple and probable, it had never entered her head that Mr. Tilney could be married; he had not behaved, he had not talked, like the married men to whom she had been used; he had never mentioned a wife and he had acknowledged a sister. From these circumstances sprang the instant conclusion of his sister's now being by his side; and therefore, instead of turning of a deathlike paleness, and falling in a fit on Mrs. Allen's bosom, Catherine sat erect, in the perfect use of her senses, and with cheeks only a little redder than usual. (*NA*, 36)

When she sees Eleanor and Henry together, Catherine does not even think to panic; she is calm and reasonable, although such an overreaction would be fairly understandable in a smitten inexperienced young woman. Although Catherine is engaged by *Udolpho* at this time, her reading of this novel does not prompt her to fanciful elaborate conjectures, and she is able accurately to assess the situation.

Neither does Catherine's reading color her perceptions of the company she keeps. Just as she is able to understand the relationship between Eleanor and Henry, she is able to judge the characters of those around her. While attempting to stifle her dislike of John Thorpe for the sake of her friend and brother, Catherine "could not entirely repress a doubt . . . of his being altogether completely agreeable" (*NA*, 48). She also has no romantic illusions concerning his attentions to her. When Isabella accuses Catherine of knowing of John's amorous intentions, Catherine is honestly astonished. Nothing in his attentions to her resembles genuine attachment. Unlike Charlotte Lennox's Arabella (in *The Female Quixote*), Catherine is not looking for the Romance Suitor or the Gothic Abductor. She assesses each situation and each individual separately rather than working them into an overarching scheme of romance.

Catherine does notice Isabella's infidelity when the latter begins to flirt with Captain Tilney: "Catherine, though not allowing herself to suspect her friend, could not help watching her closely. The result of her observations was not agreeable. Isabella seemed an altered creature" (*NA*, 116). In addition, she recognizes the Captain's gallantries to her friend for what they are, inappropriate attentions. Isabella's subsequent jilting of James proves Catherine's observations correct. Catherine's suspicions concerning General Tilney, though mocked by Henry and many critics, are not completely unfounded. As Wilt points out, "Catherine's arithmetic is faulty. But not too far faulty."[15] The General is a gothic villain, a Radcliffean Montoni[16] manipulating everyone heedlessly in order to fulfill his own whims. Catherine's reading does not obstruct her ability to understand this.

Because she reads, Catherine is not submerged in gloom when Henry disappears from Bath: "while I have Udolpho to read, I feel as if nobody could make me miserable" (*NA*, 25). Her interest in Blaize Castle, stimulated by her reading of *Udolpho*, threatens to unseat her romantic interests: "Her passion for ancient edifices was next in degree to her passion for Henry Tilney—and castles and abbeys made usually the charm of those reveries which his image did not fill" (*NA*, 110). She does not obsess about men and romance because there are more important things to think about and discuss.

In a similar fashion, Catherine's reading largely detaches her from the mindless "worldly concerns of dressing and dinner" (*NA*, 34) belonging to a rather frivolous, although harmless, Mrs. Allen, whose only passion is "dress" (*NA*, 7) and whom Austen describes as "one of that numerous class of females, whose society can raise no other emotion than surprise at there being any men in the world who could like them well enough to marry them" (*NA*, 7). Not only does Mrs. Allen have no interest in reading, but she continues to chatter away at Catherine while the latter is obviously engaged in a book. Consequently, Catherine learns to ignore Mrs. Allen's pointless "remarks and ejaculations" (*NA*, 346) while she is reading and thus avoids participating in this mindless monologue.

Isabella is another character who loves to talk. The subject of her conversation revolves around "dress, balls, flirtations, and quizzes" (*NA*, 18). Unlike Mrs. Allen, she pretends to be interested in reading, going so far as to draw up a tentative book list for Catherine: "'. . . when you have finished Udolpho, we will read the Italian together; and I have made out a list of ten or twelve more of the same kind for you'" (*NA*, 23). And although, in inclement weather, she and Catherine ostensibly "shut themselves up, to read novels together" (*NA*, 21), it quickly becomes clear that Isabella would much rather talk than read. Each time Catherine attempts to discuss *Udolpho*'s finer points with her, Isabella quickly changes the subject to clothes or men. In fact, Catherine discovers that Isabella has adopted all her literary opinions from her friend Miss Andrews. While discussing Richardson's *Sir Charles Grandison*, Isabella can only profess, "That is an amazing horrid book is it not?—I remember Miss Andrews could not get through the first volume" while Catherine, who actually has read the book, can decisively reply "It is not like Udolpho at all; but yet I think it is very entertaining" (*NA*, 25). For Catherine, books are the subject worthy of discussion, and Isabella's reluctance to participate in this conversation becomes a foreshadowing of her traitorous behavior toward the end of the novel.

John Thorpe, Isabella's overbearing brother, also does not read, and plagues one instead with his frivolous conversation. Like his sister, he pretends to have an opinion on books and when Catherine attempts to discuss *Udolpho* with him, he proclaims: "I never read novels; I have something else to do. . . . Novels are all so full of nonsense and stuff" (*NA*, 31). It is soon revealed, however, that this opinion has no basis for Thorpe has no idea what he is talking about. His disgust with the idea of reading *Udolpho* followed by the claim that only Mrs. Radcliffe's novels "are worth reading" (*NA*, 32) indicates that his knowledge of books, like Isabella's, is completely superficial. Instead he also prefers to talk heedlessly, shocking and offending Catherine with his "rattle" full of "idle assertions and impudent falsehoods" (*NA*, 47). In *Northanger Abbey*, those who do not read and cannot talk about what they read must instead resort to conversation that is at the least frivolous and at the most offensive.[17]

Although both Isabella and her brother attempt to control Catherine's behavior, she is able to resist their influence. When brother and sister try to force Catherine into breaking her appointment with the Tilneys', she vigorously resists their influence: "It does not signify talking. If I could not be persuaded into doing what I thought was wrong, I never will be tricked into it" (*NA*, 77). Here the conversation of Isabella and John is presented as aggressive and deceitful. However, their conversation cannot sway her. Empowered by her rigorous reading, Catherine removes herself from the sphere of the Thorpe's influence.

In Radcliffe's *Mysteries of Udolpho* there is a similar distrust of conversation uninformed by reading. The Quesnels intrusion into the St. Aubert family home is resented by the St. Auberts because it intrudes upon the contemplative pursuits of their country life: "Emily returned, with delight, to the liberty which their [the Quesnels] presence had restrained, to her books, her walks, and the rational conversation of M. and Madame St. Aubert, who seemed to rejoice, no less, that they were delivered from the shackles, which arrogance and frivolity had imposed" (137). The reading of books encourages "rational conversation" while the conversation of M. Quesnel is constructed as the polar opposite, frivolous and simultaneously confining. Equally harmful are Annette's fanciful "marvellous" stories of "fairies" and "ghosts." Perpetuating the motif of confinement, Emily's eventual participation in these conversations occur while she is imprisoned in Udolpho and simultaneously imprisoned by the threat of moral corruption.

Reading in *Udolpho* is important because it removes one from the temptation of moral folly. It is thus that St. Aubert believes that the reading of certain texts will prevent immorality: "A well-informed mind . . . is the best security against the contagion of folly and of vice. The vacant mind is ever on the watch for relief, and ready to plunge into error, to escape from the languor of idleness. Store it with ideas, teach it the pleasure of thinking: and the temptations of the world without, will be counteracted by gratification derived from the world within" (6). St. Aubert's disease metaphor presents the written text as an antibiotic: prescriptive reading prevents "contagion" or moral corruption. When Emily, within Udolpho's walls, no longer reads but indulges in Annette's "wonderful" stories, she is infected with terror (239).

The texts that Emily reads, however, are a set of "best books in the ancient and modern languages" (3), a controlled list, those with which St. Aubert has stocked his private library. Emily is to receive "a general view of the sciences, and an exact acquaintance with every part of elegant literature" (suggesting that literature is more suitable for women than is science) as well as in Latin and English "chiefly that she might understand the sublimity of their best poets" (6). She is not allowed the freedom Catherine has to pick her own reading material. For in *Northanger Abbey* it is not so much the actual text, but the act of reading itself that is so important. What is dangerous about *Udolpho* is not its gothic terrors, which propose that women should be rationally educated so they will not succumb to them, but the manner in which women are educated: relying on a reading list constructed by men.

The fact that Henry Tilney has actually read *Udolpho* and enjoyed it, as well as the rest of Mrs. Radcliffe's works, strengthens his connection to Catherine. Like Catherine, Henry was completely engaged by *Udolpho*: ". . . when I had once begun it, I could not lay down again,—I remember finishing it in two days—my hair standing on end the whole time'" (*NA*, 82). Henry, like Catherine, is a reader, and thus their conversations are not frivolous, obnoxious "rattle" but neither are they completely innocent. While Catherine wishes to earnestly engage him in a conversation about *Udolpho*, Henry soon begins mercilessly to tease her earnestness. In response to Catherine's query, whether he does not think *Udolpho* the "nicest book in the world" he teases her for her use of the word: ". . . and this is a very nice day, and we are taking a very nice walk, and you are two very nice young ladies. . . ." (NA, 83-84). Despite his sister Eleanor's admonitions, he persists much to the confusion of Catherine. Although, as in this case, Henry often seems to be joking, his ironic comments have a decidedly cruel aggressive thrust that Catherine does not expect.

But Catherine is capable of resisting Henry's words. While sitting together in the Abbey's breakfast parlor one morning, Henry reacts to Catherine's claim that she is "naturally indifferent about flowers" (NA, 138): "a taste for flowers is always desirable in your sex, as a means of getting you out of doors, and tempting you to more frequent exercise than you would otherwise take. And though the love of a hyacinth may be rather domestic, who can tell, the sentiment once raised, but you may in time come to love a rose?" (NA, 138). Despite her feelings for Henry, Catherine resists his assumption that she would rather sit still inside: "But I do not want any such pursuit to get me out of doors" (NA, 462). She again rejects his assertions when, earlier in the novel, Henry assures Catherine that he knows what Catherine will and should write in her journal because he is "not so ignorant of young ladies' ways" (NA, 13). Catherine, by suggesting that she keeps no journal, refuses to admit that she subscribes to his definitions of women. She vigorously rejects his characterizations of her and her sex.

Yet Catherine is eager to adopt his ideas when he lectures her on the picturesque while walking with her and Eleanor: "In the present instance, she confessed and lamented her want of knowledge; declared that she would give any thing in the world to be able to draw; and a lecture on the picturesque immediately followed, in which his instructions were so clear that she soon began to see beauty in every thing admired by him, and her attention was so earnest, that he became perfectly satisfied of her having a great deal of natural taste. . . . Catherine was so hopeful a scholar, that when they gained the top of Beechen Cliff, she voluntarily rejected the whole city of Bath, as unworthy to make part of a landscape" (NA, 86-87). Catherine's readiness to adopt Henry's ideas on the picturesque follows on the heels of a conversation of Udolpho that Catherine desires to continue. Henry's persistent teasing leads the three of them off the subject, and Catherine's desire for a literary conversation is frustrated: "The Tilneys were soon engaged in another [subject] on which she had nothing to say" (NA, 86). Her lack of resistance to Henry's influence is thus linked to her desire to converse about reading.

While Catherine is not influenced by the conversation of Mrs. Allen, Isabella, or John, she is unable to remain so independent from Henry's conversation when books are discussed. Although Daniel Cottom argues that in Austen's novels "[c]onversation is almost always a matter of aggression and appeasement,"[18] I would like to further specify that this aggressive conversation arises particularly because Henry is a reader. His discussions about reading participate in, and are a product of, the aforementioned broader cultural discourse concerning the reading material of young women. The role of the novel in a young woman's education was particularly contested at this historical moment. Although by the end of the century one branch of this genre, the polite novel,[19] was considered acceptable for young women, novel reading had been looked at over the course of the century as a frivolous and potentially corruptive activity. Countless educational treatises and conduct books written at this time were ostensibly written for women but spoke to a largely male audience.[20] These texts posited women as inherently emotional and irrational, an impression emphasized by the fact that the generation of numerous texts to instruct women defined women as textually sensitive, incapable of rising above representational influence in order to exercise their own judgment. So powerful was (and is) this primarily male discourse concerning women and reading that fuels Henry's conversation that Catherine, as the defiant woman reader, is unable to resist his opinions completely.

This link between textual influence and conversations about reading becomes glaringly apparent on the ride to Northanger Abbey. Henry, teasing once again, proceeds to present a gothic scene for Catherine of what she should expect to encounter at his family home: "And are you prepared to encounter all the horrors that a building such as 'what one reads about' may produce?" (*NA*, 124). He counters her reasonable answer—"Oh! yes—I do not think I should be easily frightened, because there would be so many people in the house. . . ." (*NA*, 124)—with an ensuing description of what will happen to Catherine once she arrives there. This tale appears to Catherine to be "just like a book," the book, in fact, that she and Henry had discussed together.

This conversation has a serious effect on Catherine. Admittedly, she is initially interested in visiting Northanger Abbey because of its potential resemblance to the structures "one reads about" (*NA*, 124). This fascination, however, is more of an intellectual interest spawned from reading, as is her earlier preoccupation with Blaize Castle. It is not that she imagines herself a heroine against a suitable ancient backdrop. And it is not until Henry taunts her with his own tale that Catherine begins to carve gothic fantasies out of her surroundings, that she is perplexed by the wood chest, or that she begins to fear the possible intrusions of "midnight assassins or drunken gallants" (*NA*, 132). In this light, Henry's admonishment of Catherine's "visions of romance," and her suspicions of the General, is unfounded and particularly harsh. Gothic novels do not construct Catherine, Henry's conversations do. Perhaps, rather than changing her reading habits, Catherine should stop talking to Henry.

St. Aubert, unlike Henry, is not a failed teacher.[21] His patriarchal influence is needed to supply Emily with the proper reading material. Although a young woman should receive a textual education, Radcliffe's text presents the availability of this education as relying on a male figure. This conflict becomes particularly apparent in considering the characters of St. Aubert and Count Montoni. Montoni becomes an excellent representative of a "malignant" patriarchy identified by Alison Milbank in her feminist analysis of the gothic novel as a reflection of female oppression. Milbank describes Radcliffe's novel as an Enlightenment fable that charts the shift from Montoni's chaotic world to a more settled order: "in Radcliffean Gothic the patriarchal order is revealed as malignant and in need of replacement." [22] St. Aubert purposefully provides Emily with specific edifying texts; Montoni irresponsibly allows her to read not what she should, St. Aubert's texts, which she has brought with her. Deprived of her father's guidance and lacking Montoni's encouragement, she will not read and return to that activity which formerly educated her. However, while Emily needs a male figure to educate her and cultivate her reason, male instruction for Catherine proves to be disastrous.

Male instruction is disastrous for Catherine because she does not answer Henry or defy him; rather she accepts and defines her behavior according to his accusations. She runs from him crying "tears of shame," and, as the narrator explains, Catherine is "completely awakened." But how ironic is this comment? Might it not be that Catherine only considers herself to be so: "She remembered with what feelings she had prepared for a knowledge of Northanger. She saw that the infatuation had been created, the mischief settled long before her quitting Bath, and it seemed as if the whole might be traced to the influence of that sort of reading which she had there indulged" (NA, 160). But the narration in Bath does not support this last statement. What does become clear here, however, is that Catherine has let Henry rewrite her past and has accepted the new story.

Furthermore, Henry's anger seems just to die down. Catherine does not deflect it with her own defense: "The formidable Henry soon followed her into the room, and the only difference in his behavior to her, was that he paid her rather more attention than usual. Catherine had never wanted comfort more, and he looked as if he was aware of it" (NA, 160). Because this outburst disappears as quickly as it comes, what is to stop it from flaring up again (in an equally unfair situation) appearing suddenly, like some gothic monster?

The narrative does seem to pull the reader into desiring a marriage between Catherine and Henry. Austen, after all, writes in a world that privileges domestic union; she probably cannot, or does not, want to think of an alternative. This marriage, however, is threatening for Catherine. She is married, but under what circumstances? It seems she has accepted Henry's incorrect surmises about her and her reading habits. Thus the novel's ending is highly uncomfortable, wrought with an ambiguity that Cottom identifies as an Austenian theme: "the issue in all the romantic circumstances of Austen's novels is one of trust: women trusting too much in their own power of interpretation and therefore trusting too much the men who actually have the power to determine which interpretations are allowed to be legitimate. Austen's major theme in all of her novels is the argument that women must learn distrust not only of the apparent sureties of the world around them, but also of themselves."[23] Because women have such trust in their own interpretive powers, they are not fully aware of the power embedded in men's interpretations. Austen's concern with women's potential misunderstandings of the inequities of interpretive power leaves the married Catherine, at the end of *Northanger Abbey*, in questionable happiness. To ignore the ambiguity of this novel's ending is to reinscribe a male interpretation, but to view *Northanger Abbey* as asking women not to trust themselves at all undermines Catherine's successful rational activity that she performs for most of the novel, up until Henry's gothic tale.

Northanger Abbey, then, is a book that does ask women to trust their own "power of interpretation" while warily encountering the conversations and ideas of reading men who wield much of the social power in Austen's world. Rather than existing as a parody of *Udolpho*, *Northanger Abbey* instead critiques the eighteenth-century positioning of the female reader. Austen herself asks the novel reader to "[l]et us leave it to the Reviewers to abuse such effusions of fancy at their leisure, and over every new novel to talk in threadbare strains of the trash with which the press now groans" (*NA*, 21). The text's discomfort, and resulting satire, is located in the intersection of men, reading, and conversation. It is these reading men who construct "visions of romance."

Reading men, who know how to manipulate texts, are familiar and well versed in print images and are particularly dangerous because they can construct these "visions of romance" and then dictate which "romance" women should read. General Tilney is not a reading man and consequently not such a threat to Catherine. She is never really taken in by him. Rather it is supposed "nice guys" like Henry, who do read, who pose such a threat and have moments where they echo General Tilney's (even Montoni's) behavior.

Though Austen may not believe that women should read *everything*, I think she would apply this same discretion to male readers. There are texts that can corrupt both men and women, and these should be avoided by both sexes. Women are no more corruptible than men. There should not be separate reading materials for men and women, and men do not have the right to decide what women can and cannot read. One may consider *Northanger Abbey*'s famous closing question—"whether the tendency of this work be altogether to recommend parental tyranny, or reward filial disobedience" (*NA*, 205)—in terms of daughters who should persist in reading what they choose and not what they are told to read.

Notes

1. Jane Austen, *Northanger Abbey and Persuasion*, vol. 5 of *The Novels of Jane Austen*, ed. R. W. Chapman, 5 vols., 3d ed. (London: Oxford University Press, 1932-34). Subsequent references are cited parenthetically in the text as *NA. Northanger Abbey* was originally written in 1798-99 but published posthumously in 1818.

2. So accepted is *Northanger Abbey*'s status as a gothic satire that Michael Williams opens his "*Northanger Abbey*: Some Problems of Engagement" as follows: "Everybody knows that *Northanger Abbey* is a parody of the Gothic novel" (1). (*Unisa English Studies, 25*, no. 2, (September 1987), 8-17). Or as Beth Lau puts it, "*Northanger Abbey* remains the most successful and enduring of all the Gothic satires. . . ." See "Madeline at Northanger Abbey: Keats's Antiromances and Gothic Satire," *Journal of English and German Philology* 84, no. 1, (1985), 34.

3. Many critics see Catherine as constructed by her gothic reading experience. Nancy Armstrong discusses how Mrs. Radcliffe misleads Catherine "into thinking that fiction can interpret the behavior of Abbey-owners" (237): "The Nineteenth-Century Jane Austen," *Genre* 23 (Summer/Fall 1990), 227-46. Lau believes that Austen provides "a warning of the ills that befall young women whose heads have been turned by too much romance reading and who can no longer distinguish the land of fiction from reality": "Madeline," 30.

4. For a survey of recent criticism on the gothic novel, see Terry Lovell, *Consuming Fiction* (London: Verso Press, 1987), 55-63. Also see, J. M. S. Tompkins, *The Popular Novel in England 1770-1800* (London: Constable and Company, 1932), 243-95.

5. Judith Wilt, *Ghosts of the Gothic: Austen, Eliot, and Lawrence* (Princeton, NJ: Princeton University Press, 1980), 121-72. In reference to theories that Austen made a decisive break with tradition, Wilt uses the term "imitation" primarily in reference to "setting," the gothic machinery that nineteenth-century novels inherited.

6. Ann Radcliffe, *The Mysteries of Udolpho* (Oxford: Oxford University Press, 1991).

7. Alvin Kernan, *Samuel Johnson and the Impact of Print* (Princeton, NJ: Princeton University Press, 1987).

8. Kernan, *Samuel Johnson*, 4 and 48.

9. See Clifford Siskin, "Eighteenth-Century Periodicals and the Romantic Rise of the Novel," *Studies in the Novel*, 26, no. 2 (Summer 1994): 26-42 .

10. Kathryn Shevelow, *Women and Print Culture: The Construction of Femininity in the Early Periodical* (London: Routledge, 1989), 1.

11. Anne K. Mellor, *Romanticism and Gender* (New York: Routledge, 1993), 1-2.

12. Ros Ballaster, "Romancing the Novel: Gender and Genre in Early Theories of Narrative," in *Living By the Pen: Early British Women Writers*, ed. Dale Spender (New York: Teacher's College Press, 1992), 193.

13. Lau, "Madeline," 31.

14. Williams, "Northanger Abbey," 11.

15. Wilt, *Ghosts of the Gothic*, 145.

16. Wilt, *Ghosts of the Gothic*, 127.

17. For an initial discussion of the importance attributed by the eighteenth century to conversation, see Siskin, "Eighteenth-Century Periodicals," 34.

18. Daniel Cottom, *The Civilized Imagination: A Study of Ann Radcliffe, Jane Austen, and Sir Walter Scott* (Cambridge: Cambridge University Press, 1985), 83.

19. Armstrong, "Nineteenth-Century Jane Austen," 97.

20. Armstrong, "Nineteenth-Century Jane Austen," 3 and 97. See also her *Desire and Domestic Fiction: A Political History of the Novel* (New York: Oxford University Press, 1987).

21. See Williams, "Northanger Abbey," for another discussion of Henry as Catherine's instructor.

22. See Alison Milbank's *Daughters of the House: Modes of the Gothic in Victorian Fiction* (New York: St. Martin's Press, 1992), 11.

23. Cottom, *Civilized Imagination*, 86.

9

Privacy, Privilege, and "Poaching" in Mansfield Park

Ellen Gardiner

In the struggle for power within the field of letters, the battle for critical authority and professional status became part of aesthetic representations of eighteenth-century "life" in literature. Eighteenth-century novelists often depicted characters who had both superior classical and moral educations as best suited to make public their interpretations.[1] They often created narrators whose superior powers of judgment mirrored their own capacities as authors to serve as their society's best critics. One of the reasons that Jane Austen has remained part of the twentieth-century canon is because, as omniscient narrator in various novels, she continues to convince scholars that she is not merely a writer but also a critic.[2]

In novels such as *Mansfield Park,* Austen explicitly draws our attention to issues of interpretation and gender when she calls into question society's propensity to invest individuals, whether they are real or imagined, with moral and critical authority purely on the basis of their institutional and/or professional affiliations. In particular, she treats as suspect the field of letters' tendency to represent men (and especially men of property or men of the cloth) as the moral guardians of the public domain, and its consequent tendency to represent men as therefore best suited to the profession of literary criticism.[3]

In *Mansfield Park,* she examines the power relationships that develop between women-as-writers and as-readers, and the institutions that reduce their options and make them marginal, especially in the field of letters. In particular, Austen scrutinizes exchanges between authors and their publics—both amateur and professional readers—and the critical discourse that structures the eighteenth-century project of moral education. *Mansfield Park* uncovers the ways that education can shape women as readers but implies as well that they have the power and means to resist being wholly determined by that education.

This essay focuses on the relationship between education and literary criticism that Austen develops in *Mansfield Park*. I will address the ways in which protagonist Fanny Price makes use of the education she receives from her cousin Edmund Bertram to achieve autonomy as a reader. Initially, this education appears to help her to develop into a reader who, some critics have charged, refuses to act.[4] Despite the conventional interpretation of her as a passive consumer, Fanny actually becomes an active producer who moves across the Bertram landscape, across linguistic and moral fields written most particularly by Edmund Bertram. To borrow Michel de Certeau's term, Fanny becomes a "poacher" when she learns to use for her own ends and gain the education she is provided.[5] Although her education is meant to teach Fanny her proper role and place as an upper middle-class female reader, it ultimately leads to her achieving a critical authority, and therefore a public power and status within the society of Mansfield Park that the literary culture of the period is reluctant to afford to women.

JANE AUSTEN: PROFESSIONAL AUTHOR/CRITIC

Jane Austen was "a professional author who [was] acutely conscious of her sales and eager to increase her profits."[6] While her audience was an intimate one, composed, argues Jan Fergus, of "like-minded members of her own social group,"[7] Austen also wanted to be taken seriously by a broader audience, perhaps most significantly an audience that included professional readers and other authors. She took, therefore, a great deal of interest in all aspects of the publishing of her novels. When she was halfway through the writing of *Mansfield Park*, she made the often quoted remark with regard to *Pride and Prejudice*: "Upon the whole . . . I am quite vain enough and well satisfied enough. The work is rather too light, and bright, and sparkling; it wants shade; it wants to be stretched out here and there with a long chapter of sense, if it could be had; if not of solemn specious nonsense, about something unconnected with the story; an essay on writing, a critique on Walter Scott, or the history of Buonaparte . . ."[8] Fergus reads Austen's tones as completely ironic here. She asserts that "Austen clearly had no real wish to include essays and critiques into her work . . . the passage reflects her own sense that her style had changed and deepened since she had first written *Pride and Prejudice* more than fifteen years earlier."[9] What is just as likely, if not more so, however, is that this passage reflects Austen's awareness of what is at stake in the struggle for status among eighteenth-century novel writers in the field of letters. Long chapters of "solemn specious nonsense, about something unconnected with the story," essays on writing, and critiques of rival authors are the sorts of discourse her contemporaries often include in their novels as a means to elevate themselves in the eyes or reviewers and ordinary readers. It is writing often designed to demonstrate a writer's superior, classical education, a kind of education usually denied to women. In fact, it is the sort of writing that those reviewers and indeed some academic critics of our own century will designate "masculine" (read "good") writing. It is as likely then that Austen refers to the critical double standard of judgment in the publishing world when she points to a criterion meant to exclude certain writers from the literary canon of her era. Fergus provides some evidence that Austen had some reservations about the practices of the literary establishment when she discusses Austen's frustration with powerful members of the publishing world: "She evidently had learned to prefer her own judgment of the value of her work to [her publisher] Egerton's . . . Publishing *Mansfield Park* for herself would once again give her brother Henry the task of supervising the printers, but Henry probably urged her not to sacrifice her profit to his convenience."[10] Notably, because of her involvement and business sense, the novel *Mansfield Park* reaped for Austen her greatest profit, despite the fact that it was not reviewed.[11]

Recent cultural criticism warns us against viewing individuals as historically overdetermined subjects of the ideological forces that interpellate them.[12] Austen's attitudes about women writers were said to be fairly traditional: "In accordance with feminine dutifulness and deference, she generally hid her work and kept silent about it."[13] This seems a problematic statement, however, given that "in 1809 Jane Austen aggressively renewed her attempts to publish"[14] and given Austen's niece's reminiscence that when "Austen stayed with the Knights in Kent, she shared her manuscripts with Fanny, Marianne's eldest sister, and probably with Lizzy . . . As Marianne tells it, "I remember that when Aunt Jane came to us at Godmersham she used to bring the MS of whatever novel she was writing with her, and would shut herself up with my elder sisters in one of the bedrooms to read them aloud. I and the younger ones used to hear peals of laughter through the door, and thought it very hard that we should be shut out from what was so delightful."[15] While this scene demonstrates that Austen appeared to be keeping her work private by retreating to an even more private realm within the domestic sphere in order to share it, reading aloud one's writing is not keeping silent. Deborah Kaplan herself admits that "by sharing work in progress, [Austen] was not only acknowledging the fact of her products but the labor of creating them, and she was welcoming her female audience's participation in that labor. They laughed, but they also offered suggestions and criticisms."[16]

A better explanation for Austen's reading aloud behind closed doors is that she made use of the privilege of privacy, which the domestic sphere afforded her, as an intermediate zone within which to prepare her words for public consumption. First, in the privacy of this space Austen's novels became a private hunting reserve for these women as socially unauthorized readers, who by their laughter and jesting introduced "plurality and difference into the written system of a society and text."[17] The bedroom, that is, constituted a secret, discursive space within which the women could themselves poach upon Austen's writing and, alongside her, resist for a time the rules of the field of letters. We might see these women as reading outside of the law given by socially authorized professionals and intellectuals.

Second, despite her desire to keep her identity as a writer private, she wished her writing to be public; remember that she "aggressively [attempted] to publish" her novels. And as a final caveat on Austen's ambivalence about publishing her work and her desire for privacy, she was annoyed enough about the lack of critical notice for *Mansfield Park* that she wrote a letter in protest.[18] At best, Austen seems to have been torn between a desire for privacy versus publicity; hence, her attitude toward women's reading and writing must be described as more complex than recent critics have allowed.

As a general characterization of the novel, Fergus writes, "power is central to *Mansfield Park.* "[19] To be sure, Fergus refers primarily to domestic power, but Austen also considers the power of texts and, more specifically, texts as tools of education within that domestic space. As Austen's bedroom readings demonstrate, literary criticism plays an important role in the private sphere. The home is where children and particularly female children learn to behave publicly. Books are often a part of that domestic education.

To that end, a standard premise of eighteenth-century literature was that all professionals who wrote as part of their labor, including those in the new profession of literary reviewership or criticism as well as those who were members of the clergy, must convince their respective audiences that they could author morally instructive texts. Austen suggests that in order to enter either the profession of criticism or the profession of the clergy, individuals must not only write moral texts, such as the ones she herself writes, they must also demonstrate a consistency in their ability to read morally. She treats ironically the notion that men of the upper classes are better prepared as readers to take on the role of moral arbiters, such as clergy or critics do, than women or members of the laboring classes. Hence, Austen insists that her audience consider whether clergy or critic should have sole authority for deciding how society ought to receive and interpret texts.

THE LEARNED DIVINE REVISITED

In eighteenth-century periodicals such as Addison and Steele's *The Spectator,* aesthetic judgment, or taste, became a privilege of an aristocratic sensibility, a matter of privacy.[20] Paradoxically, aesthetic judgment or private sensibility became a privilege for those who could express it with authority, publicly, as was the case for the fictional Mr. Spectator. While reading literature was linked for both men and women to the development of a private sensibility, for women this privatization was represented, for the most part, as an opportunity for their taking refuge from the world. Proper women did not make either public spectacles or spectators of themselves. In effect, popular discourse encouraged women to cloister themselves, to eschew taking a more active role in the public sphere. Consequently, taste was no privilege for those women who had no power to express with any authority the refined and private sensibilities that they had developed as readers.

In *Mansfield Park,* Austen reacts in part to cultural restrictions on women's linguistic productions when she creates Fanny Price, a protagonist whose perspective appears to other characters (and more important to extratextual readers) to be that of a detached and tasteful reader[21]: "In a way there is a little of the artist about her: she speaks for the value of literature, of memory, of fancy; she alone reveals a true appreciation of nature. More important, [Fanny] is in a way the supreme consciousness of the society she moves in. Like many Jamesian figures, she does not fully participate in the world but as a result she sees things more clearly and accurately than those who do."[22] Indeed, Fanny's gaze recalls the gaze of such earlier eighteenth-century social critics as Addison and Steele's Mr. Spectator and Eliza Haywood's Female Spectator.[23] As such she can be read as Austen's reaction to and appropriation of that popular trope for reader in the eighteenth century, that of "spectator." Austen brings her novel into dialogue with these earlier representations of readers both as a means to reveal the shortcomings of the spectator trope and to transform it into an image that gives women better access to the critical authority as readers, which, by the end of the eighteenth century, the trope represents for men.

As the century progressed, midcentury novelists such as Samuel Richardson and Charlotte Lennox adopted Spectator-like personas and represent themselves as narrator-critics "[beholding] all Nature with an unprejudiced Eye; and having nothing to do with Mens Passions or Interests,"[24] in order to compete better with one another for authority and status. Moreover, in their novels proper, a judgment was not usually given any weight until it had been voiced by a character who had socially sanctioned power in the public domain. It was not usual for this socially sanctioned individual to be represented as female in the discourse of the period, because proper women were so very private—that is, silent. Within their novels proper, novelists such as Richardson and Henry Fielding created critics such as Belford and Allworthy, who have power and status in the public realm but who also demonstrate superior morality—either by virtue of their reading of the Bible, like Belford, or by virtue of their belief in secularized Christian doctrine, as in the case of Allworthy. But even women novelists such as Charlotte Lennox also and often created male characters to represent socially sanctioned critics in their novels proper.[25] In Lennox's novel *The Female Quixote*, for example, it is the learned divine, a clergyman, who alone has the power to reform Arabella's behaviors and ethics.

Like Lennox, in *Mansfield Park* Austen-as-narrator also adopts a Spectator-like persona; she also apparently shares Lennox's position that the professions of clergyman and literary critic are very similar, both in form and in function.[26] Her private writings certainly suggest as much. Austen once noted that "A classical education, or at any rate a very extensive acquaintance with English literature, ancient and modern, appears to me quite indispensable for the person who would do any justice to your clergyman."[27] But she does not believe that education alone makes a person a more suitable social critic, any more than she believes that a woman's education ought to force her to develop such an intensely private sensibility that she has no power or is of no public use to the society within which she moves. Austen creates Fanny Price, then, a version of female "spectator" considered proper in this period, as a means to uncover shortcomings of cultural metaphors of both male and female readers.

She casts soon-to-be-ordained clergyman Edmund Bertram in the role of Fanny's primary instructor and socially sanctioned critic for the novel's society. Importantly, in doing so Austen yokes the term "education" with that of literary criticism. Edmund is provided a literary education at Oxford like the one Austen described in her letter. At least initially, therefore, Edmund seems the most logical choice to be Mansfield Park's moral and aesthetic arbiter and Fanny's teacher. Austen is interested, however, not only in issues of the literariness or interpretability of texts but in the (largely unspoken) professionalism of the field. She therefore looks closely at both Edmund's and Henry Crawford's (who, however whimsically, considers taking vows) motivations for choosing the clerical profession. As the second son in the family who will not inherit a fortune, Edmund needs to "do something for [himself],"[28] he needs a profession in order to provide himself with an income. While the popular opinion of many (as expressed by Mary Crawford) is that those in the upper classes seek a literary education because of their "indolence and love of ease—[and their] want of all laudable ambition" (*MP*, 110), Edmund believes that only an education like the literary one he receives at Oxford can best prepare him for work that will be "of the first importance to mankind, individually or collectively considered, temporally and eternally— which has the guardianship of religion and morals, and consequently of the manners which result from their influence" (*MP*, 92). Too, Edmund chooses this profession because it will allow him to serve others. As an individual whose "strong good sense and uprightness of mind, bid most fairly for utility, honour, and happiness to himself and all his connections" (*MP*, 21), Edmund sees this profession as providing him with more than money or leisure.

In contrast, when Henry Crawford considers the profession of clergy, he considers how it will allow him to serve himself. He believes that the qualifications for the profession of clergyman are not unlike those for other aesthetic or artistic enterprises. If he were to join the professional ranks of the clergy, he would do so in order to show off his superior education and aesthetic sensibility: "A thoroughly good sermon, thoroughly well-delivered, is a capital gratification . . . There is something in the eloquence of the pulpit, when it is really eloquence, which is entitled to the highest praise and honor . . . I never listened to a distinguished preacher in my life, without a sort of envy. But then I must have a London audience. I could not preach but to the educated; to those who were capable of estimating my composition" (*MP*, 341). Henry Crawford assumes that a clergyman's goal is not unlike that of many a literary professional's: to write beautiful and entertaining texts for an elite audience who can praise and honor him for his skills, rather than to write, as reputable clergy or literary men would admonish, beautiful and moral works whose primary purpose is to instruct, even as they entertain.

Given his ethics, then, Edmund seems an eminently more worthy spokesman for his society's moral values, and so he plays a large role in Fanny's education. Early on, he "[recommends] the books which [charm] her leisure hours, he [encourages] her taste, and [corrects] her judgment." Over time he "[makes] reading useful by talking to her of what she read, and [heightens] its attraction by judicious praise" (*MP*, 22). As an adult, Fanny attributes her aesthetic appreciation of Nature to Edmund: "you taught me to think and feel on the subject [of Nature]" (*MP*, 88). In other words, his purpose and labor as Fanny's teacher mirrors that of the period's literary critic: to shape her aesthetic sensibility in order to help her to become a better person. But

Edmund begins to lose his status as teacher/critic when he fails to understand the necessity of consistency in his readerly behavior.

A central incident in the novel involves the inappropriate attempt of the Bertrams, Crawfords, and Mr. Yates to stage *Lovers' Vows* in the Bertram home, an act that goes against all the rules of polite society. One of Edmund's objections to their group's performance of the play *Lovers' Vows* is initially the impropriety of his sisters acting, though he hedges by deferring to patriarchal authority: "[His father] would never wish his grown-up daughters to be acting plays" (*MP*, 127). Knowing that the play signals "the end of all the privacy and propriety" (*MP*, 153), and still apparently on the surface eager to uphold Spectator-like principles of proper aristocratic decorum, Edmund goes to Fanny's room to ask her opinion of his joining in the action. Mary Crawford has coyly suggested that only Edmund is suited to play the role of Anhalt in the play. Edmund's infatuation with Mary makes him willing to do just about anything that will give him the opportunity to get closer to and to please her. Edmund plans therefore to renege on his initial refusal to act in such an inappropriate drama.

Fanny stews: "To be acting! After all his objections—objections so just and so public! After all that she had heard him say, and seen him look, and known him to be feeling. Could it be possible? Edmund so inconsistent. Was he not deceiving himself? Was he not wrong? Alas! it was all Miss Crawford's doing. She had seen her influence in every speech, and was miserable" (*MP*, 156). Edmund loses credibility as a critic because he fails to repress his emotions and instead allows his passions to interfere with his ability to author and to interpret texts properly. In acting the part of Anhalt, he reproduces an immoral text; in agreeing to read the part, he submits to read as well a text that he knows to be immoral. The best clergy and the best critics of the day would not set such a bad example for their respective congregations. It is important to point out at this juncture that not one member of the Bertram circle who behaves badly throughout the novel ultimately changes his or her ways due to Edmund's influence. Because Edmund fails as a reader he also fails to achieve the ultimate goal of both clergy and critics alike: the moral reformation of society. Through her characterization of Edmund Bertram, Austen challenges the ideology that a clergyman's education and professional affiliation alone gives him more power and authority in literate and literary culture.

In Addison and Steele's *The Spectator*, Fanny's position as female spectator would have simply been that of an outsider, but in *Mansfield Park*, it is in her position as outsider that Austen first reveals Fanny's aptitude for poaching. As a spectator who poaches, Fanny becomes a nomad who travels across the linguistic and moral fields of the Bertram circle of actors, "always walking from one room to another and doing the lookings on" (*MP*, 166) at her ease. She "derive[s] as much innocent enjoyment from the play as any of them" (*MP*, 165) because in refusing an active part in it, she escapes its law. "Emancipated" from the Bertram stage, Fanny's body as reader is "freer in its movements."[29] It was "a pleasure to her to creep into the theatre, and attend the rehearsal of the first act" (*MP*, 165). She combines the play's scenes and "creates something unknown in the space organized by their capacity for allowing an indefinite plurality of meaning."[30] The other characters begin to recognize her capacity, as cultural consumer, to perform that activity of "reading" normally reserved for the literary critic or professional intellectual (cleric).

To reiterate an earlier quotation, "In a way there is a little of the artist about [Fanny] in *Mansfield Park*: she speaks for the value of literature, of memory, of fancy; she alone reveals a true appreciation of nature,"[31] and her fellow characters in the novel as well as a variety of extra textual readers seem to recognize as much. During play rehearsals, all of the *Lovers' Vows* players turn to Fanny for directorial guidance (which requires not only knowledge of the lines but an ability to interpret how they should be delivered) and judgment. Austen remembers what many critics would forget: "a director is the author of [a play's] production"[32]; while acting in this capacity, Fanny "takes neither the position of the author or the author's position,"[33] but she does become an active producer of meaning.

Furthermore, at several junctures in the text, Austen alludes to Fanny's "delicacy of taste, of mind, of feeling" (*MP*, 81). Fanny admires "all that was pretty . . . [in] nature, inanimate nature" (*MP*, 80-81). "As far as she could judge, Mr. Crawford was considerably the best actor" (*MP*, 165), and she greatly appreciates his skill at reading speeches from Shakespeare's *Henry VIII*: "in Mr. Crawford's reading there was a variety of excellence beyond what she had ever met with" (*MP*, 337). That is, it is Fanny, rather than Edmund or Henry Crawford, who demonstrates better than any other character proper aesthetic appreciation for all sorts of texts. Given Fanny's perspective as critic, it would seem to be a paradox, then, that she is considered to be one of Austen's most problematic characters.[34]

KEEPING PRIVATE, OR HOW TO PRIVILEGE REPRESSION

Nina Auerbach argues that Fanny refuses stubbornly to act, either in the famous play *Lovers' Vows* that the Bertrams improperly decide to stage, or in general.[35] I have suggested, however, that Fanny plays a very active role in the drama for other characters as well as a very active role in the rest of the novel—if only as an interested listener. In the world of *The Spectator* journals,

Fanny Price's education as reader and spectator in *Mansfield Park* has appropriately produced the kind of interiority—or private sensibility—in Fanny that, especially in her case, often impels her to her tiny room where she takes refuge from the world. Fanny's refusal to act a more public part in the various dramas of the novel seems a predictable outcome of her education.

A case in point: When Edmund seeks Fanny's advice prior to his accepting the role of Anhalt in *Lovers' Vows*, he does so because, presumably, he knows her to be a good and proper judge of what she reads and witnesses. While Edmund solicits Fanny's judgments, he does not necessarily take them very seriously. When he sees that Fanny's "judgment is not with [him]" (*MP*, 154), for instance, he immediately interrupts her and rationalizes that "if I can be the means of restraining the publicity of the business, of limiting the exhibition, of concentrating our folly, I shall be well repaid." Fanny is not convinced; Edmund allows "If you are against me, I ought to distrust myself— and yet . . ." (*MP*, 155). He then proceeds to try to pressure Fanny into supporting his decision to contradict himself. He implies that Fanny is being selfish: "I thought [you would have entered more into Miss Crawford's feelings" (*MP*, 155). Like many people of the period, Edmund believes that women like Fanny should be seen and not always heard, particularly in a public forum. Hence, as his pupil, it is little wonder that Fanny plays so well the role of a proper eighteenth-century woman reader, that she takes the part, to quote Marylea Meyersohn, of a "quiet auditor of the whole."[36]

Rather than being a reader who passively absorbs texts, however, Fanny ultimately rewrites the trope of woman reader that Edmund has recommended. She becomes instead the sort of reader who insists upon independent thinking, who does not look to others—as do Edmund or Henry Crawford—for approval, but finds the authority for her interpretations within: "We have all a better guide in ourselves, if we would attend to it, than any other person can be" (*MP*, 412). Much of her new sense of her own critical authority develops in Portsmouth.

After she refuses Crawford's offer of marriage, Sir Thomas sends her to Portsmouth because he believes "that a little abstinence from the elegancies and luxuries of Mansfield Park, would bring her mind into a sober state, and incline her to a juster estimate of the value of that home of greater permanence, and equal comfort, of which she had the offer" (*MP*, 369). Fanny's trip to Portsmouth teaches her, however, not so much the value of elegance and luxury as it teaches her the value of the kind of education that members of the upper class typically receive: "The living in incessant noise [in Portsmouth] was . . . an evil which no superadded elegance or harmony could have entirely atoned for . . . At Mansfield, no sounds of contention, no raised voice, no abrupt bursts, no tread of violence was ever heard; all proceeded in a regular course or cheerful orderliness, everybody had their due importance; everybody's feelings were consulted. If tenderness could be ever supposed wanting, good sense and good breeding supplied its place" (*MP*, 392). As this quotation illustrates, Austen certainly shares some of the biases of the educated class to which she belongs. One of the privileges of polite society is that one moves in a circle where others have learned to edit themselves, to keep certain emotional responses private and the expression of others restrained. In Austen's mind or, at the very least, in Fanny's mind, while the inhabitants of Mansfield Park may suffer severely from moral malaise, at least their expression of it is tastefully subdued.

Be that as it may, Fanny comes to realize in Portsmouth that Edmund is not solely responsible for her own good sense when she develops a strong relationship with her sister Susan; "the intimacy thus begun between them was a material advantage to each" (*MP*, 398). With surprise, Fanny realizes that even though Susan has been deprived of an education like her own, she has "so much better knowledge, so many good notions." Moreover, having been "brought up in the midst of negligence and error, [Susan has] formed such proper opinions of what ought to be—she, who had no cousin Edmund to direct her thoughts or fix her principles" (*MP*, 397-98). Acknowledging that, despite her lack of patriarchal education, Susan has innate good judgment, Fanny must also acknowledge that Edmund cannot be totally responsible for her own proper opinions and notions.

Her material distance from the seat of patriarchal authority and institutions that Mansfield Park represents allows Fanny to evaluate this knowledge in light of Edmund's moral inconsistency. His inconsistency undermines his status as a representative of the clerical and educational professions and institutions; "the creativity of the reader grows as the institution that controlled it declines."[37] Fanny seeks books on her own without Edmund's help or sanction: "She became a subscriber—amazed at being anything in *propria persona*, amazed at her own doings in every way; to be a center, a chuser of books" (*MP*, 398). In selecting books for herself, she also serves as a literary reviewer for Susan: "Susan had read nothing, and Fanny longed to give her a share in her own first pleasures, and inspire a taste for the biography and poetry which she delighted in herself" (*MP*, 398).

Fanny reforms Susan, to be sure, but it is not so much a moral reformation as it is an aesthetic one. Susan has already "proper opinions of what ought to be"; what she lacks is a private sensibility like Fanny's. Education trains Susan to repress her emotions properly, to behave with more decorum. A literary education can be a "useful influence, [can have] a moral effect on the . . .

understanding and manners," but only if an individual has learned first "the necessity of self-denial and humility" (MP, 463). Mansfield Park suggests that in Austen's view, children's dispositions are their parents' responsibilities, rather than those of authors, critics, or clergy for that matter. Ordinary people, that is, play as important a role, if not a more important role, in the moral education of society as those in the business of moral education, be it literary or religious. In terms of Austen's position on literary or social criticism, that means that a self-denying and humble disposition as well as a literate education gives one authority as a reader. Only Fanny fits the bill in Mansfield Park.

Whereas Charlotte Lennox's novel ends with the woman reader being reformed by the clergyman so that she can marry the middle-class man chosen by her father, Austen's novel ends with the woman reader marrying the reformed clergyman, her cousin, a match initially considered by all to be "morally impossible" (MP, 6). Fanny thereupon acquires as her home the Parsonage, a discursive space within which Edmund will prepare morally edifying texts for the public consumption of his parishioners—with Fanny acting, presumably, as his best reader and critic. The novel ends with a situation not unlike the one within which Austen herself prepares her texts. Fanny and Austen both accomplish the "morally impossible" by poaching, by their making use of the privileges of privacy in order to earn their respective society's sanction as readers.

Historically, authors and critics have often constructed women-as-readers as passive consumers, unable to make powerful use of their reading within their writing and unable to use their experience as readers to transform their experience as people. I have suggested here that the new direction in Jane Austen scholarship lies in a cultural studies approach. Both Fergus's and Kaplan's characterizations of Austen depend on: twentieth-century understandings of the terms "private" and "privacy"; twentieth-century understandings of eighteenth-century distinctions between private and public spheres; and our belief that eighteenth-century education inculcated in women a proper understanding of their roles or lack thereof in each respectively, and that many women quietly and wholeheartedly accepted this assessment. Austen's gender and class certainly influenced her writing, but as an "ordinary" person, so too did her idiosyncratic experiences. Like other ordinary people, she too was as capable of resisting the institutions she examined as she was of reproducing them.

Further, Austen should be read as an author rather than as a professional-but-female author. Like any other author writing at that social moment, male or female, Austen was engaged in an ongoing debate with other writers for authority and status. That is, Austen's literary career depended as much on the male novelists as it did on other female novelists; likewise it depended as much on male readers as it did on female readers. Like many literary professionals, male and female, Austen felt society's bias against novel writers strongly enough to wish to keep her identity private but saw too that privacy was one of her rights and privileges as a member of the educated classes.

Austen disliked many of the practices of professionals within the field of letters, perhaps particularly their treatment of women authors. So while Austen appears at times to have been traditional, deferent and intensely private, I have interpreted her as a writer who takes the role of female author imposed on her and makes something quite different from what those in power in the literary field had in mind. To cite de Certeau once again, Austen's use of the dominant literary critical order, represented by Edmund Bertram in *Mansfield Park*, deflects its power.[38] Fanny escapes his power without leaving Mansfield Park. In fact, she acquires better access to it. In *Mansfield Park*, Austen capitalizes on the private zone to which women have been consigned and depicts criticism as a viable activity and profession for women.

Notes

1. See my book *Writing Women Reading: Gender and Literary Criticism in the Eighteenth-Century Novel* (forthcoming) for a further explication of this line of thought. See also Linda Zionkowski, "Territorial Disputes in the Republic of Letters: Canon Formation and the Literary Profession," *The Eighteenth Century: Theory and Interpretation* 31 (1990): 3-22. This essay also suggests that eighteenth-century novels debate critical standards of judgment.

2. See, for example, James Thompson, "Jane Austen," in *The Columbia History of the British Novel*, ed. John Richetti et al. (New York: Columbia University Press, 1994), 275-99.

3. In *Writing Women Reading*, I examine this issue in more detail in chapters 3 to 6.

4. See, for example, two of the essays in Janet Todd's *Jane Austen: New Perspectives* (New York: Holmes and Meier, 1983): Nina Auerbach's "Jane Austen's Dangerous Charms: Feeling as One Ought About Fanny Price," 208-23; and Marylea Meyersohn's "What Fanny Knew: A Quiet Auditor of the Whole," 224-30.

5. Recently, Michel de Certeau has defined readers as poachers: "travellers [who] move across lands belonging to someone else, like nomads poaching their way across fields they did not write, despoiling the wealth of Egypt to enjoy it themselves." See *The Practice of Everyday Life*, trans. Steven Rendall (Berkeley: University of California Press, 1984).

6. Jan Fergus, *Jane Austen: A Literary Life* (London: Macmillan, 1991), ix.

7. Fergus, *Jane Austen*, 22.

8. See R. W. Chapman, ed., *Jane Austen's Letters to Her Sister Cassandra and Others.*, 2d ed. (London: Oxford University Press, 1952), quoted in Fergus, *Jane Austen*, 139.

9. Fergus, *Jane Austen*, 140.

10. Fergus, *Jane Austen*, 141.

11. Fergus, *Jane Austen*, 142

12. See, for example, John Fiske, *Understanding Popular Culture* (Boston: Unwin Press, 1989), or Russell Reising, "Can Cultural Reading Read Culture: Toward a Theory of Literary Incompetence," *Tulsa Studies in Women's Literature* 10, no. 1 (1991): 67-91.

13. Deborah Kaplan, *Jane Austen Among Women* (Baltimore: Johns Hopkins University Press, 1992), 103.

14. Kaplan, *Jane Austen*, 100.

15. Kaplan, *Jane Austen*, 103.

16. Kaplan, *Jane Austen*, 103.

17. de Certeau, *Practice of Everyday Life*, 173.

18. See Chapman, ed., *Jane Austen's Letters*, 453.

19. Fergus, *Jane Austen*, 145.

20. See Daniel Cottom, *The Civilized Imagination: A Study of Ann Radcliffe, Jane Austen, and Sir Walter Scott* (Cambridge: Cambridge University Press, 1985), for a more thorough discussion of the issues of private sensibility and aesthetic taste.

21. See also Laura Mooneyham, *Romance, Language and Education in Jane Austen's Novels* (New York: St. Martin's Press, 1988), 86.

22. Tony Tanner, *Jane Austen* (Cambridge, MA: Harvard University Press, 1986), 157.

23. Among other things, Cottom argues that as a figure, Addison and Steele's Mr. Spectator had embodied "a kind of higher literacy that excludes the common crowd from its discourse." Mr. Spectator never entered "into the Commerce of Discourse with any but [his] particular Friends, and not even in publick with them." See *The Spectator*, ed. Donald Bond, 5 vols. (Oxford: Clarendon Press, 1965), vol 1, 21. He only communicated his judgments, whether social, literary, or aesthetic, in writing—a practice that helped to further separate him as a reader from a readership comprised primarily of nobility and gentry. They endorsed as well the need for certain members of the audience who did not share his status to keep their readings private and therefore marginal. Women were particularly discouraged from making public their judgments, literary or otherwise.

  Later on in the century when Eliza Haywood appropriates Addison and Steele's trope of social critic, she seems to circumvent this problem as an author who wished to come across as a proper woman by asserting that the Female Spectator is an amalgamation of female voices: her own; Mira, the wife of a gentleman wit; "a daughter of a wealthy merchant," whom she calls Euphrosine, "since she has all of the cheerfulness and sweetness ascribed to that goddess." See *The Female Spectator: Being Selections from Mrs. Eliza Haywood's Periodical [1744-1746]*, ed. Mary Priestley (London: John Lane, 1929).

Unlike *The Spectator*, *The Female Spectator* lacks a singular self-conscious narrative voice; rather than asserting explicitly that these were her own views of such matters as education, in effect, Haywood created a dialogue among women.

Still, Haywood creates an image of a female "spectator" of the world of texts whose morals and manners are improved by her reading of the world of Nature or, more specifically, by the study of natural philosophy ("it will occur and prove to a demonstration that the study of nature is the study of divinity"). Fanny is also such a female spectator in *Mansfield Park*.

24. Addison and Steele, *Spectator*, 19.

25. Given society's suspicions about women writers in particular, those struggling to be seen as acceptable more often created characters whose moral stature their readership would not normally question. Significantly, Charlotte Lennox's learned divine reforms Arabella by repeating verbatim the review of *Clarissa* that Samuel Johnson published in *The Rambler*. When Lennox has the learned divine reeducate Arabella to read novels like *Clarissa* instead of romances as a means to achieve her moral reformation, she demonstrates how close in the function the professions of the clergy and the literary critic are seen to be. Further, she demonstrates why clergymen become such apt symbols of the ideal literary critic for writers such as herself and Jane Austen. By and large, the clergy's and the literary critic's missions of social reformation as seen by society to be very similar.

26. Austen had read and thought highly of Lennox's *The Female Quixote*. See Chapman, ed., *Jane Austen's Letters*, 173.

27. See Chapman, ed., *Jane Austen's Letters*, 443.

28. *Mansfield Park*. vol. 3 of *The Novels of Jane Austen*, ed. R. W. Chapman, 5 vols., 3d ed. (London: Oxford University Press, 1932-34), 92. Subsequent references are cited parenthetically in the text as *MP*.

29. de Certeau, *Practice of Everyday Life*, 176.

30. de Certeau, *Practice of Everyday Life*, 169.

31. Tanner, *Jane Austen*, 157.

32. Jill Dolan, *The Feminist Spectator as Critic* (Ann Arbor, MI: UMI Research Press, 1988), 23.

33. Dolan, *Feminist Spectator*, 23.

34. In *Jane Austen's Novels: The Art of Clarity* (New Haven, CT: Yale University Press, 1992), Roger Gard notes that Fanny "provokes feelings in critics that range from constrained and dutiful pity and admiration to positive repulsion" (123). See also Auerbach, "Jane Austen's Dangerous Charms" and John Halperin, *The Life of Jane Austen* (Baltimore: Johns Hopkins University Press, 1989).

35. In *Writing Women Reading*, I examine this issue in more detail in chapters 3 to 6.

36. Meyersohn, "What Fanny Knew," 224.

37. de Certeau, *Practice of Everyday Life*, 172.

38. de Certeau, *Practice of Everyday Life*, xiii

10

"The Different Sorts of Friendship": *Desire in* Mansfield Park

Misty G. Anderson

Midway through *Mansfield Park*, Edmund Bertram makes a surprising claim about Fanny Price, the shy heroine, and Mary Crawford, an energetic foil to Miss Price. He says to Fanny, "I would not have the shadow of coolness arise between the two whose intimacy I have been observing with the greatest pleasure, and in whose characters there is so much general resemblance in true generosity and natural delicacy as to make the few slight differences, resulting principally from situation, no reasonable hindrance to a perfect friendship."[1] Most readers have taken this kind of comment from Edmund as self-deception inspired by his infatuation with Mary. But it is worth taking his words at face value, for a moment, to see how they can change our understanding of these two women. Many critics have discussed Mary and Fanny as opposites in a satire on manners, contrasting Fanny's passivity to Mary's activity, Fanny's silence to Mary's chattiness, and so forth. But no one, it seems, has taken Edmund's point of view and discussed the remarkable ways in which Mary and Fanny are drawn to one another.

Fanny's relationship to Mary represents the most significant source of the heroine's subjectivity as a desiring adult. Austen defines Fanny's character both against and in terms of Mary, and in the process creates an intimacy between them that can be termed homoerotic.[2] Because of the erotic potential that remains just beneath the surface of the text, this relationship also creates the greatest crisis of the novel for the heroine and, perhaps, for the author. By examining the points of hesitation and ambivalence that suggest more than Austen can say, we can see the signs of protest against a tradition that constrained content, mandated closure, and repressed alternative modes of sexuality.

HAPPILY EVER AFTER

Modern literary scholarship points out that sexuality has always been a significant factor in literary texts, but that sexual drives are often repressed or sublimated in texts, just as they are in human behavior. Peter Brooks offers a reading of the parallel functioning of text and psyche that enables a discussion of desire in terms of narrative movement. The plot of a novel, which Brooks compares with the death drive from Freud's *Beyond the Pleasure Principle*, seeks the stasis of fulfillment by achieving closure. This movement toward the ending may be supplemented by digressive "counterplots" or detours that the plot makes before reaching its end.[3] From this perspective, we can discuss *Mansfield Park* as a novel with a marriage plot that is carried by an explicit desire for heterosexual union. The misguided desires of the characters that appear as detours in the narrative (Edmund's desire for Mary, Maria's desire for Henry) provide a locus for a discussion of alternative sexual desires and endings in *Mansfield Park*.

To understand the nature of Fanny and Mary's attachment as it relates to sexual desire, we must look to the manifestations of desire in literature for a more historically specific account to supplement narrative theory.[4] Eve Kosofsky Sedgwick, informed by a Foucaultian schema, points out that homoerotic, physical expressions of desire, particularly those between women, could not constitute a lesbian "identity" at the time of Austen's writing.[5] Catharine R. Stimpson had earlier made a related point, claiming that a lesbian identity is not identifiable in English language and literature until 1890.[6] Yet history and literature show that women did choose other women as companions and sexual partners throughout the eighteenth and nineteenth centuries. The few female couples willing to make a life together publicly did so at the peril of their inheritances and social status. In spite of the many impediments to happiness, it was possible to overcome the paralyzing force of censure through self-imposed exile and determination, as Elenor Butler and Sarah Ponsonby proved with their elopement in 1778.[7] Their case is a historically specific example of the possible alternative modes and public expressions of desire. Butler and Ponsonby's record of their relationship interrupts the smooth parallel between desire and its social expression in narrative by pointing to sexuality that must resist acknowledged gender roles and cultural prescriptions for social and sexual behavior. These behaviors were not part of a culturally recognizable identity and as such could not constitute a corporate voice. Understanding the role of homoerotic desire through the literature of the late eighteenth and early nineteenth century, then, depends on reading the individual protests within narrative.

Theorists of gender in literary studies have incorporated narrative theories such as the structure outlined by Brooks as a means of reading the organization of a novel.[8] One such theorist, Joseph Boone, examines the deferrals of plot and closure that at once make any narrative act possible and also mark the ideological conflicts inscribed in the generic definitions of marriage fictions. He observes that the novelistic techniques of the eighteenth and nineteenth centuries—such as linearity, repetition, and the closed ending—created the illusion of a hierarchically ordered and whole novelistic world. Narrative techniques that examine the structure and movement of plot "shed invaluable light on the way in which the marriage tradition successfully managed, for so many years, to circumscribe its thematized desires and curtail its narrative energies in the name, ironically, of readerly satisfaction."[9] Through his model, the possibility of a sexual option other than heterosexual marriage emerges as a protest against a narrative mandate of heterosexual closure as well as a social and political act countering the tyranny of the culturally prescribed ending of marriage.

An illuminating result of such a reading of narrative and tradition in relation to desire is the agency that it discovers in Fanny. Many critics consider Fanny to be Austen's most "proper" heroine, modeled on the ideals of passive, passionless femininity found in eighteenth-century conduct books. This view of Fanny defined in terms of her passivity precludes her agency as a character with specific desires. As the heroine, Fanny is an agent of the plot in that she provides the subject of the story being told and a focus for the various narratives of the novel. This central position makes her responsible for the progress of the plot, an active role even when it is carried out in the form of negation or resistance.[10] The tendency to read Fanny as only a demure, patient character is an example of what D. A. Miller terms "one effect of the novelist's ideology. . . to infect—even to intimidate—our reading with its own good manners."[11] With this caution in mind, we can look beyond Fanny's propriety to observe her feelings and desires, most important her sexual desires, which are the narrative fuel of *Mansfield Park.*

Austen expresses Fanny's agency in the novel by granting her "authorial" power within it. A reading attuned to this significant distance between authorial and narrative voices in the text reveals attitudes of ambivalence toward and resistance to socially mandated structures of closure that govern the text. Fanny gains authorial power in *Mansfield Park* as a morally superior if somewhat less vibrant character than Mary Crawford. In this sense, her authorial function within the text depends on the degree to which she reflects socially approved ideas of propriety and morality. But as the author function within the text, Fanny has a hand in the counterplots of the novel, including her complex relationship to Mary. Functionally, alternatives to the approved ending (heterosexual marriage) are woven into any novel dealing with the closure of marriage. But with an understanding of the ideological mandates inscribed in narrative that Boone discusses, the possibilities of romantic friendships and homoerotic relationships emerge as social and political protests in late eighteenth-century novels. As the heroine and agent of the author, Fanny authorizes both the conventional plot of marriage and the counterplots of sexual and textual diversion.

BROTHER LOVE AND OTHER LOVE

Mansfield Park develops as the narrative of Fanny's experiences, which include her near-incestuous attachment to her brother William.[12] The young Fanny confesses to Edmund her love for William above all her other brothers and sisters. He was "her advocate with her mother (of whom he was the darling) in every distress" (*MP*, 15). He takes the place of the mother as the character most longed for by the young Fanny and provides the familiar, familial affection that she desires. He stands as the metonymic representation of the family as well as an eroticized object in her young adult life. During his first visit to Mansfield, Fanny "was with him as he entered the house, and the first minutes of exquisite feeling had no interruption and no witnesses" (*MP*, 233). Their reunion resembles a meeting of young lovers after a long separation, as they revel in their "equal, fearless [verbal] intercourse" (*MP*, 234). The qualities of romance that surround the interaction of William and Fanny suggest that this narrative, were it not for the incestuous content, could be a viable plot line leading to marriage.

The incestuous overtones of Fanny's feelings are anticipated in the talk of incest that precedes her arrival at Mansfield. Sir Thomas thinks not of Fanny's beloved William but of Tom and Edmund, "his two sons—of cousins in love, etc." (*MP*, 6). Mrs. Norris quickly addresses his fears: "do not you know that of all things upon earth *that* is the least likely to happen; brought up as they would be, always together like brothers and sisters?" (*MP*, 6). Incest remains unspoken as a narrative possibility under the title of "that." The prohibition against incest does not actually apply to Fanny and Edmund, who are only first cousins and legally free to marry. It is evoked, however, reminding us that Fanny and Edmund are *like* brother and sister and that Edmund is *like* William in Fanny's emotional economy. Fanny holds her affection for the two as equal as she examines, the day of the ball, their gifts, "having, with delightful feelings, joined the chain and the cross, those memorials of the two most beloved of her heart" (*MP*, 271). The egalitarian nature of Fanny's feelings admits no intrinsic difference between fraternal and erotic love.[13] This lack of differentiation between brother love and other love redefines for Fanny the erotic impulse as one that seeks familiarity and family rather than the exotic and exogamous, a redefinition that is not necessarily at odds with the closure of marriage.

William proposes to save some of his prize money from his naval escapades "to make the little cottage comfortable, in which he and Fanny were to pass all their middle and later life together" (*MP*, 375). He offers her an alternative to the marriage plot (reminiscent of William and Dorothy Wordsworth's situation) that still includes the comforts of home, family, and financial security. As Peter Brooks notes of eighteenth-century literature, "it is perhaps most notably the image of incest (of the fraternal-sororal variety) that hovers as the sign of passion interdicted because its fulfillment would be too perfect . . . the very cessation of narrative movement."[14] William's proposed cottage is a conventional, idyllic offer that would threaten the narrative by erasing the tensions that create it. Through his offer and Fanny's delighted reaction, one can see the unifying element in her object choices: the desire for home and family. It is a desire that seeks beginnings through the re-creation of an idyllic family unit of intimacy and affection. Her love for William would take a narrative shortcut and reach the end too quickly, by reaching back to the familial source of her desires, were it not for a socially mandated displacement of desire from William onto Edmund. By means of the eroticization of Edmund as the older brother who could become a lover, Fanny overcomes the narrative prohibition against the incestuous "shortcircuit" and the social prohibition against incest to create a plot with her own too-perfect ending. While she cannot have the cottage with William, she can have the Parsonage with Edmund—who presses her to his heart and calls her "my only sister" (*MP*, 444)—and remain safely within the bounds of propriety, family, and the novel.

"A SORT OF INTIMACY"

Fanny's intense attachment to William can be sublimated as love for Edmund, but another narrative of desire cannot be rerouted so easily. The system of relationship that develops between Mary and Fanny endangers the closure of heterosexual marriage with an erotic alternative that threatens social and narrative convention. Mary Poovey notes that the real temptation of Fanny lies in Mary Crawford's appeal and Fanny's fascination with her charms.[15] This fascination and Fanny's ambivalence toward it mark the most radical aspects of *Mansfield Park*. Fanny feels an attraction to Mary, but unlike her affection for William, which can be rechanneled laterally, attraction to another woman can never be articulated. Fanny's silence permits Mary to function as a dangerous, sexual other by whom Fanny is enchanted. Homoerotic attraction remains an unspoken possibility, not unlike the "that" of incest that cannot be named. Indeed, it is precisely the inability to name homoerotic desire, to bring it to the level of consciousness in the text, that maintains its threat to the official plot, a dangerous narrative other that moves freely in the text.

Mary and Fanny share "a sort of intimacy which took place between them within the first fortnight after the Miss Bertrams' going away" (*MP*, 207). Fanny, who receives real attention for the first time after her cousins Julia and Maria leave, comes to visit Mary and Mrs. Grant at the Parsonage during a heavy rain. For Mary, "the sight of Miss Price dripping wet in the vestibule, was delightful" (*MP*, 206). Admittedly, Mary is pleased to have any company on an otherwise lonely day, but her pleasure at the wet Fanny smacks of something more sensual. Fanny is "obliged to submit to the attention" of mistresses and maids, given dry clothing (presumably Mary's) and entertained by Mary's harp playing. In Fanny's life, devoid of female friendship or sensual comforts, such pleasures could not go unnoticed: "Fanny went to her every two or three days; it seemed a kind of fascination; she could not be easy without going, and yet it was without loving her, without ever thinking like her" (*MP*, 208). The ambivalent nature of Fanny's relationship to Mary is in itself an attraction for Fanny, who is compelled to act out a friendship with the woman she sees as her antithesis. Likewise, Mary's attentions suggest an attraction, or at least an interest, in Fanny. The character who should be the foil to Fanny's goodness and purity becomes the "fascination" that Fanny (as well as many readers) cannot resist. This attraction to her "other" jeopardizes the clarity of Fanny's desires, which otherwise remain true to the goal of marital union with Edmund.

Fanny and Mary's relationship depends heavily on language, in the form of Fanny's speeches and Mary's letters. Language constitutes their narrative capabilities and offers a temptation away from the directness and honesty of Fanny's plot. During one of their many walks in the garden, Fanny engages in her longest speech, discoursing freely about her views on nature and memory: "There seems something more speakingly incomprehensible in the powers, the failures, the inequalities of memory, than in any other of our intelligences" (MP, 208). Although she is not particularly touched by Fanny's discourse on memory, an expansive 350 words for the quiet heroine, Mary is the only female character to whom Fanny can speak openly. Mary gives Fanny the chance to become a *narrator* within the novel. Fanny assumes the "authorial function" of the heroine as a result of her superior moral sense that guides the plot, but with Mary she has the chance to create more expansive counterplots. As the textual diversion from the plot, her alternative narratives provide pleasure in the delay they create. In these terms, Mary offers Fanny not only free access to her own voice but also empowers her to express her own desires, two freedoms she does not have with any of the other characters in the novel.

Mary writes to Fanny repeatedly during Fanny's exile to Portsmouth, although Fanny declares that her "style of writing, lively and affectionate, was itself an evil" (MP, 376). Mary has no compunction about identifying the subtext of everyday affairs and about including a worldly, gossiping honesty in her letters. She says of Mrs. Rushworth (Maria), "we *seemed* very glad to see each other, and I do really think we were a little" (MP, 393). Mary insists on the meaning beyond polite edifices of address by underscoring the word *seemed* to illustrate the superficiality of their affection. Later in the same letter, Mary indecorously discusses the monetary situation of Julia and Mr. Yates. Mary remarks, "a poor honourable is no catch . . . take away his rants and the poor Baron has nothing. What a difference a vowel makes! If his rents were equal to his rants!" (MP, 394). Mary accentuates her authorial prowess by pointing out the "difference a vowel makes" and remarking on the delicate yet pliable nature of language. Earlier in the novel, Mary's scandalous pun on *"Rears* and *Vices"* removes any doubt as to her sexual knowledge. The male homoeroticism of the joke suggests that it is a man's joke and that Mary transgresses the lines of gender by repeating the pun and thus making herself a subject. Her coquettish protest "Now, do not be suspecting me of a pun, I entreat" (MP, 60) only reinforces her awareness of sexuality. Her joke indicates the relationship between playing with language and a sort of worldliness, not only through the pun's content but also through the gesture that encourages the reading that it seems to dismiss. Her version of authorship is more dangerous because of her ability to manipulate language on several levels. But her play with language is at once "affectionate" and "evil," accenting the moral paradox that Fanny finds in Mary's narrative abilities.

Mary's irony disrupts the text's surface with evidence of a language that is not always truthful or plainly understood. This disturbing activity threatens Fanny's marriage plot most effectively by pointing out the possibilities of play in language. It deconstructs the monological character of Fanny's story by displaying the art of reading that finds multiple levels of meaning within a text. Mary admits the possibility of substitution in language that leaves meaning as a variable or a matter of interpretation. It is a gesture toward an authorial voice (Austen's) that is not without subtext. When read as a protest against fixed subject matter and meanings, which were dictated by the novelistic genre and by conventional morality at the turn of the century, Mary's risqué language games provide a venue for Austen's more iconoclastic views. Fanny, far from rejecting this form of communication, finds "great food for meditation in this letter. . . with all the uneasiness it supplied" (*MP*, 394). D. A. Miller notes that Fanny's rereading of Mary's letters "indulges and perpetuates forbidden topics in the inverted mode of denial."[16] Fanny's meditation on the content of Mary's letters shows her interest in and attraction to Mary's use of language. Although she finds unpleasantness, uneasiness, and even "evil" in her letter, she is still fascinated by the duplicitous narrative of which Mary is mistress.

PLAYING THE PART

Mary's textual ambidexterity corresponds to a sexual ambidexterity that has not been discussed in Austen studies but that is illustrated as Mary reads *Lovers' Vows* with Fanny. Acting, a pursuit shared by her brother, involves a protean quality in contrast to Fanny's more stable sense of personal identity. The imitative quality of performance, however, gives way to the actuality that the players in *Lovers' Vows* are not acting but bringing their fantasies to life. Mary is aware that Edmund, "playing" a clergyman, is the object of her forward proposals. As she points out to Fanny "I do not think I could go through it with *him* till I have hardened myself a little, for really there *is* a speech or two—you will be so kind, won't you?" (*MP*, 168). She asks Fanny to read Edmund's part with her "that I may fancy *you* him, and get on by degrees. You have a look of *his* sometimes" (*MP*, 169, Austen's emphasis). Mary makes it clear that she can imagine Fanny as Edmund, positioning her not as a character in a play but as her own would-be lover playing her fictional lover. Fanny responds to her observation with "Have I?" suggesting her pleasure at being described as being like Edmund: "[she] joined in with all the modest feeling which the idea of representing Edmund was so strongly calculated to inspire; but with looks and voice so truly feminine, as to be no very good picture of a man. With such an Anhalt, however, Miss Crawford had courage enough (*MP*, 169)." Fanny falls into the trap of the play in portraying Edmund rather than a character. In so doing, she places herself in erotic relation to Mary, who plays Amelia in order to act out her desire for Edmund.

The scene becomes more complicated with the information that Fanny is too feminine to be a good picture of a man, yet Mary "with such an Anhalt . . . had courage enough." Mary's awareness of her object's femaleness is encouraging to her. While it may be the case that Mary has an easier time speaking her lines of proposal because she is not speaking to Edmund, the possibility of a subtext with erotic overtones should not be dismissed. Mary is at ease in relating to another woman in this sexually charged scene where the notion of acting has been undermined by the fantasy play of the actors and actresses. This scene also occurs in Fanny's bedroom, an intimate, private setting. The verbal exchange between Mary and Fanny is a rehearsal of romantic interaction. It is something to "harden" Mary to the lines. The setting and the subject matter combined give the scene an air of sexual tension. Mary, as Fanny's sexualized competitor for Edmund's affections, places herself in erotic relation to Fanny and forces her to play her (Mary's) lover, Anhalt (Edmund). Mary lures Fanny into the realm of acting, which is a diversion from proper behavior and from the moral plot. By placing herself in the sexual web of relationships of *Lovers' Vows*, Fanny becomes vulnerable to the erotic and narrative deviance from the plot that Mary represents.

The illicit implications of the "scene" with Fanny and Mary are further emphasized with the entrance of Edmund. It incites "surprise, consciousness, and pleasure. . . in each of the three" (*MP*, 169). In the presence of the male gaze the intimate scene halts, suspended in time as something of which they are now "conscious." Describing consciousness as a reaction suggests an abrupt awareness of self, a being found out that acknowledges some significant activity. Mary and Fanny, under the male gaze of Edmund, become aware of the role play in which they have been engaged: "the entrance of Edmund the next moment suspended it all" (*MP*, 169). Mary and Fanny have been playing a love scene, a fact of which Edmund seems aware as soon as he sees the script they are using. They have been, in a sense, "found out" by their mutual object of affection, thus registering "surprise, consciousness, and pleasure" in that order. The description of their awareness suggests that Fanny and Mary were absorbed in their roles as lovers. While this is a normal state for a person acting, we should remember that Fanny did not want to act. Her objections centered around the scandalous subject matter of the play and the lack of differentiation between acting and the desires of the players at Sotherton. Her position on the subject of acting complicates the scene and throws a shadow of self-imposed guilt over Fanny's action. The scene suggests that, while Fanny *did* nothing wrong, she was capable of conceiving of Mary in erotic relation to herself, of envisioning such a narrative.

With Edmund in the room, Fanny "felt herself becoming too nearly nothing to both, to have any comfort in having been sought by either" (*MP*, 170). She is eclipsed as a suitable lover when the original arrives and thus is erased as a desiring subject in the circuit of erotic exchange. Her objection at being "nothing to both" includes not only her potential theatrical relationship to Edmund but also her suggestively coded relationship to Mary, both of which she prefers to the external role of prompter. She is relegated to helping the two would-be lovers with their love scene as a pitiable and unwilling pander to their exchange. This undesirable position in the erotic structure of relations forces her to recognize the complexities and the doubleness of the play. As a prompter, she quickly becomes a spectator: "watching them, she forgot herself . . . agitated by the increasing spirit of Edmund's manner" (*MP*, 170). Once again she sees that *Lovers' Vows* is not an opportunity to act but a chance to play out desires and fantasies. After participating in the play and placing herself in its tangled systems of relations, however, she is not completely free of the play's patterns.

The coalescence of two of the three members of this unusual triangle seems an integral part of its operation. Edmund, captivated by Mary but affectionate toward Fanny, notes similarities between the two women who represent such different plots for his life. Edmund claims that Mary and Fanny's characters have "much general resemblance" and calls them "the two dearest objects I have on earth" (*MP*, 264). Later, Edmund presses "[Fanny's] hand to his lips, with almost as much warmth as if it had been Miss Crawford's" (*MP*, 269). Edmund's blending of the two women betrays his desire to have elements of both the characters in one composite love object. But beyond his desire remain the sexual issues that have been raised by the relationship of Mary and Fanny. Fanny, in a reaction similar to her ruminations over Mary's 'evil' letters, "was obliged to repeat again and again that she was one of his two dearest, before the words gave her any sensation" (*MP*, 264). She repeats the unification that Edmund suggests by thinking of herself as "one of . . . two." The male gaze of Edmund throws Mary and Fanny together as friends, but also as an eroticized unit within his mind that has the potential to become part of the women's understanding of themselves. Edmund's desire pushes the two rivals closer to one another in a sexually coded subplot of female friendship.

Mary and Fanny are not merely passive participants in Edmund's plan of friendship. The women offer each other the attraction of intimacy with Edmund. Their friendship pleases him while also offering that perverse companionship so often enjoyed by rivals in an intimate setting. To invert the terms so frequently used to describe male rivals, the desire for Edmund creates a homoerotic bond between the two women. When Edmund leaves Mansfield Park after the ball, Fanny and Mary gravitate toward each other. The attraction between Mary and Fanny is problematic not only because it is mixed with a healthy dose of distaste and rivalry, but also because the late twentieth century terms for discussing same-sex relationships do not accurately represent the activities and bonds between members of the same sex as seen in late eighteenth- and early nineteenth-century texts. Sedgwick notes that any notion of sexual identity, in Austen's time as in our own, "magnetized and reoriented in new ways the heterogeneous erotic and epistemological energies of everyone in its social vicinity, without at the same time either adequating or descriptively exhausting those energies."[17] Resisting the anachronistic impulse to categorize sexuality within the modern monoliths of homosexual and heterosexual, while understanding that the notion of sexual identity does not capture the substance of erotic energy, we can illuminate a web of desires that include but refuse to be reduced to the heterosexual marriage plot. This matrix includes both the clearly identified and the suggested relations between the characters, such as the relationship of Fanny and Mary. These desires mark the lines along which the narrative of Mansfield Park is structured and make possible the tensions and intrigues necessary to arrive at a plausible closure of marriage.

THE VICTIM VICTORIAN

The clearest articulation of the homoerotic tension between Fanny and Mary occurs after Henry's proposal and just before the Crawfords are to leave Mansfield Park. Mary, coming to visit Fanny before her departure, is referred to as a "'friend.'" The quotation marks identify the term as Edmund's rather than Fanny's. The distancing of Mary is attributed to the "formidable threat" posed by Miss Crawford, of which "she lived in continual terror" (*MP*, 356). At this point in the narrative, Fanny has good reason to be afraid of Mary. The growing realization of Mary's intimacy with Edmund and of the possibility of their marriage makes her a threat in the most direct sense to Fanny's plot of marriage. Fanny fears Mary's "penetration," implying her ability to understand Fanny's private desires and thus enter her private narrative space. If Mary discovered Fanny's love for Edmund, she would likely exploit the information by revealing Fanny's desires to the family or by manipulating that knowledge to her advantage in Edmund's eyes. Mary, a skillful player with textuality, threatens Fanny's narrative power with her ability to read and retell narratives that are more "fascinating" than Fanny's direct family plot. As the amoral author and other who could potentially produce better, more interesting narratives, she is a foil to Fanny's moral narrative power.

Fanny hides from Mary throughout the morning as she previously hid from Henry: "She absented herself as little as possible from Lady Bertram, kept away from the east room, and took no solitary walk in the shrubbery, in her caution to avoid any sudden attack" (MP, 357). Mary is frightening to Fanny because she can claim intimacy as a woman and a "friend," and can thus "attack" her as Henry cannot. Mary presents herself as a replacement for Henry in the sexual economy, acting on behalf of her brother as a sexual agent in the courtship of Fanny. She has the ability and the opportunity to translate her desire for Fanny through Henry's courtship of Fanny. In spite of these terrifying qualities, Fanny also sees the power of Mary's manipulative and sexualized nature and describes this strength in somewhat glorified terms as "triumphant and secure" (MP, 356). In this light, the threatening yet attractive figure Mary represents to Fanny has sexual connotations: a woman confident of her sexuality and her power to attract in a wide variety of situations. The terrifying yet triumphant power seems to be that of a woman, Mary, capable of acting like a man in love in a world where theater and reality are not clearly separated.

The threat that Mary presents is expressed through Fanny's reaction to Mary's request. Mary "said to her tolerably soon, in a low voice, 'I must speak to you for a few minutes somewhere;' words that Fanny felt all over her, in all her pulses, and all her nerves. Denial was impossible" (MP, 357). Fanny's physical response to Mary's desire for an intimate audience, requested "in a low voice," casts an erotic, anticipatory light over the meeting. Fanny's powerful reaction registers throughout her body with a description of sensations that resembles both fear and arousal. This response with its sexual component can be seen as a reaction to the combination of culturally defined masculine agency and feminine intimacy and charm in Mary. She embodies the sexual power of a male by representing her brother but also the perceptual and social power of a woman who can understand Fanny as well as claim her private attentions without suspicion. As a proxy for Henry, Mary presents Fanny with the threat of the Crawford marriage plot through her "triumphant" powers of speech. Her ability to threaten Fanny is predicated on the culturally approved intimacy between women.

On the way to Fanny's room, Mary takes Fanny's hand and begins scolding her affectionately, but "had discretion enough to reserve the rest till they might be secure of having four walls to themselves" (MP, 357). The substance of the meeting is assumed to be about Henry's proposal, but Fanny's distress at discussing this subject with Mary seems far greater than her distress at similar interviews with Sir Thomas and Edmund, each of whom has the power of influence granted by her respect and their position as family. Mary, as external to the family structure, threatens to take Edmund away from Fanny with her more active and vocal narrative power. As Mary states later, she took great pleasure in making Edmund's "sturdy spirit bend as it did! Oh! It was sweet beyond expression" (*MP*, 358). Her narrative power runs parallel to a sexual power that tempted Edmund away from his convictions about the play. The possibility lingers that this same sexualized narrative power could tempt Fanny from her plot and into the sexual economy of the Crawfords.

The two women go to Fanny's room where Mary immediately recalls the scene of the rehearsal. "'Ha!' she cried, with instant animation, 'am I here again? The east room. Only once was I in this room before!'" (*MP*, 357-58). Mary is overtaken by the powerful act of memory that recalls the former scene and binds the two moments together in the narrative as similar occasions. By recalling the erotically coded rehearsal, Mary changes the subject from Henry to Edmund and simultaneously refers to the time when Fanny impersonated Edmund for the purposes of playing a love scene with herself. Recalling the original scene of acting where Fanny became an understudy, she admits the possibility of substitution into the present moment: that Fanny could be the object of her romantic proposals. Mary's recollection positions the two women in erotic relation to one another and gestures toward the possibility of enacting a desire that reaches beyond the text. Yet, for obvious social, cultural, and personal reasons, Austen did not carry the homoerotic plot further. Janet Todd aptly notes that while men could titillate the reading public with lesbian acts or erotic female friendships, a woman writing similar scenes would be implicated and indicted.[18] Women's homoerotic desire remains part of the palimpsestic quality of Austen's text to which Sandra Gilbert and Susan Gubar allude.[19] Insofar as such a desire cannot be reconciled with the closure of marriage, it remains unexplored and unexpressed.

After conjuring these sexualized images of the play and professing the period of the rehearsal to be her time of greatest happiness, Mary confesses, "'I believe I now love you all.' And having said so, with a degree of tenderness and consciousness which Fanny had never seen in her before, and now only thought too becoming, she turned away for a moment to recover herself" (*MP*, 358-59). Mary is no doubt pushing at Fanny's feelings (which coincide with her own for Edmund). She remembers that she came to scold Fanny, but revises her agenda: "'I have not the heart for it when it comes to the point.' And embracing her very affectionately—'Good, gentle Fanny! When I think of this being the last time of seeing you; for I do not know how long—I feel it quite impossible to do anything but love you!" (*MP*, 358). This direct appeal to Fanny's sentimental qualities affects her, and she begins to cry "as if she had loved Miss Crawford more than she possibly could" (*MP*, 359). Mary's ability to elicit strong emotions from the reserved Fanny indicates her persuasive and her narrative powers. Were there no narrator's voice interceding, one would be inclined to see her tears as a clear sign of emotional attachment to Mary. But even the voice of the narrator is equivocal; it begs the question of how much Fanny did or could possibly love Miss Crawford. As Mary talks about the friends she is going to see, Fanny meditates "on the different sorts of friendship in the world" (*MP*, 360). The ambiguity of this sentence suggests the inadequacy of language or of this genre to describe the complexities of human relationships that Fanny has begun to see. Fanny, whether unable to find the language or unable to speak what she feels because of social restrictions that edit Austen as she writes, has come to recognize the differences and nuances within the realm of desire and affection.

The question of Fanny and Mary's "different sort of friendship" can be understood in terms of the replacement and sublimation that psychically characterizes sexual desire. Their relationship is eroticized as each of the women is made in her turn to stand for a man who is a desiring subject. The construct of the erotic relation between two women illustrates the exchangeability of the object of desire but also the different systems of relation that could be generated by a woman in the place of the desiring subject. By defying traditional categorization, this kind of "different" relationship resists, even as it is subsumed by, the linearity of traditional heterosexual desire that finds closure in marriage. Brooks's notion of plot and closure is based on male physiology. Fanny's contemplation suggests the ways in which desires defy categorization. "Different sorts of friendship" must be suppressed or abandoned in order to reach a coherent, understandable ending.

WHAT CAN OTHER PENS SAY?

Fanny, of course, prevails as the true Austen heroine. The current of the plot meanders about in swirls and eddies of desire, but we reach the expected ending of reconciliation and marriage. At the end, however, we find a particularly strange narrative intrusion that breaks the mimetic illusion: "Let other pens dwell on guilt and misery. I quit such odious subjects as soon as I can, impatient to restore every body, not greatly in fault themselves, to tolerable comfort, and to have done with all the rest" (*MP*, 461). This first appearance of a general narrator, the "I," is marked both by its flippancy and its assertion of control. Austen reveals an ironic attitude toward the idea of closure in her desire to dispense with this portion of the story as quickly as possible. This attitude ostensibly springs from the ideology of settlement that governs the closure of every one of Austen's novels. The heroine's plot must end in marriage, accompanied by the necessary tying up of loose plots, the closing off of alternative desires, through secondary marriages, exile, or punishment. But unlike Austen's other novels, *Mansfield Park* contains an insistent narrative voice in a protracted ending that indicates Fanny's first pregnancy, a sign of her sexuality and her ability to create materially her longed for biological family as a mother. In this sense, the novel is a revolt against the politics of closure that hermetically seals the heroine's fate at the moment of marriage.

Austen traces the fates of the various characters in the form of a postscript to the story, engaging in an early example of what Rachel Blau DuPlessis terms "writing beyond the ending."[20] As a part of the same protest against ideology in the form of narrative stricture that looks beyond Fanny's technical moment of closure, marriage, Austen toys with alternatives to marriage and death, the two endings that govern the romance plot. Although most of the postscript endings are punishments in the form of situational comedies, Mary Crawford is spared any pain other than the separation from life at Mansfield Park. She retires to the comforts of "the kindness of her sister's (Mrs. Grant's) heart" (*MP*, 469). She achieves a notion of female community, emphasized by the repetitive structure ". . . they lived together; and when Dr. Grant had brought on apoplexy and death. . . . they still lived together" (*MP*, 469). More important than the issue of community, however, is the fact that Mary does not continue her search for a husband and the closure of marriage. She cannot satisfy the "superior tastes" she cultivated at Mansfield (for Edmund and Fanny), and for the moment at least makes no efforts to change her single status. The financial independence that these women enjoy, also suggested in the repetition of "living," marks what must have been a wish for the single Austen who on more than one occasion remarked on the economic dependence of unmarried women and their propensity for poverty.[21] Mary stands as the possibility of an ending other than marriage, although her exile points to the fact that such an ending must venture outside the morally delimited space of transmittable narratives.

The appearance of the narrative voice at the end also begs the question of what to do with the "I." The voice asserts a link with the heroine in claiming "My Fanny" as her own. This suggests an empathy with the heroine pressed by circumstance into silences about herself. But "My Fanny" also connects the narrative voice with the author, Jane Austen, who could assert ownership of a character. The authorial "I" of woman serves as a signature of the woman writer who has historically been denied the right to her own voice.[22] The desire to rewrite closure, to have another logic of plot, appears in the "I" that recalls the finality of closure that insists on the end of desire. It points us out of the text to other plots and other sexualities that could not be written in a woman's text produced for public consumption.

The "I" also awakens us to the presence of an authorial subject who wrote at a point in history that made it difficult for her to sign her own name to her novels. It also reminds us that the authorial voice has been present throughout the text, resisting identification by refraining from the use of "I." The "I" inserts a physical subject who "quits. . . subjects," who refuses to write certain things. These unwritten plots include the suppressed or interrupted narratives of *Mansfield Park* that were incompatible with its plot and with social convention. Austen breaks her silence to attempt to tell the story of the "I," which is the "desire for another logic of plot" that cannot fit in the story or its ideology. Perhaps it is the story of a woman's desires and their multifaceted forms that were edited posthumously by her sister Cassandra down to what Janet Todd called the "harmless residue" of Jane Austen's life.[23] What does remain, however, tells a story of strong ties to the women whom Austen knew. These energetic and intimate correspondences provide a supplement to the fear of the pleasures of "different sorts of friendship."

Notes

1. Jane Austen, *Mansfield Park*, vol. 2 of *The Novels of Jane Austen*, ed. R. W. Chapman, 5 vols., 3d ed. (London: Oxford University Press, 1932-34), 264. Subsequent references are cited parenthetically in the text as *MP*.

2. I separate homoerotic from lesbian here on the basis of absence of physical sexual contact. These distinctions are based on the work of Eve Kosofsky Sedgwick, Catharine R. Stimpson, and Valerie Traub. As an operative definition, this terminology allows one to speak of same-sex (homoerotic) relationships that do not engage in genital, physical sex but that do have erotic elements as opposed to lesbian relationships that do engage in physical sex. The debate over nomenclature is far from settled in the lesbian or feminist community for a variety of academic, political, and personal reasons.

3. Peter Brooks, *Reading for the Plot: Design and Intention in Narrative* (New York: Knopf, 1984), 101-2.

4. For a critique of Brooks that suggests the need for such historicizing, see Jay Clayton, "Narrative and Theories of Desire," *Critical Inquiry* 16 (1989): 33-53.

5. Eve Kosofsky Sedgwick, "Jane Austen and the Masturbating Girl," *Critical Inquiry* 17, no. 4 (1991): 823.

6. Catharine R. Stimpson, "Zero Degree Deviancy: The Lesbian Novel in English," *Critical Inquiry* 8, no. 2 (Winter 1981): 365.

7. Elizabeth Mavor, *Life with the Ladies of Llangollen* (New York: Viking Penguin, 1984).

8. Excellent examples of such work include D. A. Miller's *Narrative and Its Discontents: Problems of Closure in the Traditional Novel* (Princeton, NJ: Princeton University Press, 1981), which deals directly with *Mansfield Park* , and Rachel Blau DuPlessis, *Writing Beyond the Ending: Narrative Strategies of Twentieth-Century Women Writers* (Bloomington: Indiana University Press, 1985).

9. Joseph Boone, *Tradition Counter Tradition: Love and the Form of Fiction* (Chicago: University of Chicago Press, 1987), 71.

10. See Jay Clayton, *Romantic Vision and the Novel* (New York: Cambridge University Press, 1987), 65.

11. Miller, *Narrative and Its Discontents*, 53.

12. This discussion of incest is informed by the work of R. F. Brissenden, "*Mansfield Park*: Freedom and the Family," in *Jane Austen, Bicentenary Essays*, ed. John Halperin (Cambridge: Cambridge University Press, 1975); Glenda A. Hudson, *Sibling Love and Incest in Jane Austen's Fiction* (New York: St. Martin's Press, 1992); and Julia Prewitt Brown, *Jane Austen's Novels: Social Change and Literary Form* (Cambridge, MA: Harvard University Press, 1979).

13. Claudia Johnson, *Jane Austen: Women, Politics, and the Novel* (Chicago: University of Chicago Press, 1988), 117.

14. Brooks, *Reading for the Plot*, 109.

15. Mary Poovey, *The Proper Lady and the Woman Writer* (Chicago: University of Chicago Press 1984), 220.

16. Miller, *Narrative and Its Discontents*, 59.

17. See Sedgwick, "Jane Austen."

18. Janet Todd, *Women's Friendship in Literature* (New York: Columbia University Press, 1980), 413.

19. Sandra Gilbert and Susan Gubar, *The Madwoman in the Attic* (New Haven, CT: Yale University Press, 1979), 73.

20. DuPlessis, *Writing Beyond the Ending*, 4.

21. See R. W. Chapman, ed., *Jane Austen's Letters to Her Sister Cassandra and Others.*, 2d ed. (London: Oxford University Press, 1952), 411, 478-79, 483.

22. Nancy Miller describes the "I" of women's writing as "the iconography of desire for a revision of story, and in particular a revision of closure. This desire for another logic of plot which by definition cannot be narrated, looks elsewhere for expression." Nancy Miller, *Subject to Change: Reading Feminist Writing* (New York: Columbia University Press, 1988), 87.

23. Todd, *Women's Friendship*, 396.

Bibliography

Abrams, M. H. *A Glossary of Literary Terms*, 5th ed. New York: Holt, Rinehart, and Winston, 1988.

Addison, Joseph, and Richard Steele. *The Spectator*, ed. Donald Bond. 5 vols. Oxford: Clarendon Press, 1965.

Anderson, Benedict. *Imagined Communities: Reflections on the Origin and Spread of Nationalism*. Rev. ed. London: Verso, 1991.

Anderson, Nancy Fix. "Cousin Marriage in Victorian England." *Journal of Family History* 11 (1986): 278-97.

Armstrong, Nancy, and Leonard Tennenhouse, ed. *The Ideology of Conduct: Essays on Literature and the History of Sexuality*. New York: Methuen, 1987.

Armstrong, Nancy. "The Nineteenth-Century Jane Austen: A Turning Point in the History of Fear." *Genre* 23 (1990): 227-46.

———. *Desire and Domestic Fiction: A Political History of the Novel*. New York: Oxford University Press, 1987.

Auerbach, Nina. "Jane Austen's Dangerous Charms: Feeling as One Ought About Fanny Price." In *Jane Austen: New Perspectives*, ed. Janet Todd, 208-223. New York: Holmes and Meier, 1983.

Austen, Jane. *Catharine and Other Writings*. ed. Margaret Anne Doody and Douglas Murray. Oxford: Oxford University Press, 1993.

———. *Emma*. Vol. 4 of *The Novels of Jane Austen*. ed. R. W. Chapman, 5 vols., 3d ed. London: Oxford University Press, 1932-34.

———. *Jane Austen's Letters to Her Sister Cassandra and Others*. ed. R. W. Chapman, 2d ed. London: Oxford University Press, 1952.

———. *Mansfield Park*, Vol. 2 of *The Novels of Jane Austen*, ed. R. W. Chapman, 5 vols., 3d ed. London: Oxford University Press, 1932-34.

———. *Minor Works*, Vol. 6 of *The Novels of Jane Austen*, ed. R. W. Chapman. London: Oxford University Press, 1954.

———. *Northanger Abbey and Persuasion*. Vol. 5 of *The Novels of Jane Austen*, ed. R. W. Chapman, 5 vols., 3d ed. London: Oxford University Press, 1932-34.

———. *Pride and Prejudice*. Vol. 3 of *The Novels of Jane Austen*, ed. R. W. Chapman, 5 vols., 3d ed. London: Oxford University Press, 1932-34.

———. *Sense and Sensibility*. Vol. 1 of *The Novels of Jane Austen*, ed. R. W. Chapman, 5 vols., 3d ed. London: Oxford University Press, 1932-34.

———. *The History of England from the Reign of Henry the 4th to the Death of Charles the 1st*. Introduction by A. S. Byatt. Chapel Hill, NC: Algonquin Books, 1993.

Azim, Firdous. *The Colonial Rise of the Novel*. New York: Routledge, 1993.

Ballaster, Ros. "Romancing the Novel: Gender and Genre in Early Theories of Narrative." In *Living By the Pen: Early British Women Writers*, ed. Dale Spender, 188-200. New York: Teacher's College Press, 1992.

Barnes, Julian. *Flaubert's Parrot*. New York: Vintage, 1984.

Bazerman, Charles. "How Natural Philosophers Can Cooperate: The Literary Technology of Coordinated Investigation in Joseph Priestley's *History and Present State of Electricity*." In *Textual Dynamics of the Professions: Historical and Contemporary Studies of Writing in Professional Communities*, ed. Charles Bazerman and James Paradis. Madison, WI: University of Wisconsin Press, 1991.

Bell, Susan Groag. "Letters as Literature in Eighteenth-Century France and England." Paper presented at the annual conference for the Western Association of Women Historians. San Marino, CA: Huntington Library, May 1992.

Bloom, Harold. *The Anxiety of Influence: A Theory of Poetry*. New York: Oxford University Press, 1973.

———. *Oliver Goldsmith*. New York: Chelsea House Publishers, 1987.

Boone, Joseph. *Tradition Counter Tradition: Love and the Form of Fiction*. Chicago: University of Chicago Press, 1987.

Booth, Wayne. *The Company We Keep: An Ethics of Fiction*. Berkeley: University of California Press, 1988.

Brissenden, R. F. "*Mansfield Park*: Freedom and the Family." In *Jane Austen, Bicentenary Essays*, ed. John Halperin, 156-171. Cambridge: Cambridge University Press, 1975.

Brooks, Peter. *The Melodramatic Imagination: Balzac, Henry James, Melodrama, and the Mode of Excess*. New Haven, CT: Yale University Press, 1976.

———. *Reading for the Plot: Design and Intention in Narrative*. New York: Knopf, 1984.

Brophy, Brigid. "Jane Austen and the Stuarts." In *Critical Essays on Jane Austen*, ed. B. C. Southam, 21-38. London: Routledge and Kegan Paul, 1968.

Brown, Julia Prewitt. *Jane Austen's Novels: Social Change and Literary Form*. Cambridge, MA: Harvard University Press, 1979.

Burton, Antoinette. *Burdens of History: British Feminists, Indian Women and Imperial Culture, 1865–1915*. Chapel Hill: University of North Carolina Press, 1994.

Butler, Marilyn. *Jane Austen and the War of Ideas*. Oxford: Clarendon Press, 1975.

———. *Romantics, Rebels, and Reactionaries: English Literature and Its Backgrounds, 1760-1830*. Oxford: Oxford University Press, 1981.

Buxton, John. "Goldsmith's Classicism." In *The Art of Oliver Goldsmith*, ed. Andrew Swarbrick, 69-78. London: Vision Press, 1984.

Cavell, Stanley. *Pursuits of Happiness: The Hollywood Comedy of Remarriage*. Cambridge, MA: Harvard University Press, 1981.

Certeau, Michel de. *The Practice of Everyday Life*. Trans. Steven Rendall. Berkeley: University of California Press, 1984.

Chodorow, Nancy. "Family Structure and Feminine Personality." In *Woman, Culture and Society*, ed. M. Z. Rosaldo and L. Lamphere, 43-66. Stanford, CA: Stanford University Press, 1974.

Clayton, Jay. "Narrative and Theories of Desire." *Critical Inquiry* 16 (1989): 33-53.

———. *Romantic Vision and the Novel*. New York: Cambridge University Press, 1987.

Cohen , Jean L., and Andrew Arato. *Civil Society and Political Theory*. Cambridge, MA: MIT Press, 1992.

Colley, Linda. *Britons: Forging the Nation 1707–1837*. New Haven, CT: Yale University Press, 1992.

Cottom, Daniel. *The Civilized Imagination: A Study of Ann Radcliffe, Jane Austen, and Sir Walter Scott*. Cambridge: Cambridge University Press, 1985.

Crosby Christina. *The Ends of History: Victorians and "The Woman Question."* New York: Routledge, 1991.

Cruttwell, Patrick, ed. *Samuel Johnson: Selected Writings*. London: Penguin, 1988.

Danahy, Michael. *The Feminization of the Novel*. Gainesville: University of Florida Press, 1991.

Davidoff, Lenore, and Catherine Hall. *Family Fortunes: Men and Women of the English Middle Class 1780–1850*. London: Hutchinson, 1987.

Day, William Patrick. *In the Circles of Fear and Desire: A Study of Gothic Fantasy*. Chicago: University of Chicago Press, 1985.

Denby, David. "Does Homer Have Legs?" *New Yorker* 6 September 1993, 52-69.

Dolan, Jill. *The Feminist Spectator as Critic*. Ann Arbor, MI: UMI Research Press, 1988.

Doody, Margaret. *Frances Burney: The Life in the Works*. New Brunswick, NJ: Rutgers University Press, 1988.

Duckworth, Alistair M. "Jane Austen and the Conflict of Interpretations." In *Jane Austen: New Perspectives*, ed. Janet Todd, 39-52. New York: Holmes and Meier, 1983.

———. "Jane Austen and the Construction of a Progressive Author." *College English* 53, no. 1 (1991): 77-90.

Duncan, Ian. *Modern Romance and Transformations of the Novel: The Gothic, Scott, and Dickens*. Cambridge: Cambridge University Press, 1992.

DuPlessis, Rachel Blau. *Writing Beyond the Ending: Narrative Strategies of Twentieth-Century Women Writers*. Bloomington: Indiana University Press, 1985.

Dwyer, June. *Jane Austen*. New York: Continuum, 1989.

Elias, Norbert. *The Court Society*. Trans. Edmund Jephcott. Oxford: Blackwell, 1983.

Eliot, George. *Middlemarch*, ed. David Carroll. Oxford: Oxford University Press, 1988.

Evans, Mary. *Jane Austen and the State*. London: Tavistock Publications, 1987.

Faludi, Susan. *Backlash: The Undeclared War Against American Women*. New York: Crown, 1991.

Fergus, Jan. *Jane Austen: A Literary Life*. London: Macmillan, 1991.

Ferguson, Moira, ed., *First Feminists: British Women Writers 1578–1799*. Bloomington: Indiana University Press, 1985.

Fiske, John. *Understanding Popular Culture*. Boston: Unwin Press, 1989.

Flanders, W. Austin. *Structures of Experience: History, Society, and Personal Life in the Eighteenth-Century British Novel*. Columbia: University of South Carolina Press, 1984.

Frye, Northrop. *The Secular Scripture: A Study of the Structure of Romance*. Cambridge, MA: Harvard University Press, 1976.

Gilbert, Sandra M., and Susan Gubar. *Madwoman in the Attic: The Woman Writer and the Nineteenth-Century Literary Imagination*. New Haven, CT: Yale University Press, 1979.

Gilligan, Carol. *In a Different Voice: Psychological Theory and Women's Development*. Cambridge, MA: Harvard University Press, 1982.

Girouard, Mark. *The Return to Camelot: Chivalry and the English Gentleman*. New Haven, CT: Yale University Press, 1981.

Gluckman, Max. "Gossip and Scandal." *Current Anthropology* 4 (1963): 307-16.

Goldsmith, Oliver. *An Abridgment of the History of England, from the Invasion of Julius Caesar to the Death of George the Second*. Boston: T. Bedlington, 1825.

Grey, J. David, ed. *The Jane Austen Companion*. New York: Macmillan, 1986.

———. *Jane Austen's Beginnings: The Juvenilia and Lady Susan*. Ann Arbor, MI: UMI Research Press, 1989.

Griffiths, Ralph A. "The Later Middle Ages, 1290-1485." In *The Oxford Illustrated History of Britain*, ed. Kenneth O. Morgan, 166-222. Oxford: Oxford University Press, 1989.

Guy, John. *Tudor England*. Oxford: Oxford University Press, 1988.

Halperin, John. "Jane Austen's Anti-Romantic Fragment: Some Notes on Sanditon." *Tulsa Studies in Women's Literature* 3 (1983): 183-91.

———. *The Life of Jane Austen*. Baltimore: Johns Hopkins University Press, 1984.

———. "Rev. of Deborah Kaplan's *Jane Austen Among Women*." *Nineteenth-Century Literature* 48, no. 1 (1993): 96-99.

———. Unengaged Laughter: Jane Austen's Juvenilia," In *Jane Austen's Beginnings: The Juvenilia and Lady Susan*, ed. J. David Grey, 29-44. Ann Arbor, MI: UMI Research Press, 1989.

Handler, Richard, and Daniel Segal. *Jane Austen and the Fiction of Culture: An Essay on the Narration of Social Realities*. Tucson: University of Arizona Press, 1990.

Hardy, J. P. *Jane Austen's Heroines: Intimacy in Human Relationships*. London: Routledge & Kegan Paul, 1984.

Harris, Jocelyn. *Jane Austen's Art of Memory*. Cambridge: Cambridge University Press, 1989.

———. "Learning and Genius in *Sir Charles Grandison*." In *Studies in the Eighteenth Century*, vol. 4, ed. R. F. Brissenden and J. C. Eade, 167-91. Canberra: Australian National University Press, 1979.

————. "Richardson: Original or Learned Genius?" In *Samuel Richardson: Tercentenary Essays*, ed. Margaret Anne Doody and Peter Sabor, 188-202. Cambridge: Cambridge University Press, 1989.

Haywood, Eliza. *The Female Spectator: Being Selections from Mrs. Eliza Haywood's Periodical (1744–1746)*, ed. Mary Priestley. London: John Lane, 1929.

Hechter, Michael. *Internal Colonialism: The Celtic Fringe in British National Development, 1536–1966*. Berkeley: University of California Press, 1975.

Hill, Bridget. *The Republican Virago: The Life and Times of Catharine Macaulay, Historian*. Oxford: Clarendon Press, 1992.

Honan, Park. *Jane Austen: Her Life*. London: Weidenfeld and Nicholson, 1987.

Howells, Coral Ann. *Love, Mystery, and Misery: Feeling in Gothic Fiction*. London: Athlone, 1978.

Hudson, Glenda A. *Sibling Love and Incest in Jane Austen's Fiction*. New York: St. Martin's Press, 1992.

Hudson, Nicholas. *Writing and European Thought, 1600–1830*. Cambridge: Cambridge University Press, 1994.

Hume, David. *Essays: Moral, Political, and Literary*, ed. Eugene F. Miller, Rev. ed. Indianapolis, IN: Liberty Classics, 1985.

Jacob, Margaret C. "The Enlightenment Redefined: The Formation of Modern Civil Society." *Social Research* 58, no. 2 (Summer 1991): 475-95.

James, Henry. *The House of Fiction: Essays on the Novel*, ed. Leon Edel, Wesport, CT: Greenwood Press, 1973.

Jeffords, Susan. *The Remasculinization of America: Gender and the Vietnam War*. Bloomington: Indiana University Press, 1989.

Johnson, Claudia. *Jane Austen: Women, Politics, and the Novel*. Chicago: University of Chicago Press, 1988.

Kaplan, Deborah. *Jane Austen Among Women*. Baltimore: Johns Hopkins University Press, 1992.

Kelly, Gary. *English Fiction of the Romantic Period, 1789–1830*. London: Longman, 1989.

————. *Revolutionary Feminism: The Mind and Career of Mary Wollstonecraft*. London: Macmillan, 1992.

————. *Women, Writing, and Revolution 1790–1827*. Oxford: Clarendon Press, 1992.

Kennard, Jean E. *Victims of Convention*. Hamden, CT: Archon, 1978.

Kent, Christopher. "Learning History With, and From, Jane Austen." In *Jane Austen's Beginnings: The Juvenilia and Lady Susan*, ed. J. David Grey, 59-72. Ann Arbor, MI: UMI Research Press, 1989.

————. "'Real Solemn History' and Social History." In *Jane Austen in a Social Context*, ed. David Monaghan, 86-104. New York: Macmillan, 1981.

Kernan, Alvin. *Samuel Johnson and the Impact of Print*. Princeton, NJ: Princeton University Press, 1987.

Kestner, Joseph. *Jane Austen: Spatial Structure of Thematic Variations*. Salzburg: Institut für Englische Sprache und Literatur, 1974.

Kirkham, Margaret. "Jane Austen and Contemporary Feminism." In *The Jane Austen Companion*, ed. J. David Grey, 154-59. New York: Macmillan, 1986.

————. *Jane Austen, Feminism, and Fiction*. Totowa, NJ: Barnes & Noble, 1983.

Klancher, Jon. *The Making of English Reading Audiences, 1790–1832*. Madison: University of Wisconsin Press, 1987.

Kolodny, Annette. "Some Notes on Defining a Feminist Literary Criticism." *Critical Inquiry* 2 (1975): 75-92.

Landes, Joan B. *Women and the Public Sphere in the Age of the French Revolution*. Ithaca, NY: Cornell University Press, 1988.

Landry, Donna, and Gerald MacLean. *Materialist Feminisms*. Oxford: Blackwell, 1993.

Lau, Beth. "Madeline at Northanger Abbey: Keats's Antiromances and Gothic Satire." *Journal of English and German Philology* 84, no .1 (1985): 30-50.

Lauber, John. *Jane Austen*. New York: Twayne, 1993.

Laurenson, Diana. *The Sociology of Literature: Applied Studies*. Keele: University of Keele, 1978.

Levin, Carole. *The Heart and Stomach of a King: Elizabeth I and the Politics of Sex and Power*. Philadelphia: University of Pennsylvania Press, 1994.

Lodge, David, ed. *Jane Austen—Emma: A Casebook*. London: Macmillan, 1991.

Lonsdale, Roger, ed. *Eighteenth-Century Women Poets: An Oxford Anthology*. Oxford: Oxford University Press, 1989.

Looser, Devoney. "(Re)Making History and Philosophy: Austen's *Northanger Abbey*." *European Romantic Review* 4, no. 1 (1993): 34-56.

———. "Rethinking Women/History/Literature: A Feminist Investigation of Disciplinarity in Lucy Hutchinson, Lady Mary Wortley Montagu, Charlotte Lennox, and Jane Austen." Ph.D. diss, State University of New York at Stony Brook, 1993.

Lovell, Terry. *Consuming Fiction*. London: Verso Press, 1987.

Lynch, Deidre and William B. Warner, ed., *Cultural Institutions of the Novel*. Durham, NC: Duke University Press, 1996.

Marshall, Christine. "'Dull Elves' and Feminists: A Summary of Feminist Criticism of Jane Austen." *Persuasions* 14 (1992): 39-45.

Mavor, Elizabeth, ed. *Life with the Ladies of Llangollen*. New York: Viking Penguin, 1984.

Mayo, Robert. *The English Novel in the Magazines 1740–1815. With a Catalogue of 1375 Magazine Novels and Novelettes*. Evanston, IL: Northwestern University Press, 1962.

McAleer, John. "What a Biographer Can Learn About Jane Austen." In *Jane Austen's Beginnings: The Juvenilia and Lady Susan*, ed. J. David Grey, 7-29. Ann Arbor, MI: UMI Research Press, 1989.

McNally, David. *Political Economy and the Rise of Capitalism: A Reinterpretation*. Berkeley: University of California Press, 1988.

Mellor, Anne K. *Romanticism and Gender*. New York: Routledge, 1993.

———. "Why Women Didn't Like Romanticism: The Views of Jane Austen and Mary Shelley," In *The Romantics and Us: Essays on Literature and Culture*, ed. Gene W. Ruoff, 274-87. New Brunswick, NJ: Rutgers University Press, 1992.

Meyersohn, Marylea. "What Fanny Knew: A Quiet Auditor of the Whole." *Jane Austen: New Perspectives*, ed. Janet Todd, 224-30. New York: Holmes and Meier, 1983.

Milbank, Alison. *Daughters of the House: Modes of the Gothic in Victorian Fiction*. New York: St. Martin's Press, 1992.

Miller, D. A. "The Late Jane Austen." *Raritan* 10 (1990): 55-79.

———. *Narrative and Its Discontents: Problems of Closure in the Traditional Novel*. Princeton, NJ: Princeton University Press, 1981.

Miller, J. Hillis. "The Limits of Pluralism III: The Critic as Host," *Critical Inquiry* 3 (Spring 1977): 439-48.

Miller, Nancy. *Subject to Change: Reading Feminist Writing*. New York: Columbia University Press, 1988.

Mnthali, Felix. "The Stranglehold of English Lit." In *Literature: The Human Experience*, 6th ed., ed. Richard Abcarian and Marvin Klotz, 491-93, New York: St. Martin's Press, 1994.

Moffat, Wendy. "Identifying with Emma: Some Problems for the Feminist Reader." *College English* 53, no.1 (1991): 45-76.

Monaghan, David, ed. *Jane Austen in a Social Context*. New York: Macmillan, 1981.

Mooneyham, Laura. *Romance, Language, and Education in Jane Austen's Novels*. London: Macmillan, 1988.

Morgan, Kenneth O., ed. *The Oxford Illustrated History of Britain*. Oxford: Oxford University Press, 1989.

Morrison, Paul. "Enclosed in Openness: *Northanger Abbey* and the Domestic Carceral." *Texas Studies in Literature and Language* 33 (1991): 1-23.

Mukherjee, Meenakshi. *Jane Austen*. New York: St. Martin's Press, 1991.

Musselwhite, David. *Partings Welded Together: Politics and Desire in the Nineteenth-Century English Novel*. London: Methuen, 1987.

Myers, Sylvia Harcstark. *The Bluestocking Circle: Women, Friendship, and the Life of the Mind in Eighteenth-Century England*. Oxford: Clarendon Press, 1990.

Paine, Robert. "What Is Gossip About? An Alternative Hypothesis." *Man* 2 (1967): 278-85.

Perera, Suvendrini. *Reaches of Empire: The English Novel from Edgeworth to Dickens.* New York: Columbia University Press, 1991.

Perry, Ruth. "A Thinking Woman's Guide to British Imperialism." Keynote speech at the annual conference of the Jane Austen Society of North America, New Orleans, November 1994.

———. "Clarissa's Daughters, or the History of Innocence Betrayed: How Women Writers Rewrote Richardson." *Women's Writing* 1, no. 1 (1994): 5-24.

Pinion, F. B. *A Jane Austen Companion: A Critical Survey and Reference Book.* London: Macmillan, 1973.

Pool, Daniel. *What Jane Austen Ate and Charles Dickens Knew: From Fox-Hunting to Whist: The Facts of Daily Life in 19th-Century England.* New York: Simon & Schuster, 1993.

Poovey, Mary. "*Persuasion* and the Promises of Love." In *The Representation of Women in Fiction,* ed. Carolyn Heilbrun and Margaret R. Higonnet, 152-79. Baltimore: Johns Hopkins University Press, 1983.

———. *The Proper Lady and the Woman Writer: Ideology as Style in the Works of Mary Wollstonecraft, Mary Shelley, and Jane Austen.* Chicago: University of Chicago Press, 1984.

Quintana, Ricardo. *Oliver Goldsmith: A Georgian Study.* New York: Macmillan, 1967.

Radcliffe, Ann. *The Mysteries of Udolpho.* Oxford: University Press, 1991.

Rajan, Rajeswari Sunder, ed. *The Lie of the Land: English Literary Studies in India.* Delhi: Oxford University Press, 1992.

Raven, James. *Judging New Wealth: Popular Publishing and Responses to Commerce in England, 1750-1800.* Oxford: Clarendon Press, 1992.

Reising, Russell. "Can Cultural Reading Read Culture: Toward a Theory of Literary Incompetence." *Tulsa Studies in Women's Literature* 10, no. 1 (1991): 67-91.

Rich, Adrienne. *On Lies, Secrets, and Silence: Selected Prose, 1966-1978.* New York: W. W. Norton, 1979.

Roberts, J. M. *The Mythology of the Secret Societies.* London: Secker and Warburg, 1972.

Roberts, Warren. *Jane Austen and the French Revolution.* New York: St. Martin's Press, 1979.

Roe, Nicholas. *Wordsworth and Coleridge: The Radical Years.* Oxford: Clarendon Press, 1988.

Ross, Deborah. *The Excellence of Falsehood: Romance, Realism, and Women's Contribution to the Novel.* Lexington: University Press of Kentucky, 1991.

Rousseau, G. S., ed. *Oliver Goldsmith: The Critical Heritage.* Boston: Routledge and Kegan Paul, 1974.

Ruthven, K. K. *Feminist Literary Studies: An Introduction.* Oxford: Oxford University Press, 1984.

Said, Edward. *Culture and Imperialism.* New York: Knopf, 1993.

———. "Jane Austen and Empire." In *Raymond Williams: Critical Perspectives,* ed. Terry Eagleton, 150-64. Boston: Northeastern University Press, 1989.

Sangari, Kumkum, and Sudesh Vaid, ed. *Recasting Women: Essays in Colonial History.* New Delhi: Kali Press, 1989.

Scott, Joan. *Gender and the Politics of History.* New York: Columbia University Press, 1988.

Sedgwick, Eve Kosofsky. "Jane Austen and the Masturbating Girl." *Critical Inquiry* 17, no. 4 (1991): 818-37.

Sellers, Susan, ed. *Feminist Criticism: Theory and Practice.* Hertfordshire: Harvester Wheatsheaf, 1991.

Shapiro, Ann-Louise, ed. *Feminists Revision History.* New Brunswick, NJ: Rutgers University Press, 1994.

Showalter, Elaine. *A Literature of Their Own: British Women Novelists from Brontë to Lessing.* Princeton: Princeton University Press, 1977.

Sinha, Mrinalini. "Gender in the Critiques of Colonialism and Nationalism: Locating the 'Indian Woman.'" In *Feminists Revision History,* ed. Ann-Louise Shapiro, 246-75. New Brunswick, NJ: Rutgers University Press, 1994.

Siskin, Clifford. "Eighteenth-Century Periodicals and the Romantic Rise of the Novel." *Studies in the Novel* 26, no. 2 (Summer 1994): 26-42.

———. *The Historicity of Romantic Discourse.* New York: Oxford University Press, 1988.

————. "Gender, Sublimity, Culture: Retheorizing Disciplinary Desire," *Eighteenth-Century Studies* 28 (Fall 1994): 37-50.

Smith, Johanna H. "'My Only Sister Now': Incest in *Mansfield Park*." *Studies in the Novel* 19 (Spring 1987): 1-15.

Smith, Leroy W. *Jane Austen and the Drama of Woman*. New York: St. Martin's Press, 1983.

Sommers, Christina Hoff. *Who Stole Feminism: How Women Have Betrayed Women*. New York: Simon and Schuster, 1994.

Southam, B. C., ed. *Jane Austen: The Critical Heritage 1870–1940*. London: Routledge and Kegan Paul, 1968.

Spacks, Patricia. *Gossip*. Chicago: University of Chicago Press, 1986.

Spender, Dale. *Mothers of the Novel: 100 Good Writers Before Jane Austen*. London: Pandora Press, 1986.

Spender, Dale and Janet Todd, ed., *British Women Writers: An Anthology from the Fourteenth Century to the Present*. New York: Peter Bedrick Books, 1989.

Spivak, Gayatri. *In Other Worlds: Essays in Cultural Politics*. New York: Routledge, 1988.

Stevens, Wallace. "The Ordinary Women." In *The Palm at the End of the Mind*, 76-77. New York: Random House, 1974.

Stewart, Maaja A. *Domestic Realities and Imperial Fictions: Jane Austen's Novels in Eighteenth-Century Contexts*. Athens: University of Georgia Press, 1993.

Stimpson, Catharine R. "Zero Degree Deviancy: The Lesbian Novel in English." *Critical Inquiry* 8, no. 2 (1981): 363-79.

Sulloway, Alison G. *Jane Austen and the Province of Womanhood*. Philadelphia: University of Pennsylvania Press, 1989.

Summers, Montague. *The Gothic Quest: A History of the Gothic Novel*. London: Fortune Press, 1938.

Swarbrick, Andrew, ed. *The Art of Oliver Goldsmith*. London: Vision Press, 1984.

Tanner, Tony. "In Between—Anne Elliot Marries a Sailor and Charlotte Heywood Goes to the Seaside." In *Jane Austen in a Social Context*, ed. David Monaghan, 180-94. Totowa, NJ: Barnes & Noble, 1981.

————. *Jane Austen*. Cambridge, MA: Harvard University Press, 1986.

Taylor, Irene. "Afterword: Jane Austen Looks Ahead." In *Fetter'd or Free: British Women Novelists, 1670–1815*, ed. Mary Anne Schofield and Cecilia Macheski, 426-33. Athens: Ohio University Press, 1986.

[Telscombe, Anne.] *Sanditon*. [By "Jane Austen and Another Lady"]. Boston: Houghton Mifflin Co., 1975.

Tester, Keith. *Civil Society*. New York: Routledge, 1992.

Thompson, James. "Jane Austen." In *The Columbia History of the British Novel*, ed. John Richetti et al., 275-99. New York: Columbia University Press, 1994.

Todd, Janet. "Jane Austen, Politics, and Sensibility." In *Feminist Criticism: Theory and Practice*, ed. Susan Sellers, 71-88. Toronto: University of Toronto Press, 1991.

————. *Sensibility: An Introduction*. London: Methuen, 1986.

————. *The Sign of Angellica: Women, Writing, and Fiction, 1660–1800*. New York: Columbia University Press, 1989.

————. *Women's Friendship in Literature*. New York: Columbia University Press, 1980.

Tompkins, J. M. S. *The Popular Novel in England 1770–1800*. London: Constable and Company, 1932.

Vanita, Ruth. "*Mansfield Park* in Miranda House." In *The Lie of the Land: English Literary Studies in India*, ed. Rajeswari Sunder Rajan, 90-98. Delhi: Oxford University Press, 1992.

Vishwanathan, Gauri. *Masks of Conquest: Literary Study and British Rule in India*. New York: Columbia University Press, 1989.

Watson, Nicola J. *Revolution and the Form of the British Novel, 1790–1825: Intercepted Letters, Interrupted Seductions*. Oxford: Clarendon Press, 1994.

Watt, Ian. *The Rise of the Novel: Studies in Defoe, Richardson, and Fielding*. Berkeley: University of California Press, 1957.

Weinbrot, Howard. *The Formal Strain: Studies in Augustan Imitation and Satire.* Chicago: University of Chicago Press, 1969.

Williams, Michael. "*Northanger Abbey*: Some Problems of Engagement." *Unisa English Studies* 25, no. 2 (1987): 8-17.

Williams, Raymond. *Keywords: A Vocabulary of Culture and Society.* Rev. ed. New York: Oxford University Press, 1983.

————. *Writing in Society.* London: Verso, 1983.

Wilt, Judith. *Ghosts of the Gothic: Austen, Eliot and Lawrence.* Princeton, NJ: Princeton University Press, 1980.

Wolf, Naomi. *Fire With Fire: The New Female Power and How It Will Change the 21st Century.* New York: Random House, 1993.

Wolfram, Sybil. *In-Laws and Outlaws: Kinship and Marriage in England.* New York: St. Martin's Press, 1987.

Wollstonecraft, Mary. *A Vindication of the Rights of Woman,* ed. Carol H. Poston, 2d ed. New York: W. W. Norton, 1988.

Woolf, Virginia. *A Room of One's Own.* New York: Harcourt Brace Jovanovich, 1929.

————. *The Common Reader: First Series,* ed. Andrew McNeillie. New York: Harcourt Brace Jovanovich, 1984.

Worton, Michael, and Judith Still, ed. *Intertextuality: Theories and Practices.* Manchester: Manchester University Press, 1990.

Yeazell, Ruth. "Fictional Heroines and Feminist Critics." *Novel* 8 (1974): 29-38.

Zimmerman, Eugenia Noik. "The Proud Princess Gets Her Comeuppance: Structures of Patriarchal Order." *Canadian Review of Comparative Literature* 3 (1976): 253-68.

Zinsser, Judith P. *History and Feminism: A Glass Half Full.* New York: Twayne Publishers, 1993.

Zionkowski, Linda. "Territorial Disputes in the Republic of Letters: Canon Formation and the Literary Profession." *The Eighteenth Century: Theory and Interpretation* 31 (1990): 3-22.

Contributors

MISTY G. ANDERSON is a teaching fellow in the English and Women's Studies Departments at Vanderbilt University. She is completing her dissertation, "Laughing with Their Mouths Closed: Women Writers of Comedy, 1655-1800," which examines the representational strategies of female embodiment fostered by the tensions of comedy in writers from Cavendish to Austen. She is presently a Mellon Fellow and has contributed essays to *The Eighteenth Century: Theory and Interpretation* and *Popular Culture* (forthcoming, Ridgemont Press).

ANTOINETTE BURTON is a historian of modern Britain, empire, and feminism who is currently teaching in the History Department and the Women's Studies Program at Johns Hopkins University. She is working on a book manuscript entitled "At the Heart of the Empire: Indians and the Colonial Encounter in Late-Victorian Britain." She is the author of *Burdens of History* (1994).

ELLEN GARDINER is director of Freshman English and assistant professor of English at the University of Mississippi. She has recently completed *Writing Women Reading: Gender and Literary Criticism in the Eighteenth-Century Novel*. In addition to her work in eighteenth-century studies, Gardiner has published her work on composition and rhetoric in *Rhetoric Review* and *The Journal of Teaching Writing*. Her essay on Charlotte Lennox's *The Female Quixote* is forthcoming in *Studies in the Novel*.

JOCELYN HARRIS holds a personal chair in English at the University of Otago, New Zealand. She edited Samuel Richardson's *History of Sir Charles Grandison* (1972) and has published various articles and books, including *Samuel Richardson* (1987) and *Jane Austen's Art of Memory* (1989).

DIANE LONG HOEVELER, associate professor of English and coordinator of the Women's Studies program at Marquette University, is author of *Romantic Androgyny: The Women Within* (1990) and coeditor of the MLA volume *Approaches to Teaching Brontë's* Jane Eyre (1993). Hoeveler teaches courses on English Romanticism, the gothic novel, and women's literature, and has completed a book to be titled "Gothic Feminism: The Melodrama of Gender and Ideology from Wollstonecraft to the Brontës."

GLENDA A. HUDSON is associate professor of English at California State University, Bakersfield, where she specializes in Victorian literature and the British novel. She is the author of *Sibling Love and Incest in Jane Austen's Fiction* (1992) and coauthor of the forthcoming *Contemporary Guide to Literary Terms*. She has published articles on Austen and Katherine Mansfield and is currently working on a study of the heroine in late Victorian fiction and art.

MARIA JERINIC is a doctoral student in English and Women's Studies at the State University of New York at Stony Brook. She is working on a dissertation about the function of India in the cultural imaginary of nineteenth-century British women writers.

GARY KELLY was educated at Toronto and Oxford and taught in Canada before becoming professor and head of the English Department at Keele University in England. He has published *The English Jacobin Novel* (1976), *English Fiction of the Romantic Period* (1989), *Revolutionary Feminism: The Mind and Career of Mary Wollstonecraft* (1992), and *Women, Writing, and Revolution: 1790-1827* (1993). He has edited Wollstonecraft's novels and Sarah Scott's *Millenium Hall*. He is general editor of Longman's history of women's writing in English.

DEVONEY LOOSER is assistant professor of English and Women's Studies at Indiana State University. Her articles on feminist and poststructuralist theories, British women writers, and composition theory have appeared in *European Romantic Review, minnesota review, Rhetoric Review,* and *Style*. She is working on a book about gender, history, and literature in British women's prose writings.

CLIFFORD SISKIN, associate professor of English and Comparative Literature at the State University of New York at Stony Brook, works on problems of literary and social change in the eighteenth and early nineteenth centuries. He published *The Historicity of Romantic Discourse* (1988) and is an advisory editor for *Eighteenth-Century Studies, Literature and History,* and *Reconstructing Romanticism*. The framework for his essay on Austen is developed in *The Work of Literature: Disciplinarity and Professionalism in Eighteenth- and Early Nineteenth-Century Britain*, a forthcoming study of divisions of knowledge and labor during the long eighteenth century.

LAURA MOONEYHAM WHITE is currently visiting associate professor of English at University of Nebraska-Lincoln. The author of *Romance, Language, and Education in Jane Austen's Novels* (1988), she has also published numerous articles on nineteenth and twentieth century literature in journals such as *Twentieth-Century Literature, South Atlantic Review,* and *Genre*. She is currently working on a book about the abandonment of the comic form in the British novel from the nineteenth to the twentieth century.

Index

Abrams, W. H., 95, 100
Adorno, Theodor, 74
Althusser, Louis, 74
Armstrong, Nancy, 148n
Astell, Mary, 4
Auerbach, Nina, 159, 163
Austen, Cassandra, 38, 45-6, 98
Austen, James, 56
Austen, Jane, and education, 156; and the literary marketplace, 51-64, 113n; *Catharine*, 56, 65n; *Emma*, 29, 57, 73-7, 78, 82, 84n, 93, 101, 105-6, 107, 112; *History of England, A*, 36, 39-47; *Juvenilia*, 56, 59, 65n, 92, 95; *Letters*, 66n, 98; *Love and Friendship*, 56; *Mansfield Park*, 28-29, 78, 81, 82, 90-1, 93, 101, 104, 107-112, 151-163, 167-182; *Northanger Abbey*, 8-9, 14, 25-6, 30-1, 35-6, 47, 56, 58, 60, 61-3, 78, 92, 95, 98, 120-134, 137-148, 148n; *Persuasion*, ix, 29-30, 75, 78-80, 81, 82, 94-97; *Pride and Prejudice*, 27-8, 58, 65, 78, 82, 93, 121, 152-3; *Sanditon*, 80-3, 85; *Sense and Sensibility*, 26-7, 77-8, 89-90, 93, 95, 101, 107, 112, 121; *see also* Feminism and literary criticism
Azim, Firdous, 37

Bakhtin, Mikhail, 97
Ballaster, Ros, 139, 149
Barbauld, Anna, 92
Barnes, Julian, 72
Bell, Susan, 15n, 35
Bennett, Agnes Maria, 104
Bloom, Harold, 87, 91-3
Bluestockings, 4, 21, 22-3
Boone, Joseph, 169, 183n
Booth, Wayne, 73-5, 84n

Brontë, Charlotte, 5, 37-8, 89, 118, 134
Brooks, Peter, 76-77, 134n, 168-9, 171, 180, 182n
Brown, Charles Brockden, 105
Brown, Julia Prewitt, 112, 183n
Buonaparte, Napoleon, 80, 152
Burney, Frances, 8-9, 26, 88, 102, 121, 129
Butler, Elenor, 168
Butler, Marilyn, 3, 134n
Byatt, A. S., 41
Byron, Lord, George Gordon, 94

Cavell, Stanley, 79, 85
Chodorow, Nancy, 88, 99
Church of England, 22, 24-5, 28-31, 89, 102, 130, 157-8, 161, 165n
Class, Issues of, 21, 24, 31, 46, 83, 97, 106-7, 118, 126-7, 133, 129, 160, 162, 181
Clayton, Jay, 182n
Colley, Linda, 46
Colonialism, 4, 28, 30
Cottom, Daniel, 146, 149, 164n
Cowper, William, 90, 95

Danahy, Michael, 53
DeCerteau, Michel, 152, 163, 163n, 165n
Deconstruction, 93, 97, 122, 174
Derrida, Jacques, 93
Dickens, Charles, 53, 137
Dolan, Jill, 165n
Domesticity, 111, 129, 131, 137, 153-4
Doody, Margaret, 58-9, 61, 65, 102, 113
Duckworth, Alistair, 3, 74
Duncan, Ian, 66n
DuPlessis, Rachel, 72, 78, 181, 183n
Dwyer, June, 1